"Using the triadic analytical technique derived from the truth of the Trinity, Poythress continues his quest for an undistorted, biblical understanding of the sciences, this time zeroing in on linguistics and sociology. This is a work of first-rate thinking. Demanding yet enriching, this book is a major contribution to modern reformation and its intellectual renewal."

J. I. Packer, Board of Governors' Professor of Theology,
Regent College; author, *Knowing God*

"In the spirit of Abraham Kuyper, Vern Poythress has given us a valuable guide to thinking about godly relationships in our secular world. He develops a biblical understanding of how the distortions of sin have fractured our relationships with God and his people. I commend Poythress for his insightful thinking in this book, which joins the ranks of his similar contributions on science and literature."

J. Lanier Burns, Research Professor of Theological Studies,
Senior Professor of Systematic Theology, Dallas Theological Seminary

"It is fairly common today for preachers and theologians to speak of relationships as crucial to the gospel, and to invoke the divine Trinity as the ultimate model therein, but this point has rarely been presented in theological depth. Poythress takes up that task, showing in great detail the biblical depth of this picture. He explains that human relationships make no sense apart from God's nature, creation, and providence. Indeed, this book presents a powerful argument against the exclusion of God from sociology and psychology. And it extends the argument of his recent books (on interpretation, science, and language) that the God of Scripture is the foundation for everything human."

John M. Frame, J. D. Trimble Chair of Systematic Theology and Philosophy,
Reformed Theological Seminary, Orlando

"Vern Poythress has done thinking Christians a great service by engaging in rigorous theological reflection on relationships—that all-important facet of human existence that we are inescapably immersed in, are shaped by, and yet often take for granted. Church leaders will benefit from this fine book."

D. Michael Lindsay, Assistant Professor of Sociology, Rice University;
author, *Faith in the Halls of Power*

Redeeming Sociology

OTHER CROSSWAY BOOKS BY VERN SHERIDAN POYTHRESS

In the Beginning Was the Word: Language—A God-Centered Approach
Redeeming Science: A God-Centered Approach
Translating Truth: The Case for Essentially Literal Bible Translation
  (with C. John Collins, Wayne Grudem, Leland Ryken,
  and Bruce Winter)

Redeeming Sociology

A God-Centered Approach

VERN SHERIDAN POYTHRESS

CROSSWAY

WHEATON, ILLINOIS

This book examines human relationships in a manner analogous to a previous Crossway book that examines language: *In the Beginning Was the Word: Language—A God-Centered Approach* (2009). Where appropriate, some of the wording and structure of the previous book has been utilized in this one. This use is with permission.

Cover design: Studio Gearbox
Cover photo: Veer Inc.

First printing 2011
Printed in the United States of America

Scripture quotations are from the ESV® Bible (*The Holy Bible, English Standard Version*®), copyright © 2001 by Crossway. Used by permission. All rights reserved.

All emphases in Scripture quotations have been added by the author.

Trade paperback ISBN:　　978-1-4335-2129-4
PDF ISBN:　　　　　　　978-1-4335-2130-0
Mobipocket ISBN:　　　　978-1-4335-2131-7
ePub ISBN:　　　　　　　978-1-4335-2132-4

Library of Congress Cataloging-in-Publication Data
Poythress, Vern S.
　　Redeeming sociology : a God-centered approach / Vern Sheridan Poythress.
　　　　p. cm.
　　Includes bibliographical references and index.
　　ISBN 978-1-4335-2129-4 (tp)
　　1. Christian sociology. 2. Interpersonal relations—Religious aspects—Christianity. I. Title.
BT738.P65 2011
261.5—dc22
　　　　　　　　　　　　　　　　　　　　　　　　　　　　　2010053586

Crossway is a publishing ministry of Good News Publishers.

VP　23　22　21　20　19　18　17　16　15　14　13　12　11
14　13　12　11　10　9　8　7　6　5　4　3　2　1

To my wife and sons,
whom the Lord has given me
in precious relationships

Contents

Why Relationships?

Why a book about social relationships? We can find books with advice about devotional life, marriage, friendships, romance, and child rearing. We can also find books about large-scale social issues such as poverty, economics, politics, and law. Some of these are solidly based on the Bible. Because the Bible is God's own word, it provides us with guidance in all these areas.

The advice from these books may be wise, but as some of the books would themselves admit, mere advice is not enough. We need God's power, provided in Christ. We need fellowship with him. And we need a whole view of the world in which God is our God and is the most important and valued person in our life.

The Challenge of a Modern Worldview

A modern secular world presses in on us. If we listen to it and absorb too much of its message, we neglect to make God central. We think and act in relationships as if they were independent of God. Modern, secular thinking masters our minds instead of Christ being the Master in all areas of our life.

So we need to have a biblically based worldview that includes a sound view of our relationships. I want us to rethink the *foundations* of our relationships, and not just to offer advice or a superficial tour of those relationships. God is the Creator of the whole world in all its dimensions. He has established his own wise order for our relationships. His order and his presence are essential to life and to relationships. We need to learn how to praise God for the world of relationships that he has given us.

Linguistic and Sociological Study of the Bible

I have a second reason for considering relationships. In the last few decades, academic study of the Bible has come to include a significant body of studies using linguistic and sociological approaches. The Society of Biblical Literature, a major academic society for studying the Bible, has several "Program Units" or sections devoted to linguistic and sociological studies. In fact, linguistics and sociology and social anthropology are beginning to influence biblical studies far more broadly than just in those studies that self-consciously adopt their techniques.

In principle, these studies could make a helpful contribution. The Bible is written in language, and so linguistics is pertinent. The Bible is written to people living in particular cultural settings, and so social and cultural thinking are pertinent.

But linguistic and sociological approaches inevitably come with assumptions. Often, these assumptions are influenced by a secular view of science. According to this view, the task of science is to observe and analyze phenomena "objectively," without making religious assumptions. In the process, scientists begin to assume that God can be left out of their reckoning. If God is left out, sin is left out. And if God and sin are left out of the reckoning at the beginning, in the foundations of an academic discipline, they may be also left out at the end, in the theories and the conclusions. Or if God is not left out altogether, the god who gets brought in is not really the God described in the Bible, but a limited, tamed-down substitute.

How is God left out? Language is treated as purely human language, with God excluded from being an essential participant in the use of language. Society is treated as purely human society, with God as a person excluded from it. So sin and its effects have to be redefined, and then the remedy for sin has to be redefined.

Sin laces language with deceit and laces society with oppression and suffering. If God is not the remedy, what is? People have tried all kinds of alternatives. One possible alternative says that rather than sin being the problem, some structure in language or society or both imprisons us and keeps us from authentic living. And there is a grain of truth in what they say, since language and society, and not merely individuals, show effects from sin. These effects of sin bring untold suffering and damage, and press the lives of human beings more deeply into misery and sin.

Even our *thinking* about society becomes distorted when we lose God's illumination about our plight. For example, people may say that we cannot escape from language in order to think and see and talk about the world outside of the limitations and social effects of a language that we have inherited from our forebears. Neither can we escape from society and culture in order to think and see the world of human beings from outside the prejudices that culture has transmitted to us. In both language and culture we are trapped by the limits of our humanity. In this view, the basic problem is no longer sin but being finite (being human). And indeed being finite *is* a problem, but only when you are alienated from God who is infinite.

When people apply this view to studying the Bible, they may easily conclude that the Bible is imprisoned by the languages and cultures of its origin. Some people may still want to say that God speaks in the Bible in some sense. But they would claim that God limits himself, and his speech never rises above the prison of the cultures in which it originated. People who think in this way radically restrict the Bible's power to speak in criticism of our lives and our cultures.

How do we deal with possible biases introduced from linguistics and sociology? The task is not easy. In the end, we have to rethink all of linguistics and all of sociology, because foundational assumptions about the nature of the world and the nature of humanity and the causes of human disorders affect the disciplines as a whole. Because linguistics and sociology and our modern world are heavily influenced by natural sciences, the same concerns arise with respect to natural sciences such as physics, chemistry, and biology.

My Role

How do I fit in with these concerns? I have spent most of my career teaching New Testament at Westminster Theological Seminary in Philadelphia. I have had the privilege of studying the Bible intensely. But now I find that such study can be disrupted and distorted by assumptions that are alien to the character of the Bible and to the God who inspired its writing. These alien assumptions sometimes come from natural science, linguistics, or sociology. To have a healthy study of the Bible, we need also a healthy understanding in other areas affecting the study of the Bible. But to have a healthy view of any area of our lives, we need to receive the healthy instruction of the Bible and apply it to that area.

And so I have looked to the instruction in the Bible and thought about its implications for various areas of life. I have then found myself writing books that venture out into these areas in the modern world, and especially into areas that today affect the study of the Bible directly or indirectly. I write in order to stimulate the reconfiguration and transformation of our worldview.

The Bible gives us instruction and power that enable us to undertake this transformation. The Bible transforms the way we ought to think about and conduct natural sciences, as I have tried to show in *Redeeming Science: A God-Centered Approach* (2006). It transforms the way we think about language, as I have tried to show in the book *In the Beginning Was the Word: Language—A God-Centered Approach* (2009). It transforms the way we think about society, culture, and relationships, as I try to show in this present book. This book is therefore a sister to the book on language (*In the Beginning*). It is more like a daughter or a niece to the one about science, since social sciences and natural sciences confront somewhat different challenges.

Abraham Kuyper's Vision

The Bible's instruction has a unique role, because it is the word of God. But I have also been encouraged by a secondary source, namely Abraham Kuyper's book *Lectures on Calvinism*.[1] Abraham Kuyper observed that according to the Bible Jesus Christ is Lord—Ruler and King of the entire universe (Eph. 1:20–22; Phil. 2:9–11). His lordship and authority extend to every sphere of life. In his book Kuyper accordingly devoted a chapter each to religion, politics, science, and art. Christ, he claimed, is Lord over all these areas.

Kuyper also believed that the fall into sin made a difference. Ever since the fall, our lives and our thinking have been in disorder and rebellion. This rebellion works its way not only into religion, but also into politics, science, art, and other spheres. The Christian, who has been redeemed by Christ and has committed himself to be a follower of Christ, must loyally follow Christ in every sphere of life: religion and politics and science and art alike. Thinking in these spheres has been corrupted by sin and accordingly must be transformed. Kuyper thought that such transformation had not yet been adequately done.

In the generations after Kuyper a number of people took up Kuyper's challenge. They worked at transformation of thought. Advances took place. But along with the advances came some misjudgments, in my opinion. So work still needs to be done. And that is why I am writing. Reflection needs to continue in the natural sciences and in linguistics and sociology. So I have produced the books in these three areas. Others, I hope, will build on what I have done and will correct what I still have left amiss.

I hope that my books may contribute directly to transforming the fields of study that they address. But I hope also that they will indirectly help us in studying the Bible. We work toward healthy views of languages and of societies in order to have a healthy environment in which we study the Bible fruitfully. Through this study we grow in Christ and begin to glorify God in all of life.

---

[1] Abraham Kuyper, *Lectures on Calvinism* (Grand Rapids: Eerdmans, 1931), compiled from six lectures given in 1898 at Princeton University under the auspices of the L. P. Stone Foundation.

INTRODUCTION

Considering Personal Relationships

It is not good that the man should be alone.

—Genesis 2:18

What would it be like to live all alone on an uninhabited island? If the island had sufficient food resources, a clever person might survive for a long time. But it would not be good; he would be lonely.

We live in company with fellow human beings. God made us that way. He made us to be in relationships. First and foremost, we are designed to have a personal relationship with God himself. But God planned that we would also have relationships with other human beings, and we would benefit from the cooperation and the comradeship. We benefit as adults, but we benefited even more strikingly when we were infants. In reality, none of us is "self-made." God made us. And then we had someone to take care of us while we were young. At that point, a relationship was essential.

Human social relationships are wonderful and mysterious. They are so because they are a gift of God to us. They reflect and reveal him. How do relationships reflect God? According to the Bible, God himself is personal. God is one God in three persons. Within God, the persons—the Father, the Son, and the Holy Spirit—have rich personal relations with one another. We are made like God, and that is why we can enjoy personal relationships. When we relate to one another, we rely on resources and powers that find their origin in God. We can appreciate personal relationships more deeply, and interact more wisely, if we come to know God and see his place in these relationships.

Because I am a follower of Christ, I trust in the Bible as the word of God.[1] The Bible is a foundational resource for my thinking about personal relationships. From time to time we will look briefly at other views of humanity and human relationships. But my primary purpose is to help people increase their appreciation for relationships, using the Bible for guidance. If you as a reader are not yet convinced about the Bible, I would still invite you to think with me about relationships. The actual character of relationships does, I believe, confirm what the Bible says.

---

[1] Interested readers may consult many works that show at length that the Bible is the word of God. See, among others, Benjamin B. Warfield, *The Inspiration and Authority of the Bible* (Philadelphia: Presbyterian and Reformed, 1948); D. A. Carson and John D. Woodbridge, eds., *Scripture and Truth* (Grand Rapids: Zondervan, 1983). It is an important issue, so important that it deserves much more space than we could take here.

1

The Importance of Relationships

Two are better than one, because they have a good reward
for their toil. For if they fall, one will lift up his fellow.
But woe to him who is alone when he falls and has not another
to lift him up! Again, if two lie together, they keep warm,
but how can one keep warm alone? And though a man might
prevail against one who is alone, two will withstand him—
a threefold cord is not quickly broken.

—Ecclesiastes 4:9–12

Personal relationships have a central role in human living. We spend a lot of our time interacting with other people—talking, listening, helping, cooperating in work and in leisure. When relationships degenerate, we may feel the effects keenly: we may hate others; we may quarrel, fight, backstab, envy, covet, lie, slander, steal, and murder. We may suffer when other people hurt us. Relationships can clearly be for both good and ill.

Not only in the family but in almost every other sphere of life we experience human relationships. Education depends on relations between teacher and student and between fellow students. Businesses depend on relations of employer and employee, supervisor and subordinate, and teams of workers in cooperative effort. Communication, news, and entertainment, whether by television, radio, newspapers, or the Internet, involve relationships between communicators, news reporters, entertainers, and recipients. We can enter into relationships in friendships, social organizations, businesses, churches, charities, political parties, governmental organizations, military organizations, and sports.

Large organizations like national governments, big-business corporations, universities, and mass media organizations demonstrate the importance of relationships in another way. Their very existence is closely tied to relationships. They continue to exist because they are maintained through a vast number of internal relationships among those who work in them. And their influence on others relies heavily on what other people know and think about them. A business, for example, depends on people's trust in its reputation and their knowledge of the products that it offers for sale. A national government functions most effectively when the people freely recognize its authority, rather than regarding it as an unwelcome oppressor.

Some activities, such as gardening, do not demand the immediate presence of another human being. But even they gain significance from a larger context of human life in which relationships have an indispensable role. We practice gardening using advice and examples from other people. We may have obtained the seeds or seedlings from a nursery or gardening shop. We may work our garden with benefits in mind that extend to other people. And gardening can be more pleasant if we are talking with a friend while doing it. We could go on. Many of the most significant and precious moments in life gain significance through relationships. So examining our relationships could contribute significantly to reorienting our lives. That is why we are going to take a long look at relationships and their meaning.

The Importance of Relationships in the Bible

The Bible confirms the importance of relationships. It says that in the beginning God created human beings in his image: "Let us make man in our image, after our likeness" (Gen. 1:26). Human beings are created *like God*, and the likeness includes his personal character. Human beings thus have capability for personal relationships, involving knowing, loving, and communicating with others.

The first recorded interaction between God and man shows a personal relationship. God spoke to human beings concerning their task: "And God blessed them. And God said to them, 'Be fruitful and multiply and fill the earth and subdue it and have dominion over the fish of the sea and over the birds of the heavens and over every living thing that moves on the earth'" (Gen. 1:28). This speech showed a relationship of communication and personal responsibility between God and human beings. The personal responsibility came into focus more pointedly when God introduced a special prohibition: "And the LORD God commanded the man, saying, 'You may surely eat of every tree of the garden, but of the tree of the knowledge of good and evil you shall not eat, for in the day that you eat of it you shall surely die'" (Gen. 2:16–17). Adam and Eve, the first human beings, violated their relationship with God when they disobeyed and fell into sin. But that was not the end of their relationship with God. God gave hope to Adam and Eve through a promise of redemption, which demonstrated a continuing possibility of positive fellowship with God (Gen. 3:15).

Among human beings, family relationships play an important role. God established the relationship of marriage even before the beginning of human rebellion (Gen. 2:18–25). The human race grows through families who bear children and raise them (Gen. 4:1–5:32). Parents have a responsibility to train their children (Deut. 6:6–7; Eph. 6:4). Children must maintain a relationship of respect toward their parents (Ex. 20:12; Eph. 6:1–3).

God also established the beginning of civil government when he gave instructions on how to deal with cases of murder (Gen. 9:5–6). We can see more complex governmental organization in Egypt (e.g., Gen. 41:37–57), in the kings of Israel (1 Chronicles 22–29), and in Babylon (Daniel 1–6). God established these governments and accomplished his will through them, even though they did not always act justly (Gen. 45:5; 50:20; Dan. 2:36–45; 4:34–35; 7:17–27; Rom. 13:1–3).

In the Old Testament God's relations to human beings come to particular expression in *covenants*. We will look at covenants more closely at a later point. Roughly speaking, a covenant is a kind of pact, an agreement that establishes a relationship between two parties. God made a covenant with Abraham and his descendants (Genesis 17), and later with the nation of Israel through Moses (Exodus 24). Jesus inaugurated a covenant at the Last Supper (Matt. 26:28). God's covenants with human beings express a commitment on God's part to a special people, and they look forward to a time when God will accomplish final and definitive redemption. Redemption includes the healing of the relation between God and mankind that was broken by human rebellion.

The healing of the relationship was accomplished when Jesus Christ came into the world and carried out his work. Jesus acted to restore a proper relationship of love between God and human beings, and a relation of love among human beings. His teachings have much to say about human relationships in their many dimensions. But his *actions*, especially his death and his resurrection from the dead, took place in order to effect reconciliation in the relation between God and man, and then, as a further result, reconciliation in human relationships with one another: "A new commandment I give to you, that you love one another: just as I have loved you, you also are to love one another" (John 13:34).

The "gospel" or good news that the Bible proclaims tells how Jesus's work restored relationships, and what we are to do in responding to God and what he accomplished. The Bible's message addresses relationships in all their dimensions.

Our response to the message in the Bible includes a response in changing our relationships. First of all, we need to be reconciled to God, against whom we have rebelled. In other words, our relationship with God needs to be restored. In addition, reconciliation with God has implications for our future relationship to God and to others. Jesus summarizes our obligations to God in two central commandments, both of which involve relationships:

> "Teacher, which is the great commandment in the Law?" And he [Jesus] said to him, "You shall love the Lord your God with all your heart and with all your soul and with all your mind. This is the great and first commandment. And a second is like it: You shall love your neighbor as yourself. On these two commandments depend all the Law and the Prophets." (Matt. 22:36–40)

Living your life as God designed you to live it means living fruitfully in relation-ships. If you are genuinely carrying out God's two commands—for relationship with God and relationship with other people—you are pleasing God and fulfilling the true goal of your existence. So relationships are vital in your life.

PART 1

God's Involvement with Relationships

2

Relationships and the Trinity

The Father loves the Son and has given all things into his hand.

—John 3:35

How do we go about understanding human relationships? Human relationships have a close relation to the Trinitarian character of God. In fact, the Trinitarian character of God is the deepest starting point for understanding personal relationships. So we need to look at what the Bible teaches about God in his Trinitarian character.

The Trinity

The Bible teaches that God is one God, and that he exists in three persons, the Father, the Son, and the Holy Spirit. I will not undertake to defend orthodox Trinitarian doctrine in detail, because this has already been done many times.[1] Let me mention briefly only a small number of evidences. In addressing the polytheism of surrounding nations, the Old Testament makes it clear that there is only one true God, the God of Israel, who is the only Creator (Genesis 1; see Deut. 6:4; 32:39; Isa. 40:18–28). The New Testament introduces further revelation about the distinction of persons in God, but it everywhere presupposes the unity of one God as revealed in the Old Testament. The New Testament does not repudiate but reinforces the Old Testament: "Hear, O Israel: The Lord

---

[1] For a recent discussion, see John M. Frame, *The Doctrine of God* (Phillipsburg, NJ: P&R, 2002), 619–735.

our God, the Lord is one" (Mark 12:29). "You believe that God is one; you do well" (James 2:19).

Second, the New Testament dramatically affirms the deity of Christ the Son of God by applying to him Old Testament verses that use the tetragrammaton, the sacred name of God: "Everyone who calls on the name of the Lord will be saved" (Rom. 10:13; from Joel 2:32, which has the tetragrammaton).[2] We also find explicit affirmations that Jesus is God in John 1:1 ("... and the Word was God") and John 20:28. The Holy Spirit is God, according to Acts 5:3–4.[3] The distinction between the persons is regularly evident in John, when John expresses the relation of two persons as that of Father and Son, and when the Spirit is described as "another Helper," indicating that he is distinct from the Son (John 14:16).

God Has Personal Relations within Himself

The New Testament indicates that the persons of the Trinity speak to one another and enjoy profound personal relations with one another. These relationships within God show us the ultimate foundation for thinking about human personal relationships. God establishes a personal relationship with us, but, in addition, the persons of the Trinity have personal relations to one another. Personal relationships exist not solely among human beings, but also in divine-human relationships, and even in divine-divine relationships. Approaches that conceive of personal and social relationships only with reference to human beings are accordingly one-sided, reductionistic.

What evidence does the Bible give for divine-divine personal relationship? Divine relationships crop up again and again in the Gospel of John where Jesus talks about his relation as Son to the Father. For example, "The Father loves the Son and shows him all that he himself is doing" (John 5:20). "And I will ask the Father, and he will give you another Helper [the Spirit]" (John 14:16). The relationship between the Father and the Son includes asking, commanding, loving, and each "glorifying" the other (John 13:31–32; 17:4–5).

The statements recorded in the Gospel of John mostly focus on Jesus's relation to the Father during his time on earth. But they reflect eternal truths. The Son, the second person of the Trinity, always existed, according to John 1:1. He became a human being at a specific point in time, which was the beginning of Jesus's life on earth: "The Word became flesh and dwelt among us, and we have seen his glory, glory as of the only Son from the Father" (John 1:14). This becoming human is called the *incarnation*.

---

[2] The tetragrammaton is *YHWH* (Hebrew, יהוה, "Jehovah"), often translated in Greek as *kyrios*, "Lord".

[3] Acts 5:3–4 indicates that to lie to the Holy Spirit is to lie to God.

What Jesus said and did on earth, he said and did as both God and man. So his work on earth was in harmony with his eternal relation to the Father. The statement "the Father loves the Son" (John 5:20 and 3:35) applies to Jesus's earthly life; but it also applies eternally. The Father has always loved the Son, even before his incarnation. The language about the Father "sending" the Son implies that the Father was Father and the Son was Son even before he was "sent" to earth in the incarnation (see John 5:23, 37; 10:36; Gal. 4:4; and elsewhere). And it implies that the Father and the Son already had together a plan for sending the Son before the moment when the sending took place in his incarnation.

So far we have considered two persons of the Trinity, the Father and the Son. There is also a third, the Holy Spirit. The designation of the Holy Spirit as "another Helper" (John 14:16) indicates that the Holy Spirit is a person distinct from the Son and from the Father. The fact that the Holy Spirit "proceeds from the Father" and that the Son "sends" him from the Father indicates that the Spirit enjoys personal relations with both the Father and the Son (see John 15:26). The three persons agree in their purposes, and one carries out the intentions of another.

The Spirit's relation to the Father and the Son also comes to light in the communication and sharing of knowledge among them:

> When the Spirit of truth comes, he will guide you into all the truth, for he will not speak on his own authority, but whatever he hears he will speak, and he will declare to you the things that are to come. He will glorify me [Jesus], for he will take what is mine and declare it to you. All that the Father has is mine; therefore I said that he will take what is mine and declare it to you. (John 16:13–15)

Distinct Roles of the Persons of the Trinity in Personal Relations

Since the Father, the Son, and the Spirit are three distinct persons, we may expect rich, many-dimensional personal relations among them. They know one another; they love one another; they are in harmony in their purposes; as divine persons, they share in the divine characteristics, such as omnipresence, omniscience, omnipotence, immutability, righteousness, holiness, truth, and eternality. They dwell in one another ("coinherence").

But we can also see distinctions among the persons in the relations that they have with one another. As we observed, the Father is Father and the Son is Son. The Father has a fatherly relation to the Son, and the Son has a filial relation to the Father. These are distinct personal relations.

The Father and the Son enjoy their Father-Son relation from all eternity. But it is also expressed or made manifest in time when the Son becomes incarnate. The angel who announces the virgin birth of Christ to Mary says, "The Holy Spirit will come upon you, and the power of the Most High [God] will overshadow you; therefore the child to be born will be called holy—the Son of God" (Luke

1:35). Note the word *therefore*. The child will be called "the Son of God" because God himself—God the Father—will "overshadow you," and the child will be conceived by the special exercise of God's power, without a human father. God himself is the child's father, and so the child is definitely "the Son of God."

We have already affirmed that the Son of God was always Son of God in relation to the Father who was always the Father. The virgin birth of Christ is not in tension with this eternal reality. Rather, the virgin birth is an appropriate manifestation in its particular time and place of what was always the case in God, but it becomes newly manifest to humanity because the Son has now become "flesh," a human being.

In addition the third person of the Trinity, the Holy Spirit, has a distinctive role in the virgin birth. "The Holy Spirit will come upon you," says the angel, in an expression parallel to "the power of the Most High will overshadow you." The power of the Most High, the power of God the Father, operates through the coming and presence of the Holy Spirit. God the Father is the divine Father who fathers the Son in the virgin birth. And the Holy Spirit is present as the power of God who empowers the conception of the Son. Both Father and Spirit are present, but in distinctive ways.

Since the virgin birth and conception are in harmony with who God always is, we may infer that the Father fathers the Son eternally and that in this act of fathering the Holy Spirit is the empowerer. The old-fashioned word for fathering is *begetting*, and accordingly the Nicene-Constantinopolitan Creed uses the term to express the relations of the persons of the Godhead: "I believe . . . in one Lord Jesus Christ, the only-*begotten* Son of God, *begotten* of the Father before all worlds, God of God, Light of Light, very God of very God, *begotten*, not made, being of one substance with the Father; by whom all things were made. . . ."

The Bible also uses the term *beget* to designate the resurrection of Christ:

> And we bring you the good news that what God promised to the fathers, this he has fulfilled to us their children by raising Jesus, as also it is written in the second Psalm,
>
> "You are my Son,
>   today I have *begotten* you." (Acts 13:32–33; quoting Ps. 2:7)

Acts 13 applies the language of "begetting" in Psalm 2 to the resurrection of Christ ("raising Jesus"). In the resurrection the sonship of Jesus was displayed openly, and as the representative man he entered into a new phase of the exercise of his sonship. Romans 1:3–4 indicates the new phase: the gospel concerns "his Son, who was descended from David according to the flesh and was declared to be the Son of God in power according to the Spirit of holiness by his resurrection from the dead, Jesus Christ our Lord." Christ's resurrection took place through the power of the Holy Spirit: "If the Spirit of him who raised Jesus from the dead dwells in you, he who raised Christ Jesus from the dead will also give life to your mortal bodies through his Spirit who dwells in you" (Rom. 8:11). The resurrection of Christ, like the virgin conception of Christ, was in harmony with the eternal personal relations among the persons of the Trinity (see fig. 2.1).

Figure 2.1. The Son in Eternity and in Time

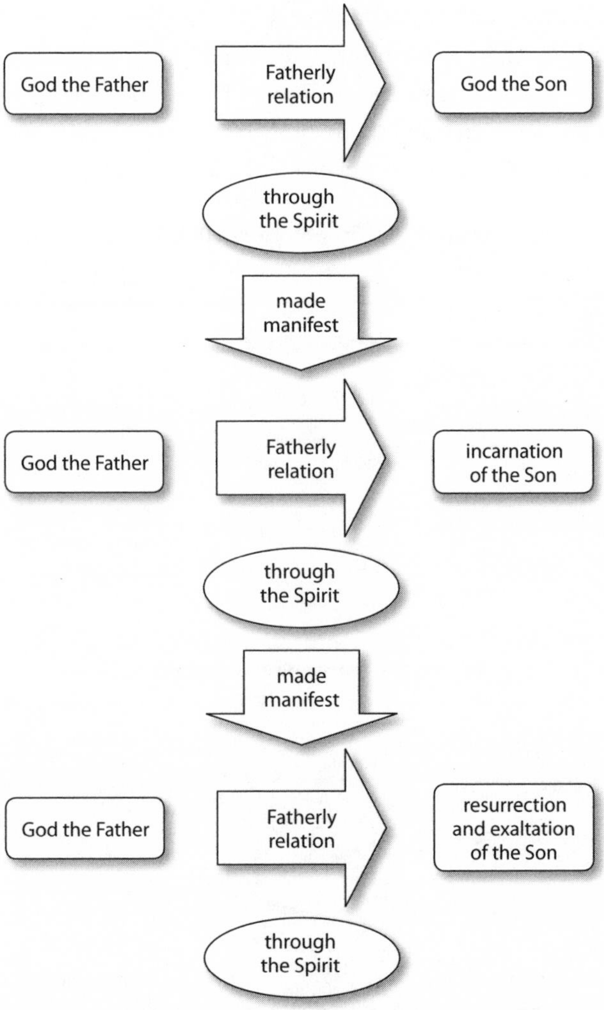

The Father has a fatherly personal relation to the Son through the Spirit. These relations among the divine persons are of deep importance to us because they are the ultimate foundation for human personal relations. You and I have the capacity for personal relationships because God gave us an ability analogous to his own personal relationships among the persons of the Trinity.

Many people take their starting point from human personal relations. They reason that we first know about earthly fathers and earthly sons. Then, by some kind of leap or extension, we project the earthly personal relationship of father-and-son into the sky, and we talk in a metaphorical way about God as "Father." Similarly, they would say that the spirit of a human being functions as the starting point for talking about the Spirit of God. But we should rather think through our own human relationships with God as our starting point. After all, *he* is the original. We are derivative. The original father is God the Father. Any earthly father is "father" only by analogy to the ultimate Father. Human beings have a spiritual aspect because the Holy Spirit exists eternally (1 Cor. 2:11; see fig. 2.2). Human fathers and human sons exist and their family relations exist only because we are made in the image of God, who is the original Father (see fig. 2.3).

Figure 2.2. God-Spirit Relations

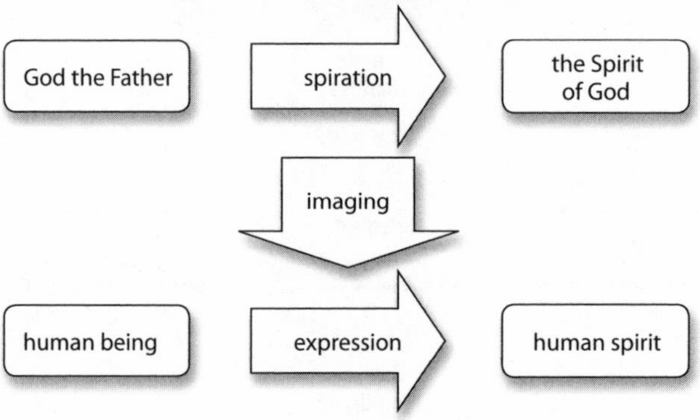

God the Father	spiration →	the Spirit of God

imaging ↓

human being	expression →	human spirit

Figure 2.3. Father-Son Relations

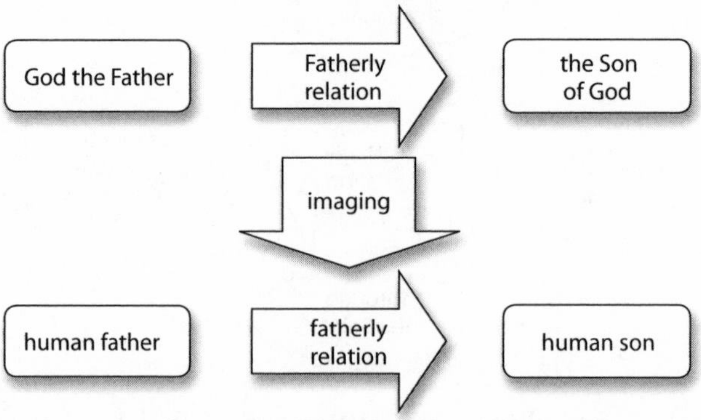

God the Father	Fatherly relation →	the Son of God

imaging ↓

human father	fatherly relation →	human son

The Gospel of John talks about other aspects of the personal relations within the Godhead. One such aspect is mutual love. "The Father *loves* the Son and has given all things into his hand" (John 3:35). This reality shows that the Father-Son relation involves not merely "begetting" but also a continuing activity of loving.

In addition, the Son loves the Father (John 14:31). The love that the Father has for his Son is expressed by the Father giving the Spirit to the Son: "He gives the Spirit without measure" (John 3:34). This verse about the giving of the Spirit describes the bounty of the Father to the Son immediately before the affirmation about the Father's love (v. 35). The Father also expresses his relationship to his Son by giving "all things" to him, according to John 3:35. Another aspect of the relationship is communication. "For I [Jesus] have given them [the disciples] the words that you [the Father] gave me" (John 17:8). The Spirit also participates in a relationship of hearing the Father and the Son (John 16:13).[4]

We can add still more aspects. The Father "sends" the Son and the Spirit. This sending indicates a personal sharing of purposes, and the Son doing "as the Father commanded me" (John 14:31) indicates a relation of command and commandment keeping. The language of the dwelling of the persons of the Trinity in one another indicates a deep sharing. Knowledge of one person in the Trinity involves knowledge of the others.[5] The giving of life and the giving of judgment are also activities in which the persons share (see John 5:22, 26).

The Uniqueness of God

We have seen many kinds of analogy between God and human beings, and between divine persons and human persons. But God is unique in his infinity. God is God, and there is no other. The three persons of the Trinity are all one God, and it is a mystery that only God comprehends. No analogy from creatures and creaturely relationships captures or explains thoroughly who God is.

The personal relationships within the Trinity are infinitely deep. In their depth they exceed what we as creatures know. Human relationships do not have this same depth, but they do derive from a divine foundation. So our relationships both with God and with fellow human beings have a weight and a significance. They reflect the goodness and the wisdom and the love of God. They are not just tacked on as an afterthought. Human relationships, when rightly ordered, reflect the glory of God. If we understand the personal character of God, we ought to be motivated to thank God for who we are as personal creatures with a capacity for relationships. And when we grasp the weightiness of our relationships, we should be motivated to try to serve God in the way we conduct relationships.

---

[4] See Vern S. Poythress, *In the Beginning Was the Word: Language—A God-Centered Approach* (Wheaton, IL: Crossway, 2009), especially chap. 2.
[5] Ibid.

3

God Creating Human Beings

Then God said, "Let us make man in our image, after our likeness.
And let them have dominion over the fish of the sea
and over the birds of the heavens and over the livestock
and over all the earth and over every creeping thing
that creeps on the earth."
So God created man in his own image,
in the image of God he created him;
male and female he created them.
And God blessed them. And God said to them,
"Be fruitful and multiply and fill the earth and subdue it
and have dominion over the fish of the sea and over the birds
of the heavens and over every living thing that moves on the earth."

—Genesis 1:26–28

Human personal activities are possible because human beings are created to be like God ("God created man in his own image," Gen. 1:27). We are able to love, to give, to communicate, to share purposes, to obey commandments, and so on. We do these things because God made us in a way that reflects his own character and the eternal relations among the persons of the Trinity (see fig. 3.1). Of course there are also differences between God the original and man the image. God is infinite and we are finite. God knows all things and we do not. Saying that human beings are God's image does not deny the differences; but it does invite us to note the analogies.

Figure 3.1. Imaging

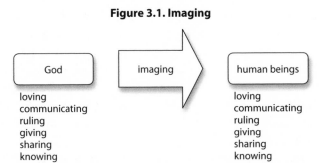

God not only has created us to be who we are but also sustains who we are. The Holy Spirit sustains human creational life, as well as redemptive life:

> The Spirit of God has made me,
>   and the *breath* of the Almighty gives me life. (Job 33:4)

> If he [God] should set his heart to it
>   and gather to himself his spirit and his breath,
> all flesh would perish together,
>   and man would return to dust. (Job 34:14–15)

God is present through his Spirit, sustaining our everyday activities of living and breathing. It follows also that he is present in sustaining and empowering our activities of loving, giving, communicating, commanding, and obeying.

God has impressed his Trinitarian character on our relationships. Whenever we interact in relationships, we rely on what he has given us. We also rely on the mutual indwelling of the persons of the Trinity. Because of this indwelling, our relationships hold together. In our relationships, we live in the presence of God, who through the Spirit gives us life and empowers us. Tacitly, we are trusting in God's faithfulness and consistency and wisdom.

This is true even when non-Christians have relationships. But they have suppressed awareness of their dependence on God, as Romans 1:19–21 indicates:

> For what can be known about God is plain to them, because God has shown it to them. For his invisible attributes, namely, his eternal power and divine nature, have been clearly perceived, ever since the creation of the world, in the things that have been made. So they are without excuse. For although they knew God, they did not honor him as God or give thanks to him, but they became futile in their thinking, and their foolish hearts were darkened.

We saw in the previous chapter that the Father expresses his love for the Son by giving the Holy Spirit. This loving relationship is the archetype or original pattern for God's relationship with human beings. Through the Son of God, God has opened the way to be reconciled to him and to have a relationship of love with him. In this relationship he has taken the initiative by showing his love to us through Christ: "God shows his love for us in that while we were still sinners, Christ died for us" (Rom. 5:8). God sends us the Spirit of Christ to enable us to respond to his love (Rom. 8:9–17). The response includes learning to listen to God's voice and learning to pray to him. In this response we reflect the love that Christ has for the Father.

Relationships among human beings also reflect divine relationships. In a human relationship one person may take the initiative. If Abe gives Bill a gift or an order, Abe is the initiator. In an unfallen world, this initiative would always be an expression of love. Abe the human initiator is like God the Father. Bill the recipient is like the Son. And the giving from one person to another that takes place in the relationship is like the Spirit. These three aspects must hold together in order for a relationship to have integrity. Abe and Bill and the actions within the relationship must all be in harmony.

Think of some of the relationships you have. First, you have a relationship with God, either broken or restored. You have a relationship with a spouse, or parents, or children, or employer. How do you conduct these relationships? You do not have the power to change the other person in any way you wish. But you do have a responsibility "to walk in love, as Christ loved us and gave himself up for us" (Eph. 5:2). You should be desiring to reflect in each relationship to another person, whether family member or friend, the harmony in love among the persons of the Trinity.

4

God's Covenants

On that day the LORD made a covenant with Abram,
saying, "To your offspring I give this land . . ."

—Genesis 15:18

The Bible indicates that in the course of history God establishes relationships with human beings. These are sometimes called *covenants*. Theologians have extensively reflected on covenants, because they embody God's redemptive plan for the human race. For our purposes, we need only to look at a few highlights that are most relevant to human relationships. The covenants express relationships between God and man. But in addition they provide significant insight into human relationships because human beings can make covenants with one another (e.g., Gen. 26:28; 31:44).

A covenant (Hebrew, *berit*) is a binding agreement between two parties. One or both of the parties commit themselves to specific obligations, and penalties or benefits may attach to keeping or violating the obligations. For example, in the covenant in Genesis 17:1–14, God required Abraham to "walk before me, and be blameless" (v. 1). God promised on his part that Abraham would be "the father of a multitude of nations" (v. 4). God also imposed the specific requirement of circumcision for Abraham and his descendants (v. 10). The uncircumcised male would forfeit his position (v. 14), which represents a penalty for violating the obligations of the covenant.

Human beings have the capacity to enter into a covenantal relation with God or with another human being. They are persons, capable of binding personal relationships. And it is clear from Genesis 1–2 that God intended from the begin-

33

ning to have a covenantal relation with human beings. God specified an obligation for Adam in Genesis 2:17 when he forbade him from eating from the tree of the knowledge of good and evil. God also indicated that the penalty for violation would be death. The relation between God and man at this point is not explicitly called a covenant, but it clearly has some of the features that characterize later covenantal arrangements. It has been called "the covenant of works."[1]

Authority, Control, and Presence

God's covenantal arrangements with human beings naturally reveal many aspects of God's character. And by implication they often reveal aspects of human character because human beings are analogically related to God through being created in his image. God shows himself to be the Lord in his relations with human beings. John Frame has observed that God's lordship expresses itself in three aspects, which he has denominated authority, control, and presence.[2]

We can illustrate these aspects by looking at God's covenant through Moses, ratified in Exodus 24. The heart of this covenant is the Ten Commandments (Ex. 20:1–17), which God delivered to Moses in written form and which Moses put inside the ark (Ex. 24:12; 25:16, 21). The ark is called "the ark of the testimony" (Ex. 25:22; 26:33) or "the ark of the covenant" (Deut. 31:25).

Meredith G. Kline observed that the Ten Commandments and the book of Deuteronomy have affinities with ancient Near Eastern treaties, specifically the Hittite suzerainty treaties.[3] God providentially brought it about that the Hittite culture would offer an analogy to his own covenantal dealings with Israel. But because he is the God of the whole universe, his covenants surpass what took place among the Hittites. The Hittite treaties had five parts: (1) the identification of the suzerain (the great king), corresponding to the language "I am the LORD your God" in Exodus 20:2a; (2) the historical prologue, reciting past benefits of the king, corresponding to Exodus 20:2b, "who brought you out of the land of Egypt, out of the house of slavery"; (3) stipulations, corresponding to the commandments

---

[1]Westminster Confession of Faith, 7.2.

[2]John M. Frame, *The Doctrine of the Knowledge of God* (Phillipsburg, NJ: Presbyterian and Reformed, 1987), 15–18. Note the reiteration of these themes elsewhere in the same volume, and in Frame, *The Doctrine of God* (Phillipsburg, NJ: P&R, 2002). See also Vern S. Poythress, *In the Beginning Was the Word: Language—A God-Centered Approach* (Wheaton, IL: Crossway, 2009), especially chap. 3, where the triad consisting of meaning, control, and presence is a variation on Frame's triad. Lanier Burns, *The Nearness of God: His Presence with His People* (Phillipsburg, NJ: P&R, 2009), focuses on the theme of presence, which is particularly important in considering our relationships. Thus his book is complementary to this one.

[3]Meredith G. Kline, *Treaty of the Great King: The Covenant Structure of Deuteronomy: Studies and Commentary* (Grand Rapids: Eerdmans, 1963); Kline, *The Structure of Biblical Authority* (Grand Rapids: Eerdmans, 1972).

themselves (Ex. 20:3–17); (4) blessings and curses, corresponding to blessings and curses attached to the second, third, and fifth commandments (Ex. 20:5–6, 7, 12); (5) provisions for public reading and for future generations, corresponding to provisions such as in Deuteronomy 27 and 31–32 (see table 4.1).

Table 4.1

Features of Hittite Suzerainty Treaties	Analogue in the Old Testament	Characteristic of God
1. Identification of suzerain	Ex. 20:2a	Presence
2. Historical prologue	Ex. 20:2b	Control
3. Stipulations	Ex. 20:3–17	Authority
4. Blessings and curses	Ex. 20:5–6, 7, 12	Control, authority
5. Provisions for reading and for passing on	Deuteronomy 31–32	Presence

The identification of the suzerain, "I am the LORD your God," indicates God's personal presence, as he presents himself to his people. It expresses the theme of presence. The provisions for future generations also imply his presence for those generations. The stipulations, the commandments, express the theme of authority. God has the right or authority to prescribe both commandments for the Israelites and consequences for their obedience or disobedience. The blessings and curses imply God's authority or right to specify consequences. But they also indicate his sovereignty over the consequences. Thus they express the theme of control. The historical prologue also expresses control, because God demonstrated his control over history in bringing the people out of Egypt.

Clearly there is some overlap between the three aspects. The blessings and curses exhibit both God's authority and his control. In fact, a deeper reflection shows that each of the three aspects implies or includes the others. The three aspects are all implications of God's lordship and his character. Authority is an implication of God's goodness and his holiness, which implies his right to set the standards for living. Control is an implication of God's omnipotence. Presence is an implication of God's omnipresence. God's attributes of goodness, omnipotence, and omnipresence operate in all that he does. So they always go together. God's presence manifests God, who always has authority and control. When God controls, he shows himself *present* in his control. His control is always rightful control and hence shows his *authority*. And so on.

All God's relations with human beings, and his relations with other creatures as well, consistently show his authority, control, and presence. We can confirm this consistency by looking at the language about covenants. The apostle Paul talks about the new covenant in 2 Corinthians 3, where he describes himself and

fellow servants of the gospel as "ministers of a new covenant" (v. 6). Such thinking shows that the entire New Testament is an expression of the new covenant.
This new covenant is analogous to but superior to the old covenant through
Moses (vv. 6–15). The core of the Mosaic covenant, as we have seen, is given in
the Ten Commandments. But these are supplemented by other material given
through Moses and then deposited beside the commandments (Deuteronomy
31). Moreover, the Mosaic covenant fulfills God's covenantal promises made
earlier to Abraham and the patriarchs (Ex. 6:4), and the prophets build on Moses
(Num. 12:6–8; Deut. 18:15–22). God makes a covenant with David as well (Ps.
89:34–37), which is the core for a larger body of instruction given in connection
with David and Solomon (Psalms, Proverbs, Ecclesiastes, Song of Solomon). The
whole Bible is covenantal communication. Some parts are explicitly described as
covenantal. And those parts that do not receive such an explicit description are
clearly linked, either by historical association or by content, with the rest.

God's covenants with human beings are also linked with his personal relationships within himself. Theologians have spoken of the "covenant of redemption."[4]
This covenant is an eternal pact or agreement between the Father and the Son,
whereby the Father undertook to send the Son into the world to accomplish
redemption, and the Son undertook to carry out the Father's will, especially in
the climax consisting in his death and resurrection. The very language of the
Father "sending" the Son implies a common purpose and understanding between
the two persons. This common purpose has been a reality forever. It implies a
commitment of the Father to the Son and the Son to the Father involving their
mutual love and commonality of purpose. The mutual commitment is clearly
analogous to the commitments we find in covenants discussed in the Bible. So the
word *covenant* can be applied to this commitment within the Trinity in order to
indicate the affinity. Or we may choose to use the word *covenant* more narrowly
to describe commitments—perhaps only formally ratified commitments—in
which human beings are one of the parties. Whether or not we want to call this
purpose of God a "covenant" or "pact," God's plan is a reality, and it is the foundation for the particular human covenants found in the Bible.

Human Commitments

The explicit covenants between God and man have a central role in the Bible.
But the Bible also recognizes that human beings as persons are capable of having
relationships of commitment among themselves, one human being to another.
Abraham made a covenant with Abimelech in Genesis 26:28. Jacob and Laban
made a covenant in Genesis 31:44. In these instances a formal pact helped to

---

[4]Louis Berkhof, *Systematic Theology* (Grand Rapids: Eerdmans, 1939), 265–67.

overcome previous distrust or alienation. But the word *covenant* can also be applied to a friendly, cooperative relationship. Malachi indicates that the relation between husband and wife is covenantal: "She is your companion and your wife *by covenant*" (Mal. 2:14). Husband and wife have made a binding commitment to be faithful to one another in marriage. Marriage is a covenant. Within a particular culture the husband and wife may have made specific vows or promises during the wedding ceremony. But even if a particular culture does not have such a practice, the commitment is implicit in the meaning of marriage, because God, not man, is the Lord of marriage. He established it in the beginning (Gen. 2:18–25). Jesus confirms God's continuing authority over marriage in his teaching: "So they are no longer two but one flesh. What therefore *God* has joined together, let not *man* separate" (Matt. 19:6; see 19:3–12).

Marriage has a particularly important role as a fundamental human relationship. But the principle of God's involvement—the principle of his presence, we might say—extends to other relationships. God is Lord of the whole world:

> The LORD has established his throne in the heavens,
> and his kingdom rules over all. (Ps. 103:19)

As Lord, he has *authority*. He specifies right and wrong in human attitudes and behavior.

In particular, because God himself is true and does not lie (Num. 23:19; John 17:17; 1 John 5:20), he expects us to be truth tellers (Eph. 4:25). The importance of truth also comes to expression in the ninth commandment, "You shall not bear false witness against your neighbor" (Ex. 20:16). If one human being makes a promise to another, he should keep it. That obligation rests not merely on human convention but on the character of God. God's authority stands behind the obligation. Human contracts, where explicit commitments are written out, are a special form of promise and commitment, and again God's authority stands behind the obligation. In a broad sense, promises and contracts are *covenantal*.

Promises and contracts include explicit moral commitments. Suppose a building contractor agrees to refurbishing my kitchen, and I agree to pay him a certain amount of money when he is finished. A contract spells out these obligations. Once we have both signed the contract, he is morally obligated to do what he promised, and I am morally obligated to pay him. Other kinds of relationships, such as friendships, telephone conversations, and participation in family sports activities, may not *explicitly* spell out particular moral commitments, but they still have a moral dimension. Human beings still should act in a loving way in the relationship.

For example, you are expected not to steal something from the grocery store by shoplifting, even though you never explicitly promised not to shoplift. Or suppose that you buy a bag of apples at the grocery store. God obliges you to pay what you owe and not to try to trick the cashier by underpaying, or by switching the label on the bag. God morally commits us not to steal but instead to respect and protect the property of our neighbors. He commits us to his standard whether we like it or not, and whether we agree with it or not.

That lack of human consent may sound harsh, but it is not. For one thing, God's moral rules are for our good. God made us and knows us. He knows us better than we know ourselves. And he knows what is best for us. In addition, the Bible indicates that each of us is created with a sense of right and wrong, and that our sense of right and wrong—our conscience—derives from our knowledge of God. "Though they [rebels] know God's decree that those who practice such things [moral evils] deserve to die, they not only do them but give approval to those who practice them" (Rom. 1:32). All people know God, inescapably:

> For what can be known about God is plain to them, because God has shown it to them. For his invisible attributes, namely, his eternal power and divine nature, have been clearly perceived, ever since the creation of the world, in the things that have been made. So they are without excuse. For although they knew God, they did not honor him as God or give thanks to him. (Rom. 1:19–21)

But they suppress what they know: ". . . men, who by their unrighteousness suppress the truth" (v. 18). We cannot here undertake a full exploration of how this can be.[5] But it implies both that people have a sense of right and wrong, and that their sense of right and wrong is distorted by their flight from knowing God. Take a particular case: I may make excuses for myself by telling myself that the grocery store overcharges, or that it belongs to a big, impersonal chain that will never miss the bit that I get away with. I may use such excuses to justify underpaying. But I am still responsible to God, according to his standards, not my distortion of his standards.

Our obligations to God and our sense of right and wrong follow us into every area of life. All of human life is morally colored. It is so colored because God is present. He is present as Lord, and his presence is tied to the original covenant made with Adam and Eve, a covenant that still binds all of us who are human. God is present in our moral sense of right and wrong. He is present as Judge, with authority to specify and rule concerning right and wrong. He is present as controller, who will reward us according to our deeds. We may therefore say that,

---

[5] I have been greatly helped by apologetics books in the tradition of "presuppositional apologetics": Cornelius Van Til, *The Defense of the Faith*, 2nd ed. (Philadelphia: Presbyterian and Reformed, 1963); John M. Frame, *Apologetics to the Glory of God: An Introduction* (Phillipsburg, NJ: P&R, 1994). See also Vern S. Poythress, *Redeeming Science: A God-Centered Approach* (Wheaton, IL: Crossway, 2006), and Poythress, *In the Beginning*, for applications to science and to language.

in a broad sense, all of life is covenantal. In all of life, including our relationships with other human beings, we have commitments to one another, and from those commitments follow both obligations and blessings or curses.

Without God, it is difficult for human beings even to articulate where moral obligations come from. Why not say that "whatever is, is right"? The philosophy of materialism, using a materialistic concept of evolution, can do little to oppose the observation that human beings can behave both altruistically at times and with extreme selfishness and murderous intent at other times. According to a materialistic concept of evolution, both are equally the product of mindless evolution. According to materialism, you may be "evolved" to prefer altruism. But your neighbor may be "evolved" to prefer selfishness. I may claim that I have been "evolved" to prefer shoplifting. If there is no transcendent source for moral standards, what are moral ideas except subjective preferences thrown up by our glands? Instinctively we know better than this. But the attempt systematically to exclude God leads to suppressing these God-given instincts.

Human Authority, Control, and Presence

Human beings made in the image of God exhibit a kind of derivative of divine authority, control, and presence. Human beings can exercise authority when they are in a position of authority. They issue commands that they expect to be obeyed. Or they can try to usurp authority even when it does not belong to them. They also show knowledge of authority when they obey someone else who has issued a command. The grocery store, as the proper owner of the bag of apples, has authority over the apples in relation to anyone else who wants to use them or eat them.

Second, human beings exercise control. Of course they can exercise control over the lower creation of animals, plants, and nonliving things. But they also exercise control in human relationships. This control need not take the form of trying totally to dominate a relationship and control it unilaterally. Human beings exercise the power of control any time they actively contribute to a relationship. Speaking, nonverbal signaling, cooperating in common work, competition in athletics, buying, selling, exchanging—these all involve active interaction with other human beings. We exert control in order to bring about our contribution to a larger relationship or social group. I take the bag of apples. I bring it to the checkout. And I offer cash or a credit card, which symbolically expresses my control over a certain amount of power to exchange goods.

Third, human beings exhibit presence. They are present to one another most obviously in the case of immediate bodily presence. Bodily presence is in fact presence of a whole person. We react to people as people, not merely as visual colors or audible sounds without meaning. And we can interact in some fruitful ways by telephone or video link even when bodily presence is lacking. Whether I personally go through the grocery checkout, or have someone else do it on my behalf, or put in a phone order or an Internet order for groceries to be delivered, the ones who give the groceries to me understand that I am the person who is entering into a purchasing transaction with moral norms. I have to deliver so much money, and the seller has to deliver a specific quantity of edible apples in good condition. The expression *have to* expresses a moral obligation that has its foundation in the justice of God.

In authority, control, and presence human beings show their finiteness. Unlike God, we do not have absolute authority, and we are not the final standard for moral goodness or justice. Unlike God, we do not exercise control exhaustively; our power is limited. Unlike God, we are not present everywhere, at all times. We have limited presence in our bodies. Man is made in the image of God, but he is not God. The Bible, unlike various forms of pantheism and panentheism,[6] maintains a clear distinction between God and human beings.

Human beings are nevertheless like God in these ways. Our authority is personal, bound up with moral standards. Our control is personal, tied in with personal purposes and understanding of the role of other persons with whom we cooperate or compete. Our presence is personal—we are present as persons who speak, think, and plan (see fig. 4.1). We are not reducible to a mere meaningless bundle of colors and sounds, mere sensation. All three aspects come to bear even in a simple transaction like buying apples.

Figure 4.1. Reflected Characteristics

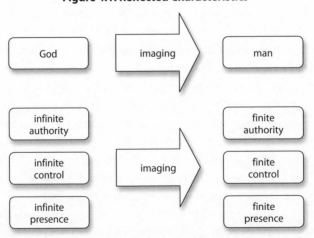

---

[6]Pantheism says that everything is God. Panentheism says that everything is "in" God. Both neglect to make a clear distinction between God and what he has made.

Human relationships depend vitally on all three of these aspects—authority, control, and presence. Without authority, we have no standard for evaluating a relationship in moral terms. In fact, we do not even have a way of classifying what *kind* of relationship we have, unless we have standards for classification. Are we dealing with marriage, friendship, a parent-child relationship, an economic, political, or educational relationship? We have to have norms in judging what kind of classification is correct.

For example, suppose Joe were caught exiting the store with a bag of apples for which he had not paid. Whether Joe is guilty depends on how we classify what he did. We have to make a judgment about it. One way of escaping obligation would be for Joe to claim that he was intending not to purchase or steal the apples but merely to admire them in the sunlight. Joe might also try to redefine the relationship he has with the store. He might say that he is a special friend of the owner, and he is sure the owner would let him just take the apples. Or he might say that despite the apples being in the store, no one really knows who owns them. Ownership, he might claim, is merely a social convention that he chose to ignore. We use norms when we evaluate arguments like these.

Second, consider the aspect of *control*. We need control. Without it, relationships do not *do* anything, and they would make no difference. I cannot accomplish a purchase of apples if I have no money or any account that represents monetary control. I cannot purchase them if I lack power to bring the apples to the checkout counter, or power to communicate to someone else who can physically help me bring them.

Finally, consider *presence*. Without presence, relationships would be disconnected from the human participants and would lose their point. A purchase is a purchase only if a person is involved. We depend on the fact that we are made in the image of God, with authority, control, and presence.

Coinherence in Human Communication

The three aspects authority, control, and presence all belong to God. But we can also see a loose association between these three aspects and the three persons of the Trinity. Authority belongs to God the Father, control to God the Son, who executes the purposes of the Father, and presence to the Holy Spirit, who indwells believers and brings the presence of God intimately to bear on their lives.[7]

The persons of the Trinity dwell in one another (see, for example, John 14:11; 17:21). This mutual indwelling is called *coinherence*. By implication, the three aspects, authority, control, and presence, belong to one another, and each implies the other. They exhibit a derivative kind of coinherence in the way in which they

---

[7]See Poythress, *In the Beginning*, chap. 3.

appear together in God. By analogy, they also have coinherence when they appear
in human relationships. For a coherent relationship even to exist, authority, control, and presence must come together coherently. You and I depend on it.

God is unique, and so the indwelling within the Godhead is also unique. But
the Trinitarian indwelling is also analogous to an indwelling in believers about
which Jesus speaks: ". . . that they [believers] may all be one, just as you, Father,
are in me, and I in you, that they also may be in us, so that the world may believe
that you have sent me" (John 17:21). Within human relationships we can see an
analogue to the unique indwelling in the Godhead. Human cooperation within
a relationship mirrors the divine unity of cooperation among the persons of the
Trinity, which is based on their coinherence.[8]

We can uncover still other ways in which human relationships reflect God in
his Trinitarian character. God is one God. But we can observe differentiation in
the roles of the persons of the Trinity in divine action. To oversimplify: God the
Father is the planner and the initiator; God the Son is the executor; and God the
Holy Spirit brings God's action to bear on its object (through his presence). We
can see that differentiation at work when we look at God speaking. The speaker
is God the Father; the speech (the Word) is associated with God the Son; and
the Holy Spirit is analogous to breath, bringing the word to bear and carrying
it to its destination.[9] Human beings made in the image of God also carry out
actions that involve plans, execution, and impact. When the plan succeeds, we
have coherence among these three.

Human relationships need human actions to support them. For example,
suppose Tammy is Carol's friend. The friendship is maintained through various
activities that involve the two. Let us say that Carol's birthday is coming up, and
Tammy gives a birthday gift to Carol. Tammy's action involves planning, execution, and reception. First, it involves planning. Tammy must have something
that she selects as a gift, or else she must make a gift or go out and purchase one.
Once Tammy has the gift in hand, the act of giving depends on Tammy having
the purpose of making a gift, not merely accidentally leaving behind some possession of hers. Second, giving involves execution. Tammy must deliver the gift.
This delivery will typically involve face-to-face explanation of its significance and
the fact that it is a gift. And the giving involves reception. For successful giving,
Carol must understand that Tammy is intending her to keep the gift rather than
just to borrow it; she must perceive that she does not have to pay Tammy for it;
and so on.

Tammy and Carol must have a common understanding of the fact of giving.
In this understanding they combine harmoniously intention, execution, and

---

[8]On coinherence, see ibid., chap. 2.
[9]See ibid.

reception. Execution intends reception. Reception of a gift is reception only if it acknowledges intention and execution. All three aspects, intention, execution, and reception, must coinhere. This coinherence depends ultimately on human capability of imitating Trinitarian coinherence in Trinitarian action.

Dorothy Sayers's View of Creativity

These reflections based on the Bible find confirmation in what Dorothy Sayers has written about artistic creation. Sayers wrote detective stories, so she had firsthand experience with artistic creation. She thought that the creation of man in the image of God was the basis for human ability to create artistic works.[10] Artistic creation imitates the creative activity of God.

Sayers finds in the process of artistic creation an analogy to the Trinitarian character of God. She observes that any act of human creation has three coinherent aspects, which she names "Idea," "Energy," and "Power." "The Creative Idea" is the idea of the creative work as a whole, even before it comes to expression. Sayers says, "This is the image of the Father."[11] "The Creative Energy" or "Activity" is the process of working out the idea, both mentally and on paper. Sayers describes it as "working in time from the beginning to the end, with sweat and passion. . . . This is the image of the Word."[12] Third is "the Creative Power," "the meaning of the work and its response in the lively soul: . . . this is the image of the indwelling Spirit."[13] Sayers uses her three terms to describe what happens within an author's mind as he works out his ideas mentally, even if they are never put to paper. In this internal process, the "Power" is the author's experience of receiving the work back, as he takes the position of an observer of his own idea and work. But Sayers also applies the terms to a work that goes out into the world, gets printed in a book, and gets read by readers. Then the readers experience its Power. At this stage, the term *Power* is obviously related most closely to the audience or readership, while the Idea is attached to the author, and the Energy or Activity to the discourse itself. Thus Sayers is advocating a variation on what we observed, namely, that the process of communication, from author to text to reader, has a Trinitarian original. Communication goes from the Father to the Word to the Spirit. Sayers also observes that each of the three aspects—Idea, Activity, and Power—is intelligible only in the context of the others. She affirms the coinherence or indwelling of each in the others.

---

[10]Dorothy L. Sayers, *The Mind of the Maker* (New York: Harcourt, Brace, 1941). See especially, "The Image of God," 19–31.

[11]Sayers, *The Mind of the Maker*, 37. The context of Sayers's work is worth reading for a fuller explanation of the distinctions among the three aspects.

[12]Ibid.

[13]Ibid., 37–38.

Sayers is thinking particularly of literary creation because that is the kind of activity in which she herself was involved. But she is aware that her observations can be generalized to apply to work of every kind.[14] Human beings in every sphere of life exercise creativity. Artistic creativity is an intense and focused form of everyday creativity. Hence, Sayers's observations about Idea, Activity, and Power apply to human work in general, and to human action in relationships. Tammy is creative when she gives her gift to Carol.

Human beings have purposes and plans—the Idea. They bring these plans to expression in particular form through actions toward others—Activity. Others receive and interpret the expressions, and in so doing experience the Power. For example, I undertake to buy a bag of apples. I have a plan, namely, to buy them and then to eat them with my family. I initiate a transaction through a series of steps in which I pick up the bag and bring it to the checkout counter. Eileen, the checkout clerk, sees the significance of my initiative and responds in harmony with the power that I put forth when I invite a response. Eileen in turn has Idea, Activity, and Power. Idea: she has a plan for helping me and others do our purchases and making sure that the store receives payment. Activity: she takes the bag and scans the label or in some other way enters the price. Power: she desires to accomplish effects. One effect is the monetary effect of transferring money from my account to the store. The other is an effect on me, namely, to cause me to acquire the apples, to have me understand that I have paid for them, and to be secure in the knowledge that they are mine. The two of us together must both have Idea, Activity, and Power. We two are not doing the very same thing. I am buying and she is the representative of the store that is doing the selling. But our Ideas, Activities, and Powers must be complementary in a detailed way in order for the buying and selling to succeed.

The exchange of apples is admittedly a prosaic exchange. But it depends in a deep and essential way on harmony and coinherence. It is an imitation or shadow or image of what we might call the ultimate exchange, the exchange of the gift of the Spirit from the Father to the Son: "He [the Father] gives the Spirit without measure. The Father loves the Son and has given [exchange] all things into his hand" (John 3:34–35). This exchange is the archetype. In accomplishing the redemption of the world, God also executed some subordinate exchanges. Christ bore our sins: "He himself [Christ] bore our sins in his body on the tree, that we might die to sin and live to righteousness. By his wounds you have been healed" (1 Pet. 2:24; see Isa. 53:5). The Father and the Son have different roles in this transaction. But their purposes are in coinherent harmony.

This divine harmony is then reflected at a lower, creational level in everyday human transactions. Human transactions do not work without harmony of

---

[14]Ibid., chap. 11.

many kinds: between Idea, Activity, and Power; between authority, control, and presence; between the contributions of one human being and the complementary contributions of another, as in the instance of buyer and seller together. These harmonies exist because man is made in the image of God. More fundamentally, they exist because God is in harmony with himself in his Trinitarian character. Out of that harmony he governs the world and its human inhabitants in harmony.

Harmony in Human Relationships, Due to God

Humans are limited; they are finite. The limitations might appear to be a problem if human beings had to make themselves self-existent, autonomous, and totally independent of God. How then could they guarantee that human relationships, in their authority, control, and presence, would function reliably? For example, how can we know that my purchase of the apples matches the purpose of the checkout clerk and the grocery story owner, and how can we know whether it is morally upright? In a God-created world, a world that God pronounced "very good" (Gen. 1:31), we know there is harmony. First of all, human beings were created to be in personal harmony with God. But in addition, God gave them the gift of relationships in complete harmony with who they were. He made the world of light and dry land and plants and animals in harmony with human nature.

A human being's knowledge of his own personal relationships is finite. He cannot remember in detail how he learned to buy a bag of apples and how he knows what the grocery clerk intends. He does not see to the very bottom. But he does not need to see to the very bottom. The key to a solution is in his personal fellowship with God. Before the fall of man and his rebellion against God, there was no barrier to personal fellowship between God and man. Adam knew God. He heard the word of God. And the sense of God's presence and God's goodness was imprinted firmly on his mind. He relied on God and trusted that God was good. And so he could confidently assume that the relationships that God gave him, and the world of his environment, were suitable for him. He could go forward in confidence not because he was omnipotent, omniscient, and omnipresent, but because God as the infinite God guaranteed the harmony of Adam's finite functioning in dependence on God.

The meanings in Adam's relationships were not meanings imposed on alien material but meanings from a mind made in the image of God, and therefore a mind in tune with the world. Adam's control in his relationships was not a distortion of the world but creative action that drew the world toward the destiny planned by God from the beginning. The presence of relationships, both with one another and with God, was not something that Adam and Eve could "climb out of" to see the world as it really is. But they did not need to climb out of it, because, on the basis of the good creating activity of God, they were already in harmony with the world as it really is. In short, difficulties that some of us modern human beings may feel very keenly, because we are alienated from God, created no substantive difficulty while human beings lived in fellowship with God—in harmony with him, with the world that he had created, and with the relationships that he had given.

Relationships as Shared

A particular human relationship involves more than one person. Other persons outside a relationship can observe and grasp what sort of relationship it is and learn how to interact with it appropriately. Relationships have a communal dimension built into them. Sociological and anthropological analyses have customarily paid attention to the community of human beings. But the Bible presents an important difference. It begins not with a human relationship but with God as the original, the Creator before whom human beings stand and with whom they have a deep relationship.

The very first recorded activity with human persons also involves God. God addresses human beings in Genesis 1:28–30 and 2:16–17. Adam and Eve experience relationships not only with each other but also with God. From the beginning, as part of God's design for creation, personal relationships include divine-human relationships as well as human-human relationships. "Society," from this point of view, includes God as well as human beings. Tellingly, there was divine-human communication in relationship even before human-human communication was possible. God communicated to Adam in Genesis 2:16–17 before Eve was created, before Adam had any other human being with whom he had a relationship. So the human capacity for relationships is not merely for human beings but for relationship with God.

God would have continued in a harmonious relationship with Adam and Eve over the years if they had not sinned. They did sin and thereby broke the relationship. They hid rather than seeking God (Gen. 3:8). Even though they did sin, God spoke a promise and thereby partially restored a relationship (Gen. 3:9–19). God continued in a personal relationship with Adam and Eve. At first the community of persons had three parties, Adam and Eve and God. When Adam and Eve had children, God had personal relationships with these children, either in a friendly way, in the case of Abel, or in an antagonistic way, in the case of Cain. God is infinitely superior to human beings, but he also continues to act in relationships to human beings. In this sense, God is part of the community or society in which human beings live in relationships.

Modern Approaches to Society

We may contrast this view with most modernist and postmodernist thinking about society.[15] In the twentieth century sociological and anthropological study of human societies has assumed, as a foundation for the discipline, that God can be left out of the account (see appendix B). Sociology and anthropology may of course study "religion" as one aspect of society. But this study focuses on human practice of religion, not on God himself.

Why this exclusion of God? One response would be to say that only by such an exclusion could these disciplines hope to be scientific. But the aspiration to be scientific is itself loaded. To begin with, it may be loaded with the assumption that somehow human beings can be treated exactly as if they were on the same level as animals or rocks or other creatures over which human beings are granted dominion. It ignores the fact that we are made in the image of God.

But even more seriously, the label *scientific* ignores the possibility that our modern conception of science, taken from the existing state of the natural sciences, has already been distorted by a systematic human flight from recognizing the presence of God in science.[16] The aspiration to be "scientific" may already have introduced biases. So, according to this modernist viewpoint, God is emphatically not a participant in social communication and personal relationships. But from a biblical point of view, the move to exclude God ignores the single most important fact about communication and the most weighty ontological fact about language. When we exclude God, we distort the subject matter that we study, so we can anticipate a multitude of repercussions when it comes to the detailed analysis of the subject.

So let us remember that God is involved in all our relationships, whether in friendships, in giving gifts, in purchasing apples, or in other kinds of relationships. We are accountable to God. Let us also remember that any harmonious functioning in relationships depends on the foundational harmony of God's relationships among the persons of the Trinity.

---

[15] See appendices A, B, and G; also Poythress, *In the Beginning*, appendix A.
[16] Poythress, *Redeeming Science*.

5

God Sustaining Relationships

The LORD has established his throne in the heavens,
and his kingdom rules over all.

—Psalm 103:19

Now let us look at God's relation to the present day and its processes. God's faithfulness guarantees that there will be a stability to the things that he has created. And this stability extends to human beings. We have the same bodies and the same memories from one day to the next—though, of course, there are also gradual changes. One aspect of this stability is that we are persons with the capacity to enter into personal relationships and to maintain them. God's governance over our world extends even to details:

> You [God] cause the grass to grow for the livestock
> and plants for man to cultivate. (Ps. 104:14)

Scientists explore the regular patterns in God's governance, regularities that are based on God's faithfulness and consistency.[1] God controls even seemingly random events:

> The lot is cast into the lap,
> but its every decision is from the LORD. (Prov. 16:33;
> see also 1 Kings 22:20, 34)

---

[1]See Vern S. Poythress, *Redeeming Science: A God-Centered Approach* (Wheaton, IL: Crossway, 2006), especially chap. 1, pp. 13–31, and chaps. 13–14, pp. 177–95.

God controls everything:

> The LORD has established his throne in the heavens,
>   and his kingdom rules over all. (Ps. 103:19)

> Who has spoken and it came to pass,
>   unless the Lord has commanded it?
> Is it not from the mouth of the Most High
>   that good and bad come? (Lam. 3:37–38)

We can conclude, then, that God's control extends to personal relationships as well, and to their details. God controls my relationship to him. He also controls the transaction in which I bought a bag of apples.

God's control over human affairs does raise a concern. How can God's control be consistent with human responsibility and human sin? The Bible nowhere fully explains how, but it does show that God is in control of human affairs. In the first sermon in the book of Acts, Peter declares, "This Jesus, delivered up according to the definite plan and foreknowledge of God, you crucified and killed by the hands of lawless men" (Acts 2:23). The expression "the definite plan and foreknowledge of God" indicates that God brought about all the events in accordance with his plan. The mention of "lawless men" indicates, however, that human beings like Herod, Pontius Pilate, and the Jewish leaders who brought about the crucifixion were responsible for their unjust deeds. God brought about salvation through Christ's crucifixion, and his purposes were wholly good. The human beings had evil motives. Acts 4:27–28 expresses similar principles: "For truly in this city there were gathered together against your holy servant Jesus, whom you anointed, both Herod and Pontius Pilate, along with the Gentiles and the peoples of Israel, to do whatever your hand and your plan had predestined to take place."

There are two levels of action here. Theologians have classically spoken of "primary cause" and "secondary cause." God as Creator and Ruler is the primary cause of the events of Christ's crucifixion. Human beings like Pilate acted on the level of secondary cause. Both of the two are real and valid. But they are not on the same level, as though God were merely another human being, with greater power, who wrestled with the other human beings in order to force things to go his way instead of their way. No, God as Creator is simply not on the level of his creatures. We are not able fully to conceptualize how he acts because we are finite and he is infinite.

We also need to distinguish between God's *decretive will* and his *preceptive will*. The *decretive will* expresses God's plan for whatever happens (including evil events like the crucifixion of Christ). His *preceptive will* expresses his moral character, as in the Ten Commandments. The injustices of Pilate were contrary to God's preceptive will. The case with the crucifixion of Christ shows that the distinction between these two kinds of authoritative will in God is valid.

We could discuss these matters at much greater length, but we must leave that to other books.[2] It is enough for the present for us to understand that God's control does not undermine the genuineness of human participation and human responsibility.

Authority, Good and Bad

We should briefly consider one other issue related to God's control. Nowadays many Americans and Europeans distrust authority. And they have some good reasons for distrust. Parents, politicians, governments, employers, advertisers, and religious leaders have grievously disappointed them. People with power have run roughshod over those under them. God is the biggest authority of all. So is his authority the most dangerous?

In one sense, yes. People can falsely appeal to God's authority in order to manipulate others. Such manipulation is particularly dangerous because people claiming to have God's authority can try to make their ideas and actions unchallengeable. Manipulation can then be all the more oppressive. But such manipulation misuses God's name.

So what should we do? Should we repudiate all authority? That is one temptation. But if we abolished governmental authorities, those who are powerful would have no governmental restraint and might further exploit the weak. Rather, we should respond by seeking good exercise of authority in order to drive out the bad. God is the ultimate good authority. But as fallen humans we start out with distorted ideas about God and distorted hopes for what we think is a good life. We have been disappointed in God because we do not know or understand or love him. I cannot here undertake to address every aspect of this disappointment with God and this alienation from him. A classic book from Billy Graham, *Peace with God*, has helped many.[3] Many other books that explain the teaching of the Bible could be cited. And of course there is the Bible itself, which I would recommend if you are struggling in this area. At the heart of the Bible is the record of Christ's life, found in the four Gospels, Matthew, Mark, Luke, and John. Knowing Christ enables us to know God as he really is and to overcome our alienation from him.

---

[2]For further discussion of God's sovereignty and providential control, see ibid., 181–83, 193–95; John M. Frame, *The Doctrine of God* (Phillipsburg, NJ: P&R, 2002), 47–79; and other Reformed theological books on God.
[3]Billy Graham, *Peace with God* (Waco, TX: Word, 1984).

6

Creativity in Relationships

Behold, the former things have come to pass,
and new things I now declare;
before they spring forth
I tell you of them.

—Isaiah 42:9

Human relationships involve creativity, and this creativity derives from God. Let us look at creativity more closely because it is an emphasis complementary to the fact that God is in control.

Creativity among Human Beings

Creativity is an important aspect of human life. As we indicated in Chapter 4, Dorothy Sayers sees a clear analogy between God's activity as Creator and the human creativity of an artist. Because we are made in the image of God, we are made to be creative, each of us in his own sphere. None of us is a carbon copy of anyone else. And we all meet challenges in our circumstances that have never before appeared in exactly the same way. When I purchase a bag of apples, I purchase one particular bag, and no one has ever done it before, with that bag in that circumstance.

Challenges arise about how to deal both with people and with material things in the environment. God expects us to be creative in meeting those challenges: "Look carefully then how you walk, not as unwise but as wise, making the best use of the time, because the days are evil. Therefore do not be foolish, but understand what the will of the Lord is. And do not get drunk with wine, for that is debauchery, but be filled with the Spirit" (Eph. 5:15–18).

God gives us moral rules for living, as summarized in the Ten Commandments. But his commandments call for application to our specific circumstances, and in the application we need God's wisdom to be insightful about the circumstances and to be creative in exercising love.[1] Human creativity, rightly understood, does not produce tension with God's rules but acts in harmony with the rules in reaching out to new situations and needs. God's rules and God's creativity are in harmony, and so likewise it ought to be with us. Being filled with the Holy Spirit, the very Spirit of God, gives us power from God both to keep his rules and to be creative, with the creativity that the Holy Spirit brings.

For example, consider Tammy's friendship with Carol. Tammy understands that being Carol's friend implies being thoughtful about Carol's needs and looking for ways to express love. Those are norms deriving from God's commandment to love our neighbors as ourselves. Tammy then gets a creative idea for a home-made birthday card or a gift. The gift expresses both Tammy's creativity and the general principle of love.

Creativity in Relationships

Creativity has a place in human relationships. In interacting with one another, we rely on a cultural context in which we share understandings of meaning. My action in bringing my bag of apples to a grocery checkout counter has a meaning supplied by a common understanding that the grocery store offers goods for sale, that the checkout counter is the proper place to make payment, and that I and the checkout clerk each have customary actions to perform.

But we also exercise creativity. We say things that have never been said before. I select a bag of apples that I have never selected before. My attitude of grumpiness or friendliness or happiness or praise to God becomes a part of what I do in my transaction. But more fundamentally, I can make choices about what stores I go to, and what kinds of relationships I enter. The relation to a grocery clerk may be stereotyped within fairly narrow bounds for the sake of economic efficiency. But friendships, marriages, educational classrooms, and some other kinds of relationships have considerable scope for creativity and individual expression. Communication in language has enormous scope for creativity.[2]

---

[1] See John M. Frame, *The Doctrine of the Christian Life* (Phillipsburg, NJ: P&R, 2008), especially with regard to the perspectival relation among rules (normative perspective), situations (situational perspective), and motives (love, the existential perspective). The existential perspective shows the value of human creativity.

[2] See Vern S. Poythress, *In the Beginning Was the Word: Language—A God-Centered Approach* (Wheaton, IL: Crossway, 2009), chap. 6.

God has provided all the richness of the millions of choices before us. Without his presence and his action, there would be no choice in language, no choice in types of relationships; more fundamentally still, there would be no human beings to make the choices. Human beings really do make these choices, minute by minute, day after day, every time they act. Their choices are real and significant. Sometimes the significance of any one choice may seem very small. But it is there, and God sees it.

> For a man's ways are before the eyes of the LORD,
>   and he ponders all his paths. (Prov. 5:21)

Sometimes the choices are weighty:

> "And if it is evil in your eyes to serve the LORD, choose this day whom you will serve, whether the gods your fathers served in the region beyond the River, or the gods of the Amorites in whose land you dwell. But as for me and my house, we will serve the LORD." . . . And the people said to Joshua, "No, but we will serve the LORD." Then Joshua said to the people, "You are witnesses against yourselves that you have chosen the LORD, to serve him." And they said, "We are witnesses." (Josh. 24:15, 21–22)

This creativity is closely related to the motif of control. We exercise control by choosing to say or do one thing and not another. Our ability to control reflects God's ability. It is God, first of all, who chooses to act creatively. He created this world and not another. He chose to create horses but not unicorns. His creativity is the basis for our own lesser creativity. Interestingly, his creativity is not at odds with his control. Rather, it illustrates his control.

God's creativity is rooted in his Trinitarian character. Passages such as John 5:19 show the Son during his incarnate state exactly carrying out the will of the Father. Hebrews 1:3 and John 1:1 imply that, even before his incarnation, the Son exactly conformed to the Father's will. In addition, the Father's actions and choices harmonize with his love for the Son. The Father purposes to glorify the Son (John 8:54; 13:31–32; 17:1–5), and to sum up all things in him (Eph. 1:10, 22). The Son purposes to glorify the Father (John 17:4). Thus two things go together in the Trinity: (1) The Son has the infinite creativity of God himself; and (2) the Son has infinite conformity to the will of his Father. These are both true whenever the Son acts.

How can this be so? We do not fully know, because we are describing the infinitude of God himself. But we know that it is so. And we can to some extent even see how it is so. The Father delights in the Son and in honoring the Son. The Son delights in the Father, and so delights in his Father's will. He has no attraction to any kind of independence that would do otherwise. "Jesus said to them, 'My food is to do the will of him who sent me and to accomplish his work'" (John 4:34). The Father and the Son are in everlasting harmony, in the presence of the Holy Spirit. Their harmony is an expression of the theme of presence. The conformity of the Son is also an expression of the theme of control—control by the Father. The Father as God sovereignly controls all things, including the actions of the Son in history. The Son as sovereign God freely decides and creatively acts, and his actions are always in harmony with the Father. We affirm the control of the Father and also the creative activity on the part of the Son.

The Son in His Humanity

Now let us begin to think about human decision making. The Son during his time on earth honored the Father in both his divine and human natures. The will of the divine Son was in full conformity to the will of his Father, and the will of his human nature submitted to the will of the Father, even when it took him to the cross:

> And going a little farther he fell on his face and prayed, saying, "My Father, if it be possible, let this cup pass from me; nevertheless, not as I will, but as you will." . . . Again, for the second time, he went away and prayed, "My Father, if this cannot pass unless I drink it, your will be done." (Matt. 26:39, 42)

> For this reason the Father loves me, because I lay down my life that I may take it up again. No one takes it from me, but I lay it down of my own accord. I have authority to lay it down, and I have authority to take it up again. This charge I have received from my Father. (John 10:17–18)

> "Now is my soul troubled. And what shall I say? 'Father, save me from this hour'? But for this purpose I have come to this hour. Father, glorify your name." Then a voice came from heaven: "I have glorified it, and I will glorify it again." (John 12:27–28)

Jesus is fully man as well as fully God. He had to be fully man in order to represent us as the last Adam and to be our sin-bearer. And he had to be a willing sin-bearer: "When he was reviled, he did not revile in return; when he suffered, he did not threaten, but continued entrusting himself to him who judges justly. He himself bore our sins in his body on the tree, that we might die to sin and live to righteousness" (1 Pet. 2:23–24). Jesus freely entered into the path that the Father laid before him. Through his work he brought into being a "new creation" (2 Cor. 5:17). At the same time, his path of suffering and the coming of new creation had been prophesied beforehand, in Isaiah 53 and other passages that predicted his sufferings and subsequent glory (Isa. 53:11–12; 59:19; 60:1; 65:17).

Human Creativity in Harmony with God

Among other things, Jesus offers a model for understanding human creativity. His work was unique. He alone was able to begin the new creation by rising from the dead. But in an analogous way we too can be creative as we enter into fellowship with him. The key to creativity is fellowship with God, who is the unique Creator. Jesus brought forth the new creation of eternal life by being in fellowship with the Father, obeying the will of the Father, and being filled with the Holy Spirit (Rom. 8:11; Acts 2:33). Through Jesus we have our fellowship restored with God (2 Cor. 5:18). Then we can be creative, in imitation of God's creativity. We are stimulated because we begin to understand God, and the vastness of God's mind opens up new directions and new thoughts. We blossom as whole people who are no longer slaves to sin (Rom. 6:20–21). And if we blossom as whole people, we blossom in our relationships as well. We learn to be creative in relationships because through renewal in the Holy Spirit we become creative in what we think. "God's love has been poured into our hearts through the Holy Spirit who has been given to us" (Rom. 5:5). The creativity of one human being in a relationship stimulates the creativity of his fellows.

By contrast, those who rebel against God like to think that creativity comes from being independent of him. But such independence is nothing more than slavery to sin (Rom. 6:20–21).

God planned beforehand the earthly life of Christ, as is evident from the way in which it fulfills many Old Testament texts. Jesus talks repeatedly about what "must" take place (Matt. 16:21; 26:54; Luke 24:26). So it is with us, by analogy. All our days are planned by God beforehand:

> In your book were written, every one of them,
>> the days that were formed for me,
>> when as yet there were none of them. (Ps. 139:16)

God planned our good works beforehand: "For we are his workmanship, created in Christ Jesus for good works, which God prepared beforehand, that we should walk in them" (Eph. 2:10). Such planning on God's part is consistent with creative human action. Jesus willingly obeyed his Father and carried out his will. He made decisions throughout his life, decisions to follow God's way rather than a selfish way. We see his creativity in the unexpected ways that he dealt with social outcasts. We see it also in the way that he rejected the typical worldly routes to power and was willing to go to the cross.

The analogy between God and a human creative artist can perhaps be helpful. If a human creative artist writes a novel, he commissions the characters in the novel to act creatively, in accordance with the personalities that they possess by virtue of his creative activity. The characters creatively make decisions and produce consequences. At the same time, the author controls the entire novel. The analogy is imperfect, but it points back to the deeper reality in which God the Father commissions his Son to make choices, and these choices always harmonize with the Father's plan. We too are called to obey willingly. The good works are prepared "that we should walk in them." In fact, the presence of God encourages and empowers our working:

> Therefore, my beloved, as you have always obeyed, so now, not only as in my presence but much more in my absence, work out your own salvation with fear and trembling, for it is God who works in you, both to will and to work for his good pleasure. (Phil. 2:12–13)

> Therefore, my beloved brothers, be steadfast, immovable, always abounding in the work of the Lord, knowing that in the Lord your labor is not in vain. (1 Cor. 15:58)

Among these good works are the good works in our personal relationships. We can become creative in enhancing relationships and bringing a blessing to those around us.

7

Exploring Examples of Relationships

The wicked borrows but does not pay back
but the righteous is generous and gives.

—Psalm 37:21

W hat does God's involvement with human interaction look like? We can illustrate by returning to a simple example.

A Sample of Interaction

Suppose I go the grocery store, pick a bag of apples off a display tray, and go to a checkout counter. I put the bag on the conveyor belt, and the checkout clerk passes it by a bar-code reader. I give a credit card to the clerk. The clerk returns the card and hands me a receipt. I put the apples into a grocery bag and depart from the store with the bag in hand.

Such purchases have become routine to many people in postindustrial cultures. But they involve complexities. We have a series of human actions in a particular order. All of these actions have particular meaning for human beings, which they would not have if done by an animal. All the actions are oriented around a process of purchasing, which an animal does not understand. The purposes in the individual human actions fit together in the overall purpose of the purchase.

Both Eileen, the checkout clerk, and I understand the significance of the bag of apples. I am buying them because I know what they are good for. Eileen knows that the apples belong to the store until we complete the transaction. She also knows that the store owner and manager have particular procedures for their clerks to follow so that the store will not lose money accidentally or by theft.

Eileen's actions have to synchronize not only with my actions, but also with the store's policies, where several people interact in a complex business relationship. I in turn understand that Eileen is not just a fellow shopper but an authorized representative of the store. If I pay Eileen at the counter, I do not expect the owner of the store to complain that I have not paid him personally, face-to-face.

Eileen and I also have to have a common understanding concerning whatever means I use to make a payment: cash, check, money order, credit card, debit card. Or will it be barter? Barter—that is, direct exchange of one set of goods for another, not using money—is common in some societies. But my grocery store expects money as the medium.

Complex meanings attach to the different methods of buying and selling. I have to share these meanings with the clerk and with the store as a whole. The transaction would not succeed if I offered French money and the store insisted on United States money, or if it did not recognize my money as money at all. What if the store does not accept credit cards?

Buying things is so natural to us that we typically do not think about all the knowledge and all the kinds of organization of human relationships on which we are relying. Once we look under the surface, however, we find astonishing complexity and astonishing detail in structure. This complexity has been established by God, as part of his overall plan for the universe and our role in it.

God's Involvement in Human Relationships

Consider the credit card in my hand. It has meaning and shape and embedded electronic information that God has given it. It also has a history behind it. It was produced by a manufacturing process. And the principles for credit card use have a twentieth-century history of development. The credit card also has a history in my personal life. I had to acquire this particular card by a series of steps, interacting with the company responsible for issuing the card. And I had to learn about credit cards and their functions as I grew up. I learned their meaning by watching others use cards and by explanations from parents or others. Thus human beings had a decisive role. Both my parents and my immediate friends, as well as the credit card company with its explanations, had a role in transmitting meaning to me. God sovereignly ruled over and controlled all these events in my past and the past of others who transmitted the meaning.

It is important to say so. Otherwise, instead of thinking in terms of the God of the Bible, we will probably be thinking in terms of an absentee god, for example the god of deism. Deism says that a god created the world and set it going at the beginning. But after that he is distant and essentially uninvolved. The world goes on simply by itself, like a clock that has been wound up and can then keep on ticking. The god of deism would be involved in our present-day human relationships only in a very indirect way, through his act of creating the world in the very distant past.

The God of the Bible, by contrast, is intimately involved with the world at all times, including the present. He is personal and immanent. As primary cause he is the one who has controlled the way in which I learned about credit cards from my parents, as well as a card's present meaning. God also gave me and other human beings the capacity to use a card. He gave me hands that can manipulate the card, motor skill to write my signature, and a mind to understand the significance of my signature and the card.

We rely on all these stabilities every time we use a credit card. God has charge not only of individual items like the credit card, but of entire transactions like the purchase of the apples. The items and the human actions fit together in a particular way, designed by God, in order to make a complete transaction. There are smaller pieces within the transaction that have an identifiable unity of their own, such as my putting the apples on the conveyor belt, and my signing the printed receipt. Ordinarily we take for granted the existence and stability of these pieces. But they can be a source for praising God. God gives us this stability. "Thank you," we can say. God gives us the resources for buying and selling and the accomplishments that come with these transactions. God is always there, always faithful, always wise, always supplying and sustaining both our bodies and our mental resources, as well as our resources for human relationship. God is involved in the details. He gave me the credit card and empowers my action in purchasing.

Perspectives on Relationships: The Wave Perspective

We have been looking at human interaction as composed of stable pieces. It depends on stable objects like a bag of apples or a credit card. From another point of view, a process of buying and selling is composed of smaller actions, such as swiping the credit card, signing the receipt, and taking up the apples in order to depart. This way of looking at human actions as composed of stable pieces is a valid one. The linguist Kenneth L. Pike has dubbed it the "particle view."[1] Within

---

[1] "The normal, relaxed attitude of the human being in most of his actions treats life as if it were made of particles" (Kenneth L. Pike, *Linguistic Concepts: An Introduction to Tagmemics* [Lincoln: University of Nebraska Press, 1982], 19). Pike's approach to language and linguistics, though not as familiar as some other approaches, is congenial to my purposes. For one thing, it explicitly acknowledges the relation of language to a larger context of human behavior, and many of its tools are designed to be useful in looking at human behavior as well as language (Pike, *Language in Relation to a Unified Theory of the Structure of Human Behavior*, 2nd ed. [Paris: Mouton, 1967]). Second, it acknowledges the importance of multiple perspectives and, in so doing, avoids reducing human action to a single one of its dimensions. I learned from personal conversations that Pike was also convinced that language contains reflections of the Trinitarian character of God. The three perspectives that we introduce here are one instance of this pattern.

academic linguistics this perspective has its uses, but there are times when linguists may adopt other perspectives, specifically the "wave" perspective or the "field" perspective.[2] These perspectives can be applied not only to language use but also to other human actions such as buying and selling.

What do these perspectives do? The wave perspective looks at human action not primarily in terms of stable pieces but also in terms of process. According to this approach, human action is dynamic. As I am buying the apples, I move gradually through the checkout line, one motion leading smoothly into another. I may be getting my credit card out of my pocket at the same time that I am depositing the apples on the conveyor belt. Even small pieces of action like signing the receipt can be broken down into a whole series of hand and finger motions. The signature gradually gets written out in a process.

And of course all these small-scale actions fit the larger purposes that we have in life. I bought the apples because we need food to sustain us, in order to carry on all kinds of activities in work, leisure, child rearing, and socializing. My particular purchase makes sense within a much larger, richer complex of human knowledge, intentions, and plans, and those in turn make sense within a world in which apples are good for food.

God is in control of all these processes. God specifies the stabilities of the pieces, as we have seen with regard to the particle perspective. He also specifies the processes. He has designed the world so that one event flows into another, and so that actions have consequences. In fact, "control" is a process in the usual way in which we think about it. God acts and causes things to happen in the world. He causes one thing, and then another thing, and then another, as the primary cause. At the same time, there are these secondary causes in human actions and even in subhuman actions, as when one billiard ball hits another. God controls the little actions, like my writing out my signature. He controls the bigger actions, like my going to the store. He controls still bigger sequences, namely, entire lifetimes:

> . . . in your book were written, every one of them,
>   the days that were formed for me,
>   when as yet there were none of them. (Ps. 139:16)

God knows all my days, including the days that are still future and unknown to me. By implication, he knows all the details in the days. He knows about each bite of food that I will eat, each time of distress or joy, each work of each cell in my intestines in the process of digestion, each work of each muscle cell in the beating of each heartbeat, each movement of my vocal chords, each movement of my tongue in making a speech.

---

[2]Pike, *Linguistic Concepts*, 19–38.

For his dominion is an everlasting dominion,
    and his kingdom endures from generation to generation;
all the inhabitants of the earth are accounted as nothing,
    and he does according to his will among the host of heaven
    and among the inhabitants of the earth;
and none can stay his hand
    or say to him, "What have you done?" (Dan. 4:34–35)

The Most High rules the kingdom of men and gives it to whom he will. (Dan. 4:32)

There is a God in heaven who reveals mysteries, and he has made known to King Nebuchadnezzar what will be in the latter days [concerning several successive kingdoms over a period of hundreds of years]. (Dan. 2:28)

The Field Perspective

A third way of looking at human interaction is the field perspective. We focus on the network or "field" of relations between various parts of human interaction. The relations are of many kinds. My signature is related in meaning to other people's signatures and to the larger cultural understanding of how signatures authenticate identity. The sale of apples has relations of similarity to sales of other kinds of groceries. Both the clerks and the customers follow common patterns in executing sales. Sales made to me as a customer have similarities to sales to other customers. In short, any one particular sale enjoys a pattern of relations to other sales.

If we like, we can represent some of the patterns of relations by constructing a grid with several dimensions, one for each type of variation in the common pattern of sales. For example, we can draw up a grid where we compare in one dimension different items for sale, and in the other dimension the clerks involved in the sale (see table 7.1). We could add a third dimension where we list different customers who are buying.

Table 7.1

	Joe	Mary	Eileen
apples	Joe sells apples.	Mary sells apples.	Eileen sells apples.
pork chops	Joe sells pork chops.	Mary sells pork chops.	Eileen sells pork chops.

We can also look at ways in which we classify items for sale in a grocery store (see table 7.2).

Table 7.2

	Canned	Frozen	Fresh
fruit			
vegetable			
meat			
fish			
dairy			
drink			

Or take a look at a credit card. My credit card is related to other credit cards, both from the same credit card company and from other companies, by the general pattern for the significance and use of credit cards. And it is related to the larger field of meaning in which monetary amounts are transferred by indirect means.

Again we can explore some of the relations through a multidimensional plot. Is a card a credit card or a debit card? Who is the issuing company (Bank of America, Citibank, etc.)? To which major type of card does it belong? Is it VISA, MasterCard, American Express, or Discover? To whom is the card issued? To how many users is the card issued (a single individual, or perhaps one card for each member of a family)? What is the credit limit? What is the expiration date? What are the penalties and what is the interest rate on unpaid balances? And so on.

Those who use credit cards know all these dimensions. Or at least they can become familiar with them when they run into trouble with a merchant who will not take American Express or when they get penalties for late payment. This knowledge is not simply an isolated piece of information but has a close relation to information about how to use credit cards other than the one a person has in hand. If you think about it, this is a very good thing. It would be burdensome, and in the end impossible, to master a distinct set of rules for Bank of America credit cards, and another set for Chase credit cards, and so on. We depend on regularities to save us from this tedium. In effect, we learn a single set of rules about how to use a credit card.

Of course there may be tantalizing variations that do not reduce completely to general rules. One card may earn gift points, while another does not. But much is the same from one card to another. God sovereignly specifies all these relations. Just as he rules over the processes that are the focus of the wave perspective, so he rules over the relations of the field perspective. Likewise, all the pieces in personal interaction and relationships, all the "particles," have a relation to God. They are what they are in relation to him. Since he is the origin of all meaning and all order, everything that exists is sustained in relation to him. Likewise, the processes are related to him as the giver of processes, and the relations between various pieces depend on him. All order in personal interaction derives from God's having given order. And so, relations to God are an indispensable aspect in accounting for any particular thing. When we study personal interaction, we are uncovering a display of the wisdom that God has in giving us this stable, complex, and flexible arena for our use. (Thank you, God!) We can praise God for his wisdom, and for his generosity and goodness in giving us the power of personal interaction.

Three Interlocking Perspectives

So we have three distinct perspectives on personal interaction, namely, the particle, wave, and field perspectives. These three perspectives are an image of the Trinity.[3] The particle perspective is closely related to stability, which is established by the unchanging stability of the plan of the Father. The wave perspective is closely related to the controlling work of the Son, who brings about action in history: "He upholds the universe by the word of his power" (Heb. 1:3). The field perspective is closely related to the Spirit's presence. Whenever we relate two pieces in human interaction to one another, we conceive of them as simultaneously present in mind, and often even as simultaneously present in space, as we lay them side by side in a pattern. The Spirit, as present to us and indwelling us who are believers in Christ (Rom. 8:9–11), expresses God's relation to us.

Accordingly, the three perspectives on personal interaction—particle, wave, and field—are coinherent. Each of the three perspectives can be applied to any part of personal interaction. They are complementary to one another and interlocking. For example, the field perspective depends on the fact that there are distinct pieces, like buying apples and buying beans, that enjoy a relation to one another. That is, the field perspective depends on the "particles," on the stable pieces. It depends also on the fact that, as analysts, we can move from one set of relations to another. This movement is itself a "wave" made by the analyst. We shift, for example, from considering the relation of frozen corn to canned corn to considering the relation of frozen ham to canned ham.

Similarly, the particle perspective depends on the field perspective. Any one piece of human interaction, like buying apples, is identified for what it is partly through its distinctive character: buying apples rather than beans, and buying rather than selling. It is related to other human actions that are similar to it or that contrast with it. And knowing about the process of buying involves knowing how to use it in practice, which is a wave process. We depend on the reality of actual examples in the process of learning how to buy.

---

[3]See Vern S. Poythress, *In the Beginning Was the Word: Language—A God-Centered Approach* (Wheaton, IL: Crossway, 2009), chap. 7.

The wave perspective likewise depends on the particle perspective. Movement from one activity to another becomes perceptible as movement precisely because there are stable endpoints. When I have collected the last item to put in my cart, the process of collecting the items is done. "Being done" is a stable endpoint. I then commence the activity of checking out. I go from one point (where I picked up the apples) to another (the checkout counter). The movement is easy to analyze because it has two stable endpoints. The endpoints can be identified as distinct wholes, as pieces. They are stable, that is, particles. And various wave movements are related to one another (field perspective) as instances of more general patterns. For example, the process of proceeding through the grocery checkout counter has relations to proceeding through the checkout at a hardware store or an office supply store, even though there may be notable differences in the details.

Dependence

The field perspective makes it evident that no one personal activity exists in absolute isolation. It exists, to begin with, as part of a particular culture. Credit card buying at a grocery store is part of modern American culture. It would be meaningless in some other culture that has no credit cards. Instead, the other culture would have its own customs and regularities. I will continue to use American culture as an example because that is where I live. But the principles apply to any culture of the world.

The significance of a particular human interaction also depends on the immediate situational context. Other customers may be standing in front of me or behind me in line. Customers may choose to interact with one another or not. In addition, buying and selling may have conditions attached—it may be understood that the buyer may return the item for a full refund if it is defective, or even if he simply changes his mind. A purchase may also sometimes take place after a trial period when the prospective buyer has used the product to see whether he wants it permanently. Buying and selling may take place in a larger context where the buyer consistently seeks out the same seller, either because he has grown to have confidence in him or because he wants his good will in other spheres of life.

The exact significance of a sale depends on the context in which it occurs. So we pay attention not only to one transaction, but also to the store in which it occurs and the personal relations that may exist between buyer and seller. These relations occur in the context of human culture. And human cultures are multiple. They arise in the context of the environment of the whole world and the whole history of the world.

To determine the meaning of a sale in a particular context, we begin with what we already know about sales in general. But we also look at its relations. We push out into the environment of the buyer, the seller, and the business of which the seller may be a part. The field of relations extends out indefinitely, from small acts of human behavior to whole human lifetimes. And the final environment is God. God is at the beginning of history as its Creator, and at the end as its consummator. And he is in between as the sustainer of the entire environment of the universe. Knowing the meaning of buying depends on knowing relations, which depends on God. We can thank God for all of this provision.

8

The Regularities of Human Relationships

Forever, O Lᴏʀᴅ, your word
is firmly fixed in the heavens.
Your faithfulness endures to all generations;
you have established the earth, and it stands fast.
By your appointment they stand this day,
for all things are your servants.

—Psalm 119:89–91

God sustains human relationships partly by sustaining regularities about relationships. Even with a small piece of human interaction, like buying a bag of apples, we meet an impressive number of regularities or rules. The clerk must accurately enter the price. If I pay by credit card, I must produce the card and sign a receipt. Through the credit card bill, I must eventually pay exactly what I owe. We need to look at the character of regularities in relationships because here also God shows his goodness and his control.

The Regularities

Each person who involves himself in personal relationships and interaction relies on regularities. For most informal relationships, a person knows many regularities tacitly, without having them explicitly taught in a classroom.[1] For example, he knows that he should put the groceries on the conveyor belt, that he should have on hand the means for paying for them, and that he should go through a series of steps in the case of credit card payment.

Breaking Rules

It should also be clear that any one particular rule can be broken. Let me introduce a fictional character, "Rebel Bob." If you give Rebel Bob a rule about personal interaction, he will show you that he can break it. He walks up to the checkout counter but refuses to put his apples on the conveyor belt or give them to the checkout clerk. Or he refuses to provide payment.

The point to notice is not that the rules are unbreakable but that, in the obvious cases, everyone is aware of the breakage. The rules are norms that specify what people normally do, and they also imply that deviations will stand out. We can say that the rules are *covenantal* because people have commitments to one another and violating those commitments results in consequences. A deviation or breakage of a rule itself serves to confirm the reality of the rule, the norm.

I should also add a technical qualification. People who analyze social behavior may sometimes distinguish descriptive analysis from prescriptive rules. For example, they may study urban gangs or people who deal in illegal drugs. The analysts may see their business as *describing* how criminals act rather than *evaluating* criminal behavior as either good or bad. Both the descriptive and the prescriptive focuses are aspects of the total situation. And prescriptive evaluations may depend on the individual or group that does the evaluating. An urban gang may have its own internal prescriptive standards about loyalty and betrayal, and at the same time disagree completely with an outside normative evaluation that sees gang behavior as bad.

The regularities extend not only to groups but also to individuals. Consider again the process of purchasing at a grocery store. Virtually all grocery stores within a given culture will share certain features about the process of checkout simply because they are stores run in a free market or some other kind of economy. Grocery store chains may add certain rules for all the stores in the chain so that they have consistent financial procedures and present a consistent image to their customers. They may prescribe a particular uniform and a dress code for the clerks. A particular store may add special rules that apply only to the clerks in the one store. And then one particular clerk may have special, consistent idiosyncrasies

---

[1] On tacit knowledge, see especially Michael Polanyi, *The Tacit Dimension* (Garden City, NY: Anchor, 1967); and more expansively, Polanyi, *Personal Knowledge: Towards a Post-critical Philosophy* (Chicago: University of Chicago Press, 1964).

in his or her manner of conducting a checkout. It is clear that there are various levels of generality on which rules function and in which regularities occur.

The more thorough the investigation, the more rules we find, and the more we find rules for accounting for the variations in the rules and the apparent and sometimes real breakage of an individual rule. We cannot escape the rules except by escaping into another culture with its own set of rules, or else escaping into insanity. And of course psychopathology investigates regular patterns (rules) found in insanity!

Rules tie in to a larger cultural setting. And the world has multiple cultures. For example, some premodern cultures do not use credit cards at all, so the rules for credit card purchasing do not apply there. We will consider the multiplicity of cultures later (chaps. 15–17). God rules over all the cultures, so it is still true that God sustains the regularities associated with any one culture.

Within a particular cultural setting, we should recognize that the rules may "fade gradually" when we enter gray areas that are difficult to classify as either fully rule obeying or overtly rule disobeying. Some grocery clerks may meticulously keep to all the manager's regulations. Others may proceed more flexibly to keep to "the spirit" of the regulations, but may make exceptions when the situation seems to warrant it. Managerial rules inevitably do not anticipate every unusual situation. Were the rules intended to apply to these special situations or not?

For example, the clerk may be told to accept a personal check only when the customer lives locally. But how locally? The clerk may be told to accept a personal check only after asking for personal identification. But what if the person in question is a regular customer and known to the clerk? Whether or not the clerk is actually within the bounds of the rules may depend on the personal judgment of the manager.

A store plagued by deadbeats who do not pay may require an adjusted set of rules in comparison to a store with responsible customers, who naturally do not want to be treated as if they were potential criminals. One can envision a chain of stores under unified management that formulates rules allowing them to adjust to the situation of a particular store.

In a business run for profit much depends on whether the stores are profitable. So we can expect to have more explicit rules with respect to handling money. But human relationships are of many kinds, not all driven by economic factors. We can make adjustments to the situation in many kinds of relationships: in friendships, in informal sports teams, in relationships among travelers on a bus or plane. You may treat a friend who has a nasty fit of anger with more sympathy if you know that he has just lost his job or broken up with his wife.

This kind of situation regularly occurs in human relationships, and we can begin to formulate rules to describe it. So it should be seen as one aspect of the way that rules actually function in personal relationships rather than a failure of relationships to conform to rules. It all depends on how we conceive of the rules. If we formulate a simple rule about grocery stores or friendships, we may sometimes find exceptions, and the exceptions are "violations" of the rule. But the problem is that our formulation fails to capture fully the complexity of social relations. The actual rules are more complex than our formulation, and so of course we are going to be disappointed.

Moral and Social Rules

We need to make a distinction between social rules and God's moral rules. God's moral rules like the Ten Commandments spell out moral and spiritual obligations that derive from God's own moral character. Violating a moral rule makes us guilty before God. But social rules or social expectations are not of this kind. American etiquette says that in formal dining situations you should eat with knife and fork, not with your fingers. There is no absolute moral commandment from God that specifies knife and fork. That rule is a cultural or social rule. God providentially controls cultures, so this kind of rule is still a rule that God caused to be in place. The rule is a product of God's *decretive* will. But it does not directly express his *preceptive* will (on the distinction, chap. 5).

Social rules can still be important. Why? God's preceptive will, his moral law, specifies that we should love our neighbors as ourselves. In many situations loving our neighbors implies keeping the social rules. But there are exceptions. Jesus ate with "with tax collectors and sinners" (Luke 5:30) even though he offended his religious opponents. He broke a social rule. In fact, his opponents thought he was breaking a moral rule, because in their minds their social rule had God's moral endorsement. Jesus showed that they were wrong: "Those who are well have no need of a physician, but those who are sick. I have not come to call the righteous but sinners to repentance" (Luke 5:31–32). Jesus here appeals to a broad principle of responding in love to human need. That principle, based on God's preceptive will, shows that Jesus was right in breaking the social rule.

Social rules have varying degrees of weight or importance within a particular culture. Many Americans would be greatly agitated by someone eating with his fingers at a formal dinner, because it suggests that the person is totally insensitive or boorish. They would be less disturbed if a man failed to have on a tie at the dinner, because that would suggest a lesser kind of carelessness and might possibly have a logical explanation (if, say, he was suffering from a painful skin condition on his neck, which prevented him from wearing a tight collar). A person who fails to write a thank-you note after being a guest at dinner or after receiving a favor has still less difficulty, because the practice of writing thank-you notes is gradually becoming more of an optional courtesy. We have gradations.

We need also to reckon with the "covenantal" dimension of human relationships. Human relationships have a covenantal dimension (chap. 4), in the sense that various moral obligations fall on various participants in the relationships. The moral obligations are real and go back to God's authority. For example, civil governments have authority deriving from God (Rom. 13:1). God commands us to submit (though there are limits to this submission, because God's authority is superior to that of the governments: Acts 4:18–20; 5:29). If two people are in a buying-and-selling relationship, God's command not to steal or defraud constrains them. They must be covenantally faithful within their relationship. Partners within marriage are covenantally bound to one another (Mal. 2:14) and must be faithful to the commandment not to commit adultery (Ex. 20:14). These covenantal obligations are moral obligations that derive from God.

People have a choice whether to enter a marriage relationship, sign a contract, or agree to a sale. Before they make an agreement, they are free of obligations. When they make an agreement, they also create a relationship. They have moral obligations because they have a kind of covenant with their spouse or with a buyer or seller. In this sense, social relationships have moral, and not merely social, rules that govern them.

God's Hand

Our major conclusion is this: God's hand is in the rules. By providing rules for personal interaction, he gives a stable basis for interaction. The rules include both God's moral rules and social rules that may have moral implications but are not themselves instances of his moral law.

9

God's Rule

For his invisible attributes, namely, his eternal power
and divine nature, have been clearly perceived, ever since
the creation of the world, in the things that have been made.

—Romans 1:20

Let us now focus on the character of the rules for personal relationships. More precisely, we focus on the rules *behind* human articulation of rules. What do we mean? Sociologists may formulate rules about human social behavior. Their formulations are guesses or approximations to the real rules, which govern the behavior "out there." We are focusing on these real rules. In addition, people themselves issue "rules," as when lawmakers make laws, or people draw up a contract, or parents give orders to children. For example, a father may say to his child, "Make your bed each morning when you get up." These are man-made rules. But there are rules governing how and when man-made rules come into being. For instance, there is an underlying regularity concerning the rules between parents and children. This regularity (or rule) says that in the parent-child relationship, rules may be issued by parents and may specify what the children are expected to do. The parent-made rules may specify either a regular practice ("make your bed *each morning*") or a one-time task ("make your bed now"). The rule that says that parents issue rules is a rule behind the rules.

Man-made rules, when they have authority, have authority that does not reside merely in the fact that someone has spoken. The particular "someone" who speaks has to have authority or to be given authority. Parents have authority over their children, according to Ephesians 6:1. The real rule is the rule together with authority, an authority that ultimately goes back to God. Real rules in this sense reveal God in some striking ways.

Omnipresence

First, the rules for personal relations hold throughout the culture or subculture that they describe. For example, consider the rule that the purchaser must supply the credit card number of a valid card for which he has purchasing authority. That rule holds wherever credit card purchasing takes place. It holds not only where such purchases actually take place, but wherever they *could* take place. Otherwise, we would not be talking about the kind of credit card purchasing characteristic of various modern cultures. The rule is at least as universal as the culture to which it attaches. And, virtually by definition, the rule would hypothetically hold in *all places* where the culture might come to function. If, for example, a group of Americans or Chinese or Nigerians were to come to reside in some other country and set up there an "enclave" of their native culture, the rules for their culture would still hold in the new location. The rules are qualified by being rules for a particular culture, but they are still *universal* in space. They hold *wherever* the culture is practiced.[1]

Eternality

The presence of a rule at different places extends easily to embrace its presence at different times. The rule about credit card purchases applies whenever such purchasing takes place, either past or future. But now we must make a qualification. American culture or any particular culture changes over time. Credit cards did not exist a century ago; and in the distant future they might be replaced with something else. There are subtle and sometimes major changes in purchasing and in other human interactions. There are changes in the surrounding cultures within which the purchases make sense. So the rules change.

But we might just as well say that the changed rules to which we point are rules with respect to somewhat different cultures and different cultural practices. If

---

[1]Some rules have built in them a restriction about circumstances. In American culture, you are supposed to use knife and fork *at a formal dinner*. The rule is restricted to the circumstance of a formal dinner; only with that qualification is it a universal rule. By contrast, you may eat a hamburger holding it in your hand if you are at an outdoor barbecue. A formal dinner held under a tent or a pavilion in the outdoors would be unusual, but would still require the usual etiquette. Of course Americans also expect knife and fork to be used in many less formal circumstances. The main clues as to what is expected come partly from the type of food (hamburgers and hotdogs and rolls can go in the hand, but not cooked vegetables) and partly from the example set by the host or hostess. These details show the complexity of rules. But the rules are *universal* within the circumstances that they actually govern.

we are talking not about the whole history of civilization (how far back would we go?) but about contemporary culture, for example, we have a suitable focus. Even here we must talk about a variety of subcultures. But that variety, properly understood, is part of the rules, rules describing differences. What is essential is that we not simply confuse our own culture with previous decades or previous centuries. There is little scope for human interaction without some stable cultural framework within the bounds of which we interact. And then we must have particular rules for a particular culture at a particular stage. These rules are applicable wherever that particular culture is the background for our interaction. And so, yes, a credit card purchaser would supply a credit card number if, thirty centuries from now, some group of learned scholars of American culture were to revive it as a living culture. More likely, they would create a culture like the American one but also subtly different, and so the rules for them would differ at some points. The rules are always to be understood as the rules for a particular culture. Those rules hold anytime that particular culture is used. And so the rules, though not the living practice of the culture, are eternal.

It may seem strange to talk about the rules of a culture being eternal, since cultures themselves change. But a similar principle holds with respect to any truth about the world. The world changes. But the truths about events in the world always hold once we make the qualification that they are truths about an event at a particular time and place. Christ was crucified under Pontius Pilate. That truth concerning a particular event can be affirmed now, or in the future, just as much as at the time it happened.[2]

Immutability

It follows also that the rules are immutable. The rule about supplying a credit card number does not change (with respect to American culture as it now exists), and indeed it cannot change, because a new rule would hold only with respect to a new state of development of a culture, rather than holding with respect to a culture as it now exists. We should also say that there are rules to describe cultural change. Introductions of new cultural practices, or new meanings ascribed to old practices, take place in various regular ways. Regularities like this can be captured to some extent by rules.

The Role of God

We have already spoken about the rules of human relationships as omnipresent, eternal, and immutable. It is not an accident that we are seeing here some of the

---

[2]See the discussion about the divine attributes of truth in Vern S. Poythress, *Redeeming Science: A God-Centered Approach* (Wheaton, IL: Crossway, 2006), chap. 14.

attributes of God. According to the Bible, God by his word governs the whole of the world:

> And God said, "Let there be light," and there was light. (Gen. 1:3)

> By the word of the LORD the heavens were made,
>> and by the breath of his mouth all their host. (Ps. 33:6)

> Who has spoken and it came to pass,
>> unless the LORD has commanded it?
> Is it not from the mouth of the Most High
>> that good and bad come? (Lam. 3:37–38)

In particular, God governs the physical and biological world through his word. Scientists in studying scientific law are actually looking into the word of God that governs the world.

A similar situation holds when we consider rules for cultural interaction. We can summarize the situation with respect to scientific law as follows:

> According to the Bible, he [God] is involved [not only in extraordinary events but] in those areas where science does best, namely areas involving regular and predictable events, repeating patterns, and sometimes exact mathematical descriptions. In Genesis 8:22 God promises, "While the earth remains, seedtime and harvest, cold and heat, summer and winter, day and night, shall not cease." This general promise concerning earthly regularities is supplemented by many particular examples:

>> You make darkness, and it is night,
>>> when all the beasts of the forest creep about. (Ps. 104:20)

>> You cause the grass to grow for the livestock
>>> and plants for man to cultivate,
>> that he may bring forth food from the earth. (Ps. 104:14)

>> He sends out his command to the earth;
>>> his word runs swiftly.
>> He gives snow like wool;
>>> he scatters hoarfrost like ashes.
>> He hurls down his crystals of ice like crumbs;
>>> who can stand before his cold?
>> He sends out his word, and melts them;
>>> he makes his wind blow and the waters flow. (Ps. 147:15–18)

The regularities that scientists describe are the regularities of God's own commitments and his actions. By his word to Noah, he commits himself to govern the seasons. By his word he governs snow, frost, and hail. Scientists describe the regularities in God's word governing the world. So-called natural law is really the law of God or word of God, imperfectly and approximately described by human investigators.

Now, the work of science depends constantly on the fact that there are regularities in the world. Without the regularities, there would ultimately be nothing to study. Scientists depend not only on regularities with which they are already familiar, such as the regular behavior of measuring apparatus, but also on the postulate that still more regularities are to be found in the areas that they will investigate. Scientists must maintain hope of finding further regularities, or they would give up their newest explorations.[3]

Similar observations hold when it comes to considering human beings. God in governing the world of human beings governs credit card transactions. The rule or regularity about supplying a credit card number is a rule from God himself as he acts in governing culture.

A number of passages in the Bible indicate that God governs the physical aspects of the world, which are the focus of natural science. The Bible supplies even more passages that talk about the personal world of human cultural interaction. The book of Proverbs is full of observations and maxims about that world. Consider this sample:

> The proverbs of Solomon.
> A wise son makes a glad father,
>   but a foolish son is a sorrow to his mother.
> Treasures gained by wickedness do not profit,
>   but righteousness delivers from death.
> The LORD does not let the righteous go hungry,
>   but he thwarts the craving of the wicked.
> A slack hand causes poverty,
>   but the hand of the diligent makes rich.
> He who gathers in summer is a prudent son,
>   but he who sleeps in harvest is a son who brings shame.
> Blessings are on the head of the righteous,
>   but the mouth of the wicked conceals violence.
> The memory of the righteous is a blessing,
>   but the name of the wicked will rot. (Prov. 10:1–7)

---

[3]Ibid., 14–15.

Proverbs 10:3 makes a direct statement about what the Lord does in interacting with human situations: "The LORD does not let the righteous go hungry." By contrast, many other proverbs make observations about life, without directly referring to the Lord. The context of the book of Proverbs as a whole nevertheless implies that all the observations about life have their ultimate root in God. God by his wisdom has made the world, including the world of human interaction (Prov. 8:22–31). Hence, the Lord God sovereignly controls human relationships. For example, he put in place the principle that

> a slack hand causes poverty,
>> but the hand of the diligent makes rich. (Prov. 10:4)

In the case of a "slack hand" we can see secondary causes. A slack hand *causes* poverty. And we can fill in some of the reasons why. If the hand is slack, that is, if the person is not working, he is not earning wages, nor is he producing things for sale, and as a result he ends in poverty. But now if we ask ourselves how it comes to be that there is a regular relation between a slack hand and poverty, it goes back to God. God in many cases exerts his control in connection with secondary causes. But it is he who, in the acts of creation, pronounced the words putting in place the regularity of the secondary causes.

We have treated the proverbs in the book of Proverbs as God's rules. They are that, but they occur in a context. The proverbs are meant to be mulled over and meditated on. Not all proverbs yield up their meaning immediately. Many may express general tendencies that may nevertheless have exceptions. Does a slack hand *always*, in every conceivable case, lead to poverty? On a spiritual level, slackness toward God always leads to ultimate spiritual poverty in the last judgment. But what about the short run? What about ordinary reckonings of how many material possessions a person has? Slackness leads to poverty in the typical case. But what about the person who, in spite of his aversion to work, comes into a sudden windfall, a million-dollar inheritance from some distant relative? What does Proverbs have to say?

Proverbs enjoins us to seek wisdom, wisdom from God:

> For the LORD gives wisdom;
>> from his mouth come knowledge and understanding.
>> (Prov. 2:6; see Prov. 1:7; 2:1–6)

Wisdom involves understanding the ways of God, or the rules of God. And that means acknowledging depths and complexities. A summary statement in Proverbs, even though it comes from the mouth of God, does not say everything that God could say. It is meant to be understood as nuanced by the other things that

God says, not only in Proverbs, but in the rest of the Bible. So, yes, there can be rich fools like Nabal (1 Sam. 25:25) and the man who was building bigger barns (Luke 12:16–21).

Violations of God's Rules

We need to add a further complexity. God's laws or rules with respect to the physical world are never violated or broken. Miracles are surprising to us because they violate our expectations concerning laws, but they are in conformity with God's plan and his word, which is the real law. On the other hand, God's rules with respect to a particular cultural practice, like credit card purchases, can be broken. They are broken when someone uses a fake credit card or a stolen credit card. In that respect the rules for human relationships are more like God's moral law. God says, "Do not steal." Rebel Bob can go ahead and steal, if he wants, just to show that he can break God's law. He does indeed break God's law. But God's law, as a moral standard, remains unchanged. Rebel Bob succeeds not in changing it, but only in violating it. And his violation also fits within God's rules in several senses. For one thing, his acts are still within the scope of God's decrees, God's words that specify the whole course of the history of the world.[4] For another, Bob is accountable for his violation. There are consequences, both on earth and after death. God's rules also specify these consequences.

Now let us return to consider the breaking of a rule for purchasing. A violation of a cultural rule may or may not be a moral violation. Suppose that the salesperson and I both forget that I am supposed to put my signature on the credit card receipt. I walk away with my purchase, with no intention of stealing. And the transaction with the credit card company will go through correctly even without the signature. So I have broken a cultural rule about signatures, but I have not committed a moral transgression.

In sum, cultural rules are norms. They can be broken, but they remain in place as norms. The rules need to remain stable and unchanged in order effectively to be broken, and in order for culture to exist without chaos.

With this understanding, let us proceed to explore further and to ask whether the rules for human relationships display other attributes of God. For convenience, I will follow the order of discussion I used in the book *Redeeming Science* to discuss scientific law.[5] Many of the observations remain the same when we focus on laws (rules) concerning human relationships.

---

[4]On God's decrees, see the discussion in ibid.; for discussion of God's decrees within Reformed theology, see, e.g., John M. Frame, *The Doctrine of God* (Phillipsburg, NJ: P&R, 2002), 313–39.
[5]Poythress, *Redeeming Science*, chap. 1.

Invisibility

Rules concerning human interaction are at bottom ideational in character. When a customer supplies a credit card, we do not literally see the rule that the purchaser must provide a credit card number. We see and hear only the effects of the rule on the purchaser's behavior. The rule is essentially immaterial and invisible but is known through its effects. Likewise, God is essentially immaterial and invisible but is known through his acts in the world.

Truthfulness

Real rules, as opposed to human approximations of them, are also absolutely, infallibly true. Truthfulness is also an attribute of God.

The Power of Rules

Next consider the attribute of power. Sociologists, anthropologists, and other students of culture formulate rules as descriptions of regularities that they observe. They would say that the purchaser must provide a credit card number. But that was already true before the rule about it was formulated. The people who originally invented the idea of using credit cards had to make rules. So did they originate the rule? In a sense yes, but of course they operate under the sphere of the sovereignty of God, who rules over all things as the primary cause. Moreover, the inventors of the credit card system did not have much choice. They had to have some way of keeping track of different cards belonging to different people with different accounts. Otherwise, the system would not work. God has made the world with constraints. The credit card people had to pay attention to those constraints.

So now, within our culture, a law or regularity holds for supplying credit card numbers. The sociologist cannot force the issue by inventing a rule that the purchaser must present double the number on his card. He cannot just force the culture to conform to his artificial rule. Social interaction rather conforms to rules already there, rules that a sociologist discovers rather than invents. The rules must already be there, and they must actually hold. They must "have teeth." Even if Rebel Bob deliberately breaks the rule by giving double the number on his card, the rule remains what it was and remains true. No purchasing event escapes the "hold" or dominion of the rules. Even Rebel Bob, when he breaks the rule, is still subject to the rule in the sense that everyone can see that he is breaking it. The power of these real laws is absolute—in fact, infinite. In classical language, a rule for human interaction is omnipotent ("all powerful").

If the rule about credit card numbers is omnipotent and universal, there are truly no exceptions. But what about Rebel Bob? He shows that the universality of a rule for human interaction is of a different kind than with physical laws like the law of gravity. The rule remains in place as a standard, a norm, to which Rebel Bob is subject, even when he breaks it. In addition, the violations of a rule are within the purpose of God for human relationships. They take place in accordance with his predictive and decretive word. So the power of any one rule about credit card numbers is to be understood in the context of other rules, including rules describing the possibility of breaking the one rule.

God's rule, as distinct from the sociologist's rule, encompasses the very possibility of breaking the sociologist's rule. Similarly the Ten Commandments, as given by God, include within their context indications from God that he knows that the Israelites may violate them. That is one of the reasons he issues the commandments in the first place. The violations do not take God by surprise, but are in fact encompassed by the commandments, some of which include consequences for disobedience as well as blessings for obedience (Ex. 20:5–7).

Transcendence and Immanence

The rules are both transcendent and immanent. The rule about credit card numbers transcends particular instances of credit card transactions, and it transcends particular human beings by exercising power over them, conforming them to its dictates. The rule is immanent in that it touches and holds in its dominion the particular occurrences of credit card transactions.[6] Transcendence and immanence are characteristics of God.

Are the Rules Personal or Impersonal?

Many agnostics and atheists by this time will be looking for a way of escape. It seems that characteristics of rules for personal interaction look suspiciously like the characteristics of God. The most obvious escape, and the one that has rescued many from spiritual discomfort, is to deny that rules of human interaction are personal. The people to whom the rules apply are of course personal, but the rules are impersonal. They are just there as an impersonal something. It just "happens to be the case" that credit card numbers are presented in purchases.

This reasoning replaces the person of God, governing personally, with a system of impersonal rules. The impersonal rules have then become a substitute for God. Is this substitution legitimate? And does it work?

In ancient times people constructed idols, which served as substitutes for God. The idols often had the form of statues representing a god—Poseidon, the god of the sea; or Mars, the god of war. Nowadays in the Western world we

---

[6]On the biblical view of transcendence and immanence, see John M. Frame, *The Doctrine of the Knowledge of God* (Phillipsburg, NJ: Presbyterian and Reformed, 1987), especially 13–15; and Frame, *Doctrine of God*, especially 107–15.

are more sophisticated. Idols now take the form of mental constructions of a god or a God-substitute. Some people make money and pleasure the ultimate goals of life. Then money and pleasure have become idols. Humanity or nature can become a God-substitute when it receives a person's ultimate allegiance. Scientific law, when viewed as impersonal, becomes another God-substitute. In both ancient times and today, idols conform to the imagination of the person who makes them. Idols have enough similarities to the true God to be plausible, but differ so as to allow us comfort and the satisfaction of manipulating the substitutes that we construct.

Rule-Giving, Rationality, and Language-Like Character

In fact, a close look at rules for personal interaction shows that this escape route is not really plausible. Rules imply a rule giver. What gives power to the rule about credit cards? Someone must think up the rule and enforce it if it is to be effective. With credit card numbers, we could say that the rules go back to the inventors of credit cards. But these inventors, as we have observed, found themselves constrained by social realities that they did not invent. They had to deal with the moral standards concerning property and theft, which they did not invent. In back of the particularities of the rules lies the very character of human nature, which we did not invent. Human nature displays regularities. We are similar in our humanity. There are regularities—rules—concerning human nature. Are these rules simply impersonal? Are we merely complicated machines made out of organic molecules?

The rules for presenting credit card numbers probably had an origin at a particular point in time, when credit cards were first invented. But other rules do not have a clear point when they were consciously invented. What about the rule, "Children, obey your parents" (Eph. 6:1)? Where did that come from? What about the prohibition against incest? What about the custom of shaking hands as a greeting in American culture? Are these rules impersonal because they had no clear point when people decided to "invent" them?

We may proceed in another, more indirect, way. Students of culture in practice believe passionately in the rationality of the rules for culture. We are not dealing with irrationality, totally unaccountable and unanalyzable, but with lawfulness that in some sense is accessible to human understanding. Rationality is a sine qua non for scientific investigation of any kind, including the social-scientific investigation undertaken by sociologists. Moreover, the ordinary person as well as the social scientist must assume that the rules for culture are fundamentally rational. Otherwise, his own behavior has no rational bottom, and his own views of culture are all irrational. And if he is analyzing a society without rational rules, he is trying to analyze chaos and not a society at all. Now, if the rules are rational, they are also personal, because rationality belongs to persons. Persons have rational capacities, but not rocks, trees, and subpersonal creatures. If the rules are rational, which social scientists assume they are, then they are also personal. God shows his personhood in making the rule for credit card numbers.

Social scientists also assume that rules can be articulated, expressed, communicated, and understood through human language. Scientific work includes not only rational thought but also symbolic communication. Now, the original, the rule "out there" about children respecting their parents, already exists even if it is not expressly articulated in a particular human language. God did use language in giving the rule, "Honor your father and your mother" (Ex. 20:12) to the Israelites. But people must have had a sense of moral obligation to their parents even before God expressly articulated the rule at a particular time. Many other social rules exist. They can be expressed in language. We can say, in English, that "a credit card number has to be presented with a credit card purchase." And this rule must be translatable into not only one but many human languages. In the new language, we may have to explain what a credit card is, if that is an unfamiliar concept with respect to the new language. We may represent restrictions, qualifications, definitions, and contexts for rules through clauses, phrases, explanatory paragraphs, and contextual explanations in human language. The rules concerning social interaction are clearly like human utterances in their ability to be grammatically articulated, paraphrased, translated, and illustrated. A rule is utterance-like, language-like. And the complexity of utterances that we find among social scientists, as well as among human beings in general, is not duplicated in the animal world.[7] Language is one of the defining characteristics that separate man from animals. Language, like rationality, belongs to persons. The rules for social interaction, being themselves language-expressed, are therefore in essence personal.

As we observed, some of the rules may have been invented by a particular person at a particular time. Or a group of people may have agreed together on a set of rules, as in the case of the meeting to draw up the United States Constitution. Or there may be a more tacit agreement, as with the custom of shaking hands. The rules are personal in these cases because persons have invented them or at least have had a role in them. But even all of these personal interactions together do not explain human nature itself. Why are people the way they are? How do they have the capability of personal interaction in relationships such as friendships and conversational interchanges? Some of the rules may be due to

---

[7] Animal calls and signals do mimic certain limited aspects of human language. And chimpanzees can be taught to respond to symbols with meaning. But this is still a long way from the complex grammar and meaning of human language. See, e.g., Stephen R. Anderson, *Doctor Dolittle's Delusion: Animals and the Uniqueness of Human Language* (New Haven, CT: Yale University Press, 2004).

human creativity and human rationality, but from where do human creativity and rationality come? The rules concerning humanity trace back to a more ultimate origin, to God as a person.

An Objection from Evolutionary Naturalism

But now we must consider an objection that could be raised from the philosophy of evolutionary naturalism.[8] Evolutionary naturalism postulates that a process of Darwinian evolution, without any personal purposes—not guided by God or any spiritual influence—has produced the human race and its social and linguistic abilities. (This view must be distinguished from "theistic evolution," which says that God used an evolutionary process and controlled the process by which he created the various kinds of living things. And of course it is even more obviously distinct from various creationist views.)[9]

According to this scenario, the rules for society and language would have originated in the end from the biological structures of the human brain and would be reducible to the brain. The apparent rationality and language-like character of the rules would somehow be a projection or effect of the more basic rationality and language-like features originating in the structure of the human brain. But this move simply postpones the question by pushing the rules back from being rules of social interaction to being rules of biology and rules for brains and for evolution. It so happens that those rules, those scientific laws, are also rational and language-like and personal, as I argue in *Redeeming Science*.[10] No, we will not escape God that way.

Finally, we might be troubled by the plurality of rules for social interaction, and more broadly about the plurality of scientific laws. Are there many gods, or is there one? There is only one God, as the unity and harmony of all the laws testify. But he has plurality in himself, the plurality of three persons in one God. The plurality of laws and rules for human relationships is no more an accident than their harmony.

Incomprehensibility of Law

In addition, rules for human relationships are both knowable and incomprehensible in the theological sense. That is, we know truths about social interaction, but in the midst of this knowledge there remain unfathomed depths and unanswered questions about the very areas where we know the most. What is it about human nature that makes us able to engage in buying and selling at all? The rules never

---

[8]Concerning evolutionary naturalism, see Poythress, *Redeeming Science*, chaps. 5, 19.
[9]On the various alternatives, see ibid., 252–58.
[10]Ibid., chap. 1, pp. 19–20.

succeed in making transparent why there are human relationships, why they are rational in the way that they are, and so on. The knowability of rules is closely related to their rationality and their immanence, displayed in the accessibility of effects. We experience incomprehensibility in the fact that the increase in understanding only leads to ever-deeper questions: How can this be? Why this rule rather than many other ways that the human mind can imagine? The profundity and mystery in human relationships can only produce awe—yes, worship—if we have not blunted our perception with hubris (Isa. 6:9–10).

Are We Divinizing Nature?

We must consider another objection. By claiming that rules behind social interaction have divine attributes, are we divinizing nature? That is, are we taking something out of the created world and falsely claiming that it is divine? Are not rules behind social interaction a part of the created world? Should we not classify them as creature rather than Creator?[11]

Man-made rules, like the rules for using credit cards, have their origin in human beings, who are creatures, and whose rules are creaturely. But behind the man-made rules are God-ordained rules about human nature, and God's governance over each particular society, including societies that use credit cards. God ordains that human beings have the authority to make their rules, and he specifies the possibilities for using credit cards.

The specificity of God's rule, with its obvious relation to the created world of credit cards, makes it tempting to infer that God's rules are a part of the created world. But such an inference is clearly invalid. The speech describing a butterfly is not itself a butterfly or a part of a butterfly. Speech referring to the created world is not necessarily an ontological part of the world to which it refers. In addition, let us remember that we are speaking of God's rules, not merely our human guesses and approximations. We are speaking about the "rules behind the rules," the rules governing human nature and the presence of authority in rules. The real rules are in fact the word of God, specifying how the world of creatures and the world of social interactions are to function. So-called rules are simply God speaking. The real mistake here is not a matter of divinizing nature but of refusing to recognize that the rules are the law of God.

The key idea that the law is divine is not only older than the rise of modern science; it is older than the rise of Christianity. Even before the coming of Christ, people noticed profound regularity in the government of the world and wrestled with the meaning of this regularity. Both the Greeks (especially the Stoics) and the

---

[11] The Bible (especially Genesis 1) shows that God and the created world are distinct. God is not to be identified with the creation or any part of it, nor is the creation a "part" of God. The Bible repudiates all forms of pantheism and panentheism (see, e.g., Ex. 20:4–6; Acts 14:15; 17:24–26).

Jews (especially Philo) developed speculations about the *logos*, the divine "word" or "reason" behind what is observed.[12] In addition, the Jews had the Old Testament, which reveals the role of the word of God in creation and providence.

Against this background John 1:1 proclaims, "In the beginning was the Word, and the Word was with God, and the Word was God." John responds to the speculations of his time with a striking revelation: that the Word (*logos*) that created and sustains the universe is not only a divine person "with God," but the very One who became incarnate: "the Word became flesh" (1:14). God said, "Let there be light" (Gen. 1:3). He referred to light as a part of the created world. But precisely in this reference, his word has divine power to bring creation into being. The effect in creation took place at a particular time, but the plan for creation, as exhibited in God's word, is eternal. Likewise, God's speech to us in the Bible refers to various parts of the created world, but the speech (in distinction to the things to which it refers) is divine in power, authority, majesty, righteousness, eternity, and truth.[13]

The analogy with the incarnation should give us our clue. The second person of the Trinity, the eternal Word of God, became man in the incarnation but did not therefore cease to be God. Likewise, when God speaks and says what is to be the case in this world, his words do not cease to have the divine power and unchangeability that belong to him. They are divine and in addition have the power to specify the situation with respect to creaturely affairs. God's word is still divine when it becomes law, a specific directive with respect to this created world.

The Goodness of Rules

Are the rules for social interaction good? Here there are difficulties. We know that terrible evils can take place through the corruption of a whole society. Social expectations may encourage not only noble accomplishments but also corrupt practices. A whole culture may normalize bribery or slavery or prostitution. And if we were to be immersed in a society filled with propaganda, as Nazi Germany once was, or as North Korea more recently has been, we would find it difficult as individuals to escape its clutches. The United States and Europe are not free from such baneful influences if modern advertising has contributed to materialism and consumerism. How can God be good, and how can his rules for social interaction be good, if the result contains evil?

---

[12] See R. B. Edwards, "Word," in *The International Standard Bible Encyclopedia*, rev. ed., ed. Geoffrey W. Bromiley et al. (Grand Rapids: Eerdmans, 1988), 4:1103–7, and the associated literature.

[13] On the divine character of God's word, see Vern S. Poythress, *God-Centered Biblical Interpretation* (Phillipsburg, NJ: P&R, 1999), 32–36.

It is not simple to escape the presence of God in these struggles. We may appeal to a standard of good in order to judge that an existing situation is evil. In doing so, we appeal to a standard beyond the confines of the empirical world. We appeal to a standard, a law. To give up the idea of moral law is to give up the very basis on which criticism of evil depends. Moral law is thus indispensable for moral evaluation, but at the same time it presupposes an absolute. And this absolute, in order to obligate us and hold us accountable, must be personal. The Bible's answer alone gives clarity here. God's character is the ultimate source of moral law. Man, made in the image of God, is aware of this law but has rebelled against it (Rom. 1:32). The existing evils are a consequence of that rebellion. We must cast moral blame not on God but on man. With respect to social interaction, we may say the same thing.

The eighth commandment says, "You shall not steal" (Ex. 20:15). It leaves the door open to the possibility that someone may in fact steal. It anticipates it; why else would it be issued as a command if not to warn against violations? But God and the rule of God do not become less good if someone steals. Likewise, the rules concerning social interaction open the possibility for stealing and even anticipate it. But God's rules for society are themselves good.

We also need to acknowledge that whole societies may go astray in a corporate devotion to immorality or idolatry. Even when they do, they cannot escape God's overall rule. The crucifixion of Christ is a key example. God controls human actions, such as those of Herod and Pontius Pilate, which are contrary to his moral law. Hence, we distinguish between God's decretive will (specifying what happens) and his preceptive will (specifying the moral standards to which Herod and Pontius Pilate are held accountable; see chap. 5). Similarly, when Jesus eats with tax collectors and sinners, or when he does not follow the Pharisaic rule about washing before eating, we distinguish between human ideas concerning morality and God's rule. Human ideas are nevertheless still part of the society. Both Jesus and his opponents know that he is breaking social expectations. In that sense, the rule is actually there. And it is there in accordance with God's decretive sovereignty.

The Rectitude of Rules

Another attribute of God is righteousness. God's righteousness is displayed pre-eminently in the moral law and in the moral rectitude of his judgments, that is, his rewards and punishments based on moral law. Does God's rectitude appear in the rules of society as well? It appears in two ways. First, God's rectitude makes it possible to judge human social rules. Second, God shows his rectitude through consequences of human actions. "Honor your father and your mother, *that your days may be long* in the land that the LORD your God is giving you" (Ex. 20:12).

We may not always see consequences within this life. There are exceptions and injustices that go unrectified. But cases where consequences do come show God's righteousness.

In addition, the rectitude of God is closely related to the fitness of his acts. It fits the character of who God is that we should worship him alone (Ex. 20:3). It fits the character of human beings made in the image of God that they should imitate God by speaking and by exercising dominion over the world (Gen. 1:28–30). Human actions fitly correspond to the actions of God. Likewise, punishments must be fitting. It is fitting that a thief should pay back double for what he has stolen (Ex. 22:9).

> As you have done, it shall be done to you;
> > your deeds shall return on your own head. (Obadiah 15)

The punishment fits the crime. There is a symmetrical match between the nature of the crime and the punishment that fits it.[14] The arena of rules for society includes issues of punishment, but it includes much more: moral standards, rules of etiquette, and social expectations. Rectitude also expresses itself in the fitness of social rules for our tasks. This "fitness" is perhaps closely related to beauty. God's attributes are involved in one another and imply one another, so beauty and righteousness are closely related. It is the same with the area of rules for social interaction.

Rules as Trinitarian

Do the rules for social interaction specifically reflect the Trinitarian character of God? Philosophers have sometimes maintained that we can infer the existence of God, but not the Trinitarian character of God, on the basis of the world around us. Romans 1:18–21 indicates that unbelievers know God, but how much do they know? I am not addressing this difficult question,[15] but rather reflecting on what we can discern about the world once we have absorbed biblical teaching about God.

Rules for social interaction—not man-made rules but God's—are a form of the word of God. So they reflect the Trinitarian statement in John 1:1, which identifies the second person of the Trinity as the eternal Word. In addition, as we saw in chapter 2, all three persons of the Trinity are present in distinct ways when God interacts personally. Man is made in the image of God, and so his

---

[14]See the extended discussion of just punishment in Vern S. Poythress, *The Shadow of Christ in the Law of Moses* (Phillipsburg, NJ: P&R, 1995), 119–249.

[15]But see the later discussion, where we deal with some of the related issues on the situation for human beings in rebellion against God.

social interaction is in the image of God. For example, human love involves a lover, the gift and bond of love, and the one receiving love. These correspond to the roles of the Father, the Son, and the Holy Spirit in the Father's love for the Son. Similarly, when Tammy gives a gift to Carol, we must have a giver, a gift, and a recipient, and these three must function together coherently. The rules of social interaction specify, among other things, that our interaction is Trinitarian. Human social interaction also displays a coinherence, which reflects the archetypal coinherence in the Trinity.[16]

---

[16]See chap. 3.

10

Responding to God's Government

> . . . they did not honor him as God or give thanks to him.
>
> —Romans 1:21

Everyone within a culture relies on the rules of that culture. Since the rules are providentially from God, everyone is relying on God. And everyone who interacts culturally relies on the coinherence of initiators, recipients, and the exchanges between them. In doing so, people rely on the coinherence of the Trinity.

But Do They Believe?

Do these participants in culture therefore believe in God? They do and they do not. The situation has already been described in the Bible: "For what can be known about God is plain to them, because God has shown it to them. For his invisible attributes, namely, his eternal power and divine nature, have been clearly perceived, ever since the creation of the world, in the things that have been made. So they are without excuse" (Rom. 1:19–20). They know God. They rely on him. But because this knowledge is morally and spiritually painful, they also suppress and distort it:

> For although they knew God, they did not honor him as God or give thanks to him, but they became futile in their thinking, and their foolish hearts were darkened. Claiming to be wise, they became fools, and exchanged the glory of the immortal God for images resembling mortal man and birds and animals and creeping things. (Rom. 1:21–23)

Modern people may no longer make idols in the form of physical images, but tacitly, in their ideas about the rules for relationships, they idolatrously twist their knowledge of God. They conceal from themselves the fact that God's rules are personal and that they are responsible to him. Or they may substitute the term *human nature*, and they talk glowingly about the wonderful character of human nature, which gives us the power for social action. They evade what they know of the transcendence of God over nature.

Even in their rebellion, people continue to depend on God being there. They show in action that they continue to believe in God. Cornelius Van Til compares it to an incident he saw on a train, where a small girl sitting on her grandfather's lap slapped him in the face.[1] The rebel must depend on God and must be "sitting on his lap" even to be able to engage in rebellion.

Do We Christians Believe?

The fault, I suspect, is not entirely on the side of unbelievers. The fault also occurs among Christians. Christians have sometimes adopted an unbiblical concept of God that moves him one step out of the way of our ordinary affairs. We ourselves may think of either "scientific laws" or "rules for social interaction" or "laws of human nature" as impersonal cosmic mechanisms or constraints that run the world most of the time, while God is on vacation. God comes and acts only rarely, through miracle. But this is not biblical.

> Even before a word is on my tongue,
>> behold, O LORD, you know it altogether.
> You hem me in, behind and before,
>> and lay your hand upon me.
> Such knowledge is too wonderful for me;
>> it is high; I cannot attain it.
> Where shall I go from your Spirit?
>> Or where shall I flee from your presence?
> If I ascend to heaven, you are there!
>> If I make my bed in Sheol, you are there!
> If I take the wings of the morning
>> and dwell in the uttermost parts of the sea,
> even there your hand shall lead me,
>> and your right hand shall hold me. (Ps. 139:4–10)

---

[1] I do not know the location of this story in print. For rebels' dependence on God, see Cornelius Van Til, *The Defense of the Faith*, 2nd ed. (Philadelphia: Presbyterian and Reformed, 1963), and the exposition by John M. Frame, *Apologetics to the Glory of God: An Introduction* (Phillipsburg, NJ: P&R, 1994).

Let us not forget it. If we ourselves recovered a robust doctrine of God's involvement in daily caring for us in detail, we would find ourselves in a much better position to dialogue with skeptics who, without admitting it, rely on that same care.

Principles for Witness

In order for those of us who believe in God to use this situation as a starting point for witness, we need to bear in mind several principles. First, the observation that God underlies the rules for human relationships does not have the same shape as the traditional theistic proofs—at least as they are often understood. We are not trying to lead people to come to know a God who is completely new to them. Rather, we show that people already know God as an aspect of their human experience in relationships. This places the focus not on intellectual debate but on being a full human being within the context of life.[2]

Second, people deny God within the very same context in which they depend on him. The denial of God springs ultimately not from intellectual flaws or from failure to see all the way to the conclusion of a chain of syllogistic reasoning, but from spiritual failure. We are rebels against God, and we will not serve him. Consequently, we suffer under his wrath (Rom. 1:18), which has intellectual as well as spiritual and moral effects. Those who rebel against God are "fools," according to Romans 1:22.

Third, it is humiliating to intellectuals to be exposed as fools, and it is further humiliating, even psychologically unbearable, to be exposed as guilty of rebellion against the goodness of God. We can expect our hearers to fight with a tremendous outpouring of intellectual and spiritual energy against so unbearable an outcome.

Fourth, the gospel itself, with its message of forgiveness and reconciliation through Christ, offers the only remedy that can truly end this fight against God. But it brings with it the ultimate humiliation: that my restoration comes entirely from God, from outside me—in spite of, rather than because of, my vaunted abilities. To climax it all, so wicked was I that it took the price of the death of the Son of God to accomplish my rescue.

Fifth, approaching people in this way constitutes spiritual warfare. Unbelievers and idolaters are captives to satanic deceit (1 Cor. 10:20; Eph. 4:17–24; 2 Thess. 2:9–12; 2 Tim. 2:25–26; Rev. 12:9). They do not get free from Satan's captivity unless God gives them release (2 Tim. 2:25–26). We must pray to God and rely

---

[2]Much valuable insight into the foundations of apologetics is to be found in the tradition of transcendental apologetics founded by Cornelius Van Til. See Van Til, *Defense of the Faith*; Frame, *Apologetics to the Glory of God*.

on God's power rather than the ingenuity of human argument and eloquence of persuasion (1 Cor. 2:1–5; 2 Cor. 10:3–5).

Sixth, we come into this encounter as fellow sinners. Christians too have become massively guilty by being captive to the idolatry in which human relationships are regarded as self-sufficient rather than dependent on God. Within this captivity we take for granted the benefits and beauties of relationships for which we should be filled with gratitude and praise to God. Does an approach to witnessing based on these principles work itself out differently from many of the approaches that attempt to address intellectuals? To me it appears so.

PART 2

From Big to Small

Relationships in the Context of History

11

Small Pieces of Human Action within the Big Pieces

Are not two sparrows sold for a penny?
And not one of them will fall to the ground apart from your Father.
But even the hairs of your head are all numbered.

—Matthew 10:29–30

Now we consider some of the ways in which human interaction occurs in bigger-sized and smaller-sized pieces, and how those pieces are designed by God to function within larger wholes in society. Consider the sample interaction when I buy a bag of apples. That interaction consists of several smaller pieces. I put the apples on the conveyor belt; the checkout clerk enters the amount in the register; the clerk does the same for whatever else I have in my cart; I present my credit card; a receipt is printed; I sign the receipt; the apples and other purchases are packed into bags. The purchase transaction is also integrated into a larger series of actions: going to the store; picking out purchases; then the checkout; taking the purchases out of the store; returning home. This one trip to the store belongs with a larger series of actions during the same day, and also with other trips to the same store. All of these trips belong to the life of a single person.

When we pay attention to the patterning of pieces within pieces, we are using the wave perspective to see what goes before and after a particular piece of human interaction. Typically, one piece of action sits alongside other activities, other human beings who are speaking and working and playing and conversing. Using the field perspective, we could focus on the relation of one human activity to its social and physical environment. Other human activities give us a human background for understanding the particular action on which we focus. To obtain a full understanding of the meaning of any one piece, we have to look at the relations. We look at context, the pieces around the one piece of action with which we start. We also reckon with the fact that there are certain identifiable pieces, that is, particles, that enjoy relations to the larger wholes. The particle, wave, and field perspectives all apply (chap. 7).

Daily human actions in turn integrate into whole lifetimes of many people interacting. Human living fits into the context of whole cultures, and cultures into the whole history of the world. And the whole history of the world begins with God, who surpasses history (see fig. 11.1). God began history by creation (Gen. 1:1) and consummates history in a glorious fulfillment (Rev. 21:1–22:5). Thus, the meaning of any one piece, however small, ultimately depends on God. God is the final context, both at the beginning of history and at the end. But God is present all along the path of history, not just at the beginning and the end. All these relationships of pieces within pieces exist according to the plan of God, according to the will of God. He specifies them; he rules over them. And his rules describe the ways in which smaller pieces combine into bigger ones.

Figure 11.1. Embedding of Actions

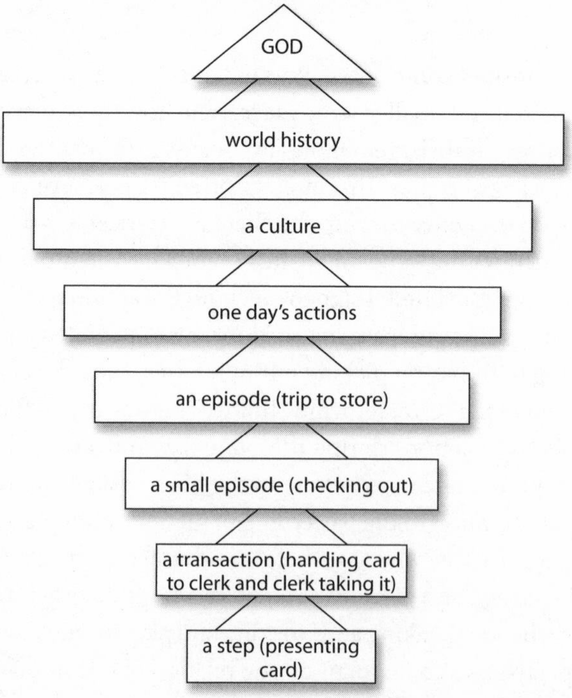

In human action, the pattern of pieces-within-pieces can be quite complex. A trip to the grocery store can involve a whole cart full of purchases rather than just a bag of apples. For the grocery story employee, a day at work has in a sense the unified purpose of a single "episode," but it includes smaller episodes in which the employee takes on various types of tasks.

Human Transcendence

As human beings we also have the capability of reflecting on our actions. We can reflect not only on a single episode at work, but also on a whole day at work, or our whole lifetime, or a whole culture, or the whole of history. How can we do this?

We have the ability not only to be aware of ourselves, but also to stand back and overlook large amounts of time and space. Within a period of ten minutes we can contemplate the meaning of the cosmos. The act of thinking or speaking about the cosmos occupies ten minutes of sitting at a desk; but it refers to a much larger whole. We transcend the particularities of our immediate space of awareness. We can also in a sense transcend our act of thinking, by thinking about what it means for us to think about the meaning of the cosmos. And we can think about thinking about thinking, and so on, indefinitely. That indefinite extension in a sense transcends any particular self-reflection. And then we can think about the process of thinking about indefinite extension. There is no stopping. We can see such transcendence illustrated either in our thinking or in language that expresses our thinking.

In this ability, human beings imitate God, who has complete knowledge of himself and of all of history. So our ability in thought and language reflects the fact that we are made in the image of God. We can put it in another way. In our minds we can imagine the whole of our situation as it might look "from above." This ability for "transcendence" imitates and reflects the greater transcendence that belongs to God. God transcends the entire created world. We are creatures, so we do not. But in our thinking and in our language we can achieve a kind of imitation of God's transcendence. In both thought and language we "package" wholes and so in a sense stand above them enough to consider them as wholes.

12

World History

It is done! I am the Alpha and the Omega, the beginning and the end.
To the thirsty I will give from the spring of the water of life
without payment.

—Revelation 21:6

We now focus on the widest vista of personal action: the whole history of the world. History is wider than any one human description. Human action has meaning within this larger context, which only God fully masters. The world did not always exist. Rather, it began when God created it (Gen. 1:1–31). The world therefore exists in a more ultimate context, the context of God and his actions. God exists eternally. The Father loves the Son and the Son loves the Father forever, in the unity of the Holy Spirit. God in his eternal being and his eternal activity is the source and foundation for activity in creation. God exists. Creatures exist in a derivative manner, dependent on God's existence. God himself acts. And creatures act in a way that analogically reflects his action.

Plan and Goal

God is also at the center in the goal of creation, namely, the consummation depicted in Revelation 21:1–22:5. The goal of history is to "unite all things in him [Christ]" (Eph. 1:10). God had a plan from the beginning (Eph. 1:11). He created the world as the first stage in the execution of his plan. The plan will reach its fulfillment when God's glory is displayed in the whole of the new heaven and the new earth (Rev. 21:1, 22–27). Both the plan and its execution involve all three persons of the Trinity: the Father (1 Cor. 8:6), the Son (the Word, John 1:1–3), and the Holy Spirit (Gen. 1:2).

The world reaches its goal in a glorification that takes place in a way that is patterned after Christ's glorification.[1] In the New Jerusalem of Revelation 21:1–22:5, the glory of God is displayed centrally in God and the Lamb, but the whole city has the glory of God: "He . . . showed me the holy city Jerusalem coming down out of heaven from God, having the glory of God" (Rev. 21:10–11). Thus the pattern of Christ's glory extends to the fullness of the new creation. Christ's resurrection is the "firstfruits" for the resurrection of believers:

> But in fact Christ has been raised from the dead, the firstfruits of those who have fallen asleep. For as by a man [Adam] came death, by a man [Christ] has come also the resurrection of the dead. For as in Adam all die, so also in Christ shall all be made alive. But each in his own order: Christ the firstfruits, then at his coming those who belong to Christ. (1 Cor. 15:20–23)

The "firstfruits" is not only first in time but the pattern for the rest. Christ's resurrection body already belongs to the order of the new creation. It is the firstfruits, the first "piece," the foundation piece, for the whole. Christ's resurrection also points to his ascension and rule. The latter two are implications of the resurrection:

> And being found in human form, he humbled himself by becoming obedient to the point of death, even death on a cross. Therefore God has highly exalted him and bestowed on him the name that is above every name, so that at the name of Jesus every knee should bow, in heaven and on earth and under the earth. (Phil. 2:8–10)

We see stages in divine action in the life of Christ. At the beginning, there is the initiative of God, both in the incarnation and in the commission of the Son by the Father. In the middle, the Son accomplishes the work of the Father. In the end, God rewards him in exaltation. These three stages involve the life of one person, the Son. But they also have cosmic significance. The Son, as 1 Corinthians 15:45 and 15:22 indicate, is the "last Adam," the representative for the new humanity. So we can stand back and see stages with respect to the whole of history (see fig. 12.1).

---

[1] See Vern S. Poythress, *In the Beginning Was the Word: Language—A God-Centered Approach* (Wheaton, IL: Crossway, 2009), chap. 12.

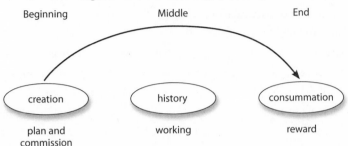

Figure 12.1. God Working in History

Stages

At the beginning of human history, God created man in his image, which corresponds to the Son's being in the image of God (Col. 1:15; Heb. 1:3). God commissioned Adam to the work of dominion (Gen. 1:28–30), corresponding to the commissioning of the Son (Gal. 4:4; John 17:4). Adam was then supposed to carry out his work in obedience to God, but he failed and disobeyed. Hence Christ, the last Adam, intervened. Christ as the last Adam achieved his goal of dominion in the ascension:

> ... he [God] worked in Christ when he raised him from the dead and seated him at his right hand in the heavenly places, far above all rule and authority and power and dominion, and above every name that is named, not only in this age but also in the one to come. And he put all things under his feet and gave him as head over all things. (Eph. 1:20–22)

Thus, for the whole of history, we have a pattern of commission, work, and reward. These three stages should have been followed by Adam. They are achieved by Christ as the last Adam. These three stages reflect in a way the three persons of the Trinity. All three persons are involved in all three stages. But the commission can be particularly associated with God the Father. The work is preeminently the work of the Son, who is, as it were, the executor of the Father's will. And glorification takes place as we are filled with the Spirit. The Spirit is "the Spirit of glory" (1 Pet. 4:14).[2] But these distinctions in role are mysterious. The persons of the Trinity dwell in one another, so that all three persons are involved in all the works of God. The Father and the Holy Spirit are present empowering the Son in accomplishing his work. The glory displayed in the new heavens and the new earth is the glory belonging to the Father, the Son, and the Holy Spirit.

The diversity in the stages of the work of God reflects the diversity within God himself. God is not a creature and is not subject to time; he is not limited by

---

[2]See, in particular, Meredith M. Kline, "The Holy Spirit as Covenant Witness," ThM thesis, Westminster Theological Seminary, 1972.

temporal development. But in view of the activities of God in time, we can also say that time, development, and climax are not out of step with the character of God. He acts in time in a manner reflective of his character, and his entire plan from beginning to end is in thorough accord with his Trinitarian nature.

We can also see distinctive modes of action that are characteristic of the three phases. In the first phase, in commissioning, the Father speaks and the Son hears. The action is verbal. In the second phase, in the accomplishing of the work, the Father and the Son are both acting in power: "The Father who dwells in me does his works" (John 14:10). In the third phase, the Father blesses and crowns the work with reward. And the heart of the reward is the presence of God himself, who is the fountain of all blessing. So the three phases could be summarized as involving first speaking, then powerful working, then blessing.

The characteristic feature in each phase is not entirely absent from the other phases. Rather, each phase shows all the features, but not with the same prominence. For example, the speaking of God can empower people and can be a source of blessing (or sometimes curse). Speaking coheres with power and blessing. So God speaks in all three phases. Likewise, the exertion of God's power is meaningful, and all God's works can be described as being accomplished by speaking:

> Is it not from the mouth of the Most High
> that good and bad come? (Lam. 3:38)

Works can be a blessing, and blessing can take the form of a work.

In fact, these three characteristic features correspond in some ways to the three aspects of God's lordship that we discussed earlier: authority, control, and presence (chap. 4). Authority corresponds to God's speech and commission; God has the authority to decide what purposes and goals are to be accomplished. The work of accomplishment shows control. And the blessing is a blessing of God's presence. These three—authority, control, and presence—are aspects that are present in all of God's lordship. They are perspectives on the whole.

Finally, we can also see a relation of the three phases to the three "offices" of Christ as Prophet, King, and Priest.[3] The role of the prophet is primarily to speak on behalf of God, and so is related to the function of speaking. The role of the king is primarily to rule on behalf of God, and so is related to the function of power and control. The role of the priest is primarily to mediate in the communion of God with man, particularly communion with his presence—presence

---

[3]All three offices appear in Heb. 1:1–3. Christ's work is compared to the Old Testament prophets in v. 1. He "upholds the universe by the word of his power" in v. 3, showing the kingly function of ruling. He made "purification for sins," which is a priestly role (v. 3). See the Westminster Shorter Catechism, 23: "Christ, as our Redeemer, executeth the offices of a prophet, of a priest, and of a king, both in his estate of humiliation and exaltation."

in blessing. And so the priest is related to the function of blessing and presence. The three offices are generally distinct from one another in the Old Testament, though some figures like Moses perform all three roles. In Christ the roles come together. They are aspects of his work rather than being strictly separable. The result of all this is that God's actions are in harmony in constituting the whole history of the world. Human action takes place in imitation of and in harmony with the larger context formed by God's actions.

Your actions and mine, when they involve planning and executing plans, imitate God and rely on him.

13

The Fall into Sin

And the great dragon was thrown down, that ancient serpent,
who is called the devil and Satan, the deceiver of the whole world.

—Revelation 12:9

We have taken a very broad viewpoint by looking at world history as a whole. Now we should look at two crucial events within history, events that have radically changed the situation for the whole of the rest of history. First we look at the fall of mankind. In the next chapter we look at the redemption accomplished by Christ.

According to the Bible, humanity today is in a state of rebellion against God. That has implications for our thinking about human relationships. We are not neutral observers. We no longer readily and joyfully acknowledge the gift of relationships by giving thanks to God. We are morally and spiritually sick—in fact, spiritually dead (Eph. 2:1). And this spiritual death has corrupted our relationships as well. Human beings today sometimes manipulate and exploit others.

How did this come about? Human beings did not retain the original harmonious communion with God that they enjoyed in the beginning. The divine-human relationship was corrupted, and that also corrupted human-human relationships. Mankind rebelled. Genesis 3 tells the story. The rebellion involved two individuals, Adam and Eve, but it was not confined to them. Not only did Adam suffer the penalty of death (Gen. 3:19; 5:5), but his descendants did too (Gen. 5:1–31). Sin multiplied in the lives of Cain and his descendants (Gen. 4:1–24), leading to increasing corruption (Gen. 6:5–7). Adam was the head and representative of the whole human race, and when he fell, he plunged the race as a whole into sin and rebellion (see Rom. 5:12–21; 1 Cor. 15:21–22, 45–49).

Ever since, we have come into the world already in a state of alienation from God. So the story in Genesis 3 has two sides. On the one hand, it is the historical record of the original fall of the first man and the first woman. On the other hand, it shows the character and meaning of the fall and in this respect has implications for understanding our present condition. We ourselves are infected with sin and rebellion against God. We find growing up in our own hearts, like a poisonous weed, the same plant that Adam and Eve grew in their hearts. That poisonous weed infects our relationships with one another, as well as other areas of life.

Deception and Confusion

The events leading to the fall did not really begin with Adam and Eve, but began with the Serpent. The Serpent said to the woman, "Did God actually say, 'You shall not eat of any tree in the garden?'" (Gen. 3:1). The fall began with an attack on Adam and Eve's relationship with God. The Serpent questioned God's word and his truthfulness in what he said to Adam and Eve. The Serpent's next utterance unveiled his bold opposition to God: "You will not surely die" (3:4).

Clearly this was no ordinary serpent. Adam and Eve themselves could have seen that, even without any further information. It should be no surprise, then, that the Bible later on lifts the veil a little more to indicate that behind the literal snake stood a more crafty, bold, and determined opponent, namely, Satan, a powerful spirit, a fallen, rebellious archangel, who is denominated "that ancient serpent" (Rev. 12:9; 20:2; see Isa. 27:1). He is "the deceiver of the whole world" (Rev. 12:9). His deceit began in the garden. But, as the book of Revelation indicates, it continues to this day. So it is worthwhile to think about deceit in this one case in order to have a framework for understanding deceit throughout history.

Satan already attempted to deceive Eve in his first question, "Did God actually say, 'You shall not eat of any tree in the garden?'" (Gen. 3:1). He insinuated that God could withhold from Eve what was good. The deceit then escalated when Satan directly contradicted God's earlier statement by saying, "You will not surely die" (3:4; contradicting 2:17).

Rebellion against God involves destroying a relationship of trust toward God. It also involves language and mind and thought that undermine and obscure knowledge of key truths about humanity's relation to God. The denial concerning the effect of eating from the tree is a denial about future events in the world. But it is also indirectly a denial concerning God and his relation to humanity. The Serpent seems to concede that Eve is correct about what God said, but insists that

God is lying. The Serpent implies that either God does not have the power or he does not have the willingness to bring the penalty of death. Probably, suggests the Serpent, God never intended to execute the death penalty in the first place, but is merely producing a vain threat in order jealously to keep some benefits for himself alone and to keep Eve from enjoying them.

Maybe the Serpent's speech is all the more effective because he does not directly blurt out all his conclusions and all his ideas about God, but allows Eve to follow the trail of insinuations herself and to arrive at her own conclusions. To arrive at her own conclusions—is not that the point? "You will be like God, knowing good and evil" (Gen. 3:5). In effect, the Serpent suggests, "You will make up your own mind about good and evil by looking at the fruit and by exercising your own independent judgment as to what seems right. This is godlike autonomy in morality, as opposed to the 'babyhood' of meekly submitting to whatever God says."

Within our fallen race, we should not be surprised to find some later thinkers reacting to the Genesis story of the fall by claiming that it was a fall "upward," from moral babyhood into moral maturity. For them, autonomy is equated with moral maturity. We could reply to this idea by pointing out that, indeed, Adam and Eve did start out in a situation where their knowledge and their experience were just beginning to grow. But God had his own plans for maturity, as he indicates in the cultural mandate to "fill the earth and subdue it" (Gen. 1:28). Adam and Eve could have chosen to mature by following the way of obedience rather than the way of disobedience.[1]

One decisive way in which Adam and Eve could have matured would have been by resisting the Serpent's temptation. If they had resisted, they would have experienced in themselves a growing knowledge of good in the very process of doing what is good. And they would have experienced a growing knowledge of evil in the process of resisting evil. Through resisting they would have seen evil more deeply for what it is. The joint effects of these experiences would have given them a growing "knowledge of good and evil." But it would have taken place in the way of obedience rather than disobedience.

Unfortunately, such reasoning tends to be lost on rebels who turn God's morality upside down by claiming that the fall went morally upward rather than downward. We should not be surprised that they do so, because they are following the same path of deceit that the Serpent laid down for Adam and Eve. They are being seduced by the very same satanic arguments. By their captivity to deceit they confirm in their own lives that, even to this day, the Serpent's strategy is indeed crafty and alluring. The processes in their own minds confirm the truthfulness of the biblical account.

---

[1]Jesus Christ, as the last Adam, followed the way of obedience perfectly, and so he undid for us the effects of Adam's rebellion (Heb. 2:10–15; 5:7–10). See the next chapter.

Now we may begin to draw out several implications from this account of the fall. First, our relationships challenge us concerning religious commitment. Will you trust God, or will you refuse to trust him? Will you serve God, or will you refuse to serve him? Will you pursue fellowship with God, or will you run away from him into would-be autonomy? The challenge confronts us in each of the three aspects of God's lordship: authority, control, and presence. First, the challenge to trust God is a challenge about authority. Does God possess the authority that he claims for himself? Does he have the right to forbid the tree of knowledge? And will you trust that he is telling you the truth? ("You will not surely die," says the Serpent.)

The challenge confronts us not only when we deal with the speech of God, but also when we deal with the speech of the Serpent. What authority does the Serpent claim? How does he know as much as he knows about what God did say? And if he knows what God did say, why does he misrepresent it? And if he has gotten confused, what does it matter to him anyway? What is in it for him? Why does he seem to be insinuating that God would withhold something good? Why is this Serpent speaking anyway? Is he claiming to be Eve's equal or superior? Can I trust the Serpent? And if, in the end, I do think that I can trust the Serpent, will my trust in him tacitly involve an abandonment of trust in God? And if it does, am I giving to the Serpent the kind of allegiance due only to God and so committing myself to an alien god and an alien worship and an alien religion?

Second, we have here a challenge either to serve God or to refuse to serve. That is a challenge concerning control. Will we continue to have God control our lives, through his commandments, or will we usurp control for ourselves? If God says, "You shall not eat," is that enough for us? Or do we insist on "making up our own minds"? Or—watch out—will we end up being controlled by our own sin and by the manipulative, deceitful rhetoric of the Serpent? Listening to the Serpent also raises the same issues of control.

Third, we have a challenge to mature in fellowship with God or to walk away from that fellowship into would-be autonomy. That is a challenge concerning presence. Will we continue to enjoy God's presence? Will we continue in fellowship with him when he is "walking in the garden" (Gen. 3:8) in a special expression of his presence? Will we also continue in fellowship when he is present with us through his word, which continues to sit in our mind and our memory all day? Will his instruction, "You shall not eat," be a continuing spiritual nourishment as we rejoice in communion with his mind and rejoice in the goodness and wisdom that his word expresses? Or will we break free from that nourishment in the hope of nourishing ourselves, by ourselves, through an autonomous, independent exploration of the moral world?

And then, when we hear the voice of the Serpent, into what sort of personal communion does that voice invite us? Who is this Serpent, and what does he represent, and can he and his words really afford us an entrance into a presence that would displace and overpower and supersede the former presence of God?

In all three aspects—authority, control, and presence—we confront the same basic issue: will we commit ourselves in a relationship of trust to God or not (see table 13.1)? The decision not to commit ourselves to God is just as religious as the decision to commit ourselves to God. Rebellion against God is a religious move, even if it is a negative one.

Table 13.1

	Serving God	Serving self (and Satan)
authority	Recognize and submit to God's authority in instructing in what is right	Become an independent authority
control	Trust in God's control over consequences	Seize control; be controlled by sin
presence	Enjoy God's presence	Ignore God; flee his presence

Moreover, it is not wholly negative. We are incurably religious. If we do not serve God, we will end up serving something, whether that is one of the false gods in ancient Israel, or the god of material success, or human pride, or simply autonomy. We will have a relationship with some god or gods of our devising. G. K. Chesterton is reported to have said, "If people do not believe in God, it is not that they believe in nothing. Rather, they believe in anything."[2] Adam's decision not to serve God is simultaneously a decision to commit himself to autonomy—"You will be like God"—and a decision to serve Satan as a substitute and usurper of the proper place of God. Adam decided to become a subject within the "domain of darkness," the kingdom of Satan (Col. 1:13; cf. Heb. 2:14–15; 1 John 5:19).

Broad Relevance

Someone may be thinking, *All this was long ago, back in the garden of Eden.* Yes. But the fundamental religious issues are the same all the way through history. The book of Revelation depicts the principles of spiritual war, a war between God and his agents on the one side, and Satan and his agents on the other. Revelation may be focusing to some degree on one particular period in history, such as the period of the Roman Empire in which it was originally written, or the period of

---

[2]These words are widely attributed to Chesterton, though their exact source is unknown. See http://chesterton.org/qmeister2/any-everything.htm.

the final crisis just before the second coming. But the principles for spiritual war remain the same, and so it has broad relevance.[3]

In this spiritual warfare, you are either for God or against him. People from time to time may change sides (as when someone is converted to faith in Christ). But there is no neutral ground. Whether you like it or not, your life involves religious commitment to one or the other side of the war.

Corruption of Human Relationships

The fall affects our relationship with God. Does it also affect our relationships with one another? We see effects of the fall in Genesis. Adam blamed Eve rather than admit his own responsibility (Gen. 3:12). Cain killed Abel (Gen. 4:8). Lamech took two wives (Gen. 4:19) and boasted about his vengeance (Gen. 4:23–24). By the time of Noah, "the earth was corrupt in God's sight, and the earth was filled with violence. . . . All flesh had corrupted their way on the earth" (Gen. 6:11–12). Corruption in relation to God leads to corruption in relationship with fellow human beings. Ephesians indicates that this pattern is general: "They [Gentiles] are darkened in their understanding, alienated from the life of God because of the ignorance that is in them, due to their hardness of heart. They have become callous and have given themselves up to sensuality, greedy to practice every kind of impurity" (Eph. 4:18–19).

We can see a connection in several ways. God as ultimate authority is the source for moral standards. If we do not acknowledge God, our sense of morality can be corrupted. We can also see a connection through covenants. Ever since Adam, we are in covenant relation to God. Corruption of that covenantal relation spills over into the corruption of covenantal and quasi-covenantal relations with human beings. Hence, all our relations are corrupted. Or we can see the same point by looking at the three aspects of covenantal lordship, namely authority, control, and presence. Rebellion against God corrupts these three in relation to God. Corruption then extends to the way that human beings exercise authority, control, and presence in relation to others.

The Challenge of Religious Commitment

Adam heard God's commandment concerning the tree (Gen. 2:17). Eve heard Satan's tempting words of deceit (Gen. 3:1, 4–5). But we do not hear such direct speeches now, do we? What about those alive today who are just hearing the voices of other human beings? Though the circumstances in the garden of Eden

---

[3]See Vern S. Poythress, "Counterfeiting in the Book of Revelation as a Perspective on Non-Christian Culture," *Journal of the Evangelical Theological Society* 40, no. 3 (1997): 411–18; Poythress, *The Returning King* (Phillipsburg, NJ: P&R, 2000), especially 16–25.

were unique, there is still permanent relevance. For one thing, God did not utterly abandon mankind when Adam rejected fellowship with God. God continued to speak. He confronted Adam with his sin (Gen. 3:9–13). More than that, he gave a promise of redemption from sin (Gen. 3:15). He continued to expand on his promises, and the Bible is his word in permanent form. God continues to confront us with his claims through the Bible and then indirectly through human beings who bring the message of the Bible to others.

Thus, people today continue to hear the voice of God. Even those who have never heard of God from the Bible do not escape. To this day, rebellious human beings, though they may flee from God's presence with enormous vigor, never escape his presence. Romans 1:18–21 is worth looking at again:

> For the wrath of God is revealed from heaven against all ungodliness and unrighteousness of men, who by their unrighteousness suppress the truth. For what can be known about God is plain to them, because God has shown it to them. For his invisible attributes, namely, his eternal power and divine nature, have been clearly perceived, ever since the creation of the world, in the things that have been made. So they are without excuse. For although they knew God, they did not honor him as God or give thanks to him, but they became futile in their thinking, and their foolish hearts were darkened.

God's voice does not come to everyone as an immediate, audible voice. Nor has it come to everyone through reading the Bible, because not everyone has read the Bible. But God has a message about himself through creation and through the very constitution of human beings, and no one escapes that message. The message is present in the very rules for human relationships because those rules are a manifestation of the character of God who provides those relationships and governs them through his word.[4] The message may not be formulated explicitly in the particular words of a particular human language, but it is still there, it is still known, and it still demands the response: Will you trust God or not? Will you serve him or not? Will you have fellowship with him or not? At this level, everyone continually confronts temptations that are the same in essence as the temptation of Adam and Eve.

The gloomy picture in Romans 1:18–21 says not only this but, in addition, that everyone succumbs to the temptation. We continue to rebel against God unless, through the gospel of Christ, God himself comes to rescue us (Rom. 1:16–17!).

God speaks to everyone through creation. Does Satan also speak? Modern snakes do not speak in audible voices. Eden was unique in that respect. But Satan is "the deceiver of the whole world" (Rev. 12:9). Deceiving involves language

---

[4] See chaps. 8–9.

or something analogically akin to language. According to the Bible, when we rebel against God, we end up in "the domain of darkness" (Col. 1:13), under the kingdom of Satan:

> And you were dead in the trespasses and sins in which you once walked, following the course of this world, following the prince of the power of the air, the spirit that is now at work in the sons of disobedience—among whom we all once lived in the passions of our flesh, carrying out the desires of the body and the mind, and were by nature children of wrath, like the rest of mankind. (Eph. 2:1–3)

It seems natural that people who have become captive in the kingdom of Satan, and whose minds have been deceived by his deceit, would often practice that deceit in their relationships. They are affected not only in their relationship with God but also in their relationships with other human beings.

What such people say is usually not going to be pure error, or pure truth, or pure deceit, but a complex mixture. A mixture can sometimes be more alluring to our own rebellious hearts than a blatant lie. A bald lie would too easily unmask its true character. When unmasked it would cease to be useful, either to Satan in his desire to lure us into evil or to us in our desire to conceal from ourselves our baser motives. For maximum contentment in deceit, we do not need the blatant lie, but we need a whole culture that has corporately drifted and led itself along through a whole series of half-truths into a situation of self-deceit. Then it can be content because everyone is deceived in the same way, and each assures his neighbor that all is well.

The Power of Culture for Evil

Culture does have enormous power to mold us. And maybe, just maybe, it has molded us in some evil ways as well as good. In fact, the Bible assures us that the "maybe" is not just "maybe" but a certainty.[5] Through propaganda, Nazism in Germany succeeded in drawing many of the German people into delusions about themselves and their enemies. Militant Islam has succeeded in drawing its adherents into its delusions. A cultural atmosphere can captivate people so that they see the world and their own duties in a distorted way. The power of human relationships—originally a good gift from God—becomes twisted to evil. Unlike totalitarian countries, in the United States and in Europe we have the protection

---

[5]Among many passages, we may cite the following: "For although they knew God, they did not honor him as God or give thanks to him, but they became futile in their thinking, and their foolish hearts were darkened" (Rom. 1:21); "Now this I say and testify in the Lord, that you must no longer walk as the Gentiles do, in the futility of their minds. They are darkened in their understanding, alienated from the life of God because of the ignorance that is in them, due to their hardness of heart" (Eph. 4:17–18); ". . . Satan, the deceiver of the whole world" (Rev. 12:9).

of freedom of speech, so we may think we are immune to propaganda. But we may still experience molding in more insidious ways. What about the power of advertising and the pressure of conformity?

Yes, advertising helps to make us aware of some new product that would be useful. But it can also tempt us to be selfish in always wanting more. We become aware of not being stylish if we fail to keep up with the latest fashions of friends and neighbors. Likewise, the major media and the major educational institutions may exert enormous social pressure to fall in line. We become like sheep, all going in one direction, and dissenting voices may be marginalized.

Challenge from the Different Voices

So what we hear in our modern environment includes a complex mix of truth and half-truth and deceit. It includes the voice of God and the voice of Satan mixed together. Each voice calls us to religious commitment. That is true not only when the voices are talking about religion in a narrow sense. It is true in all our human relationships. The meanings in human relationships are meanings that are ultimately rooted in God's meanings, and God's meanings are aspects of the plans and thoughts that he has not only with respect to himself but also with respect to the whole course of history. Human relationships, therefore, demand religious commitment. Will we conduct those relationships on the basis of the authority and power and presence of God? Or will we conduct them with each human being claiming to be himself his own ultimate standard, his own god?

Antithesis

Satan hates God.[6] He is antithetical to God and to God's word because God's word faithfully represents God. So one of his goals is to tear down God's word. This he does by contradicting it. "You will not surely die," he says (Gen. 3:4). He not only openly contradicts a specific statement from God but also attacks God's word at a general level by undermining confidence with respect to authority, control, and presence.

When he makes the direct contradiction, "You will not surely die," he implies that God's authority is not to be trusted. But indirectly he also undermines the other aspects. He denies that God controls what will happen by denying that death will ensue. And by denying that God can be trusted, he denies that God presents himself as he truly is. Satan implies that God is not present in his word but rather is presenting in his word a deceitful substitute for himself. Such is the case with Satan's initial attack on Eve. But, as usual, such will always be the case

---

[6] The opposition is vividly depicted in symbolic, pictorial form in the book of Revelation.

in Satan's strategy, because his hatred of God leaves him no other choice. He will always be antithetical to God.

Counterfeiting

This antithesis to God is not, however, the only striking feature in Satan's attack. The attack also has subtlety and craftiness to it ("Now the serpent was more crafty than any other beast of the field," Gen. 3:1). The craftiness first peeks out in the initial question, "Did God actually say, 'You shall not eat of any tree in the garden?'" (Gen. 3:1). The answer is no. The Serpent is already introducing distortion. But there is some grain of truth. God did forbid one tree. Moreover, the Serpent's speech has the form of a question and so conceals his intent later to contradict God. The craftiness comes out even more strikingly in the Serpent's next speech: "You will not surely die. For God knows that when you eat of it your eyes will be opened, and you will be like God, knowing good and evil" (Gen. 3:4–5).

What Satan says is actually uncannily close to the truth. Consider what actually happens in Genesis 3. Eve (and Adam as well) does eat the fruit (Gen. 3:6). But she does not die physically, at least not right away. Nor does Adam. In Genesis 2:17 God said, "In the day that you eat of it you shall surely die." But apparently this does not happen. Rather, what Satan said would happen is what actually happens.

What is going on? We have to ask about the meaning of both *life* and *death*. Real life, life with meaning, life with joy and growth and fruitfulness, is life in communion with God. To be cut off from God means spiritual death (see Eph. 2:1). And spiritual death is actually more significant than physical, bodily death. Hardened rebels against God will experience bodily resurrection, according to John 5:28–29. But that does them no good at all. They experience spiritual death forever, the "second death" (Rev. 20:14). This second death is the real death, the death most to be dreaded (Matt. 10:28). In comparison with it, bodily death is only a pinprick, an emblem, a shadow of the real thing to come. So God was right to say that Adam and Eve would die, and Satan was wrong. But Satan was not wrong if what he meant was physical death. He concealed his meaning. He gave them a half-truth.

Similarly Satan says, "When you eat of it your eyes will be opened" (Gen. 3:5). And what actually happens in the sequel? "Then the eyes of both were opened, and they knew that they were naked" (Gen. 3:7). Satan was right. Or was he? The opening of the eyes to more knowledge sounds like a good thing, an attractive thing. But it turns out not to be. Adam and Eve have their eyes opened only to feel shame. They have been tricked by Satan. And yet what he said was true, after a fashion. That is the kind of trickery we confront when dealing with the schemes of Satan. He offers something close to the truth, but it is a counterfeit.

Like a counterfeit twenty-dollar bill, it has to look genuine in order to trick people. But a careful inspection discloses that it is fake.

Finally, Satan says, as his climactic promise, "and you will be like God, knowing good and evil." That promise also comes true, after a fashion. In Genesis 3:22 God himself says, "Behold, the man has become like one of us in knowing good and evil." Some people see the statement in Genesis 3:22 as purely an ironic echo of Genesis 3:5. It is ironic, to be sure. But it is also true that man has come to "know good and evil" in a deeper way. That is, man has come to know good and evil experientially, in a way that he did not know before the test. He has experienced evil firsthand in the deception of the Serpent. He has also experienced it in his own succumbing to temptation. He has experienced it in the consequences of shame and flight and excuse making. He has also experienced good firsthand, in the goodness of God promising redemption (Gen. 3:15) and mitigating the punishment of death. He has also experienced good secondhand, as an alternative that he rejected in his disobedience. He has come to know both good and evil at a new and deeper level.

But if he has at all repented, he has also come, to some degree, to see that all this experience has a deep bitterness that could totally have been avoided by an experience of good and evil in the way of obedience. He could have "known" good by doing good, and "known" evil by seeing it for what it is and resisting it. So has Adam become "like one of us" in the sense of Genesis 3:22? Has he become like God? In a sense he has, and so this aspect also of Satan's alluring promise has come true. Adam aspired to be "like God" in autonomously deciding about good and evil, and autonomously making his own path in the world. God alone has true autonomy, true and absolute control over his own moral judgments and over his future. Adam could never have that. But he has achieved a kind of pseudo-autonomy by separating himself from fellowship with God.

Even in that separation, he cannot cease to be in the image of God, and therefore to imitate God. But now he imitates God by aspiring to be autonomous rather than in the legitimate way that God appointed. And what does it mean to be "like one of us"? Does it mean that Adam has become "like God"? In some sense yes, but also in some sense no. He has tried to be autonomous as God is autonomous. But he has become an imitator of Satan's own rebellion and distrust, not merely an imitator of God. And his hoped-for autonomy is a failure. He is still dependent on God, and he suffers the consequences of sin (Gen. 3:17–19).

So Satan, in all three aspects of the promise that he makes in Genesis 3:4–5, is using half-truths. He is counterfeiting. We can be the more confident about this theme of counterfeiting because it is clearly present in Revelation, when Revelation sums up the spiritual war between God and Satan. For example, Satan counterfeits God the Father, who is the planner. The Beast (described in Rev. 13:1–10) counterfeits Christ, who is the executor of the Father's will. And the

False Prophet (described in Rev. 13:11–18 and mentioned later by name in Rev. 16:13; 19:20; and 20:10) counterfeits the Holy Spirit, who draws people to worship Christ.[7] A counterfeit that is close to truth seduces people more effectively than a blatant falsehood.

Satan seduced Eve, and Adam went along with her. But that was only the beginning. Satan is still operating today, according to 1 Peter 5:8: "Your adversary the devil prowls around like a roaring lion, seeking someone to devour." He may sometimes do so through subordinate evil agents, namely, evil spirits (1 Tim. 4:1). These agents may have access to people's minds. But because the effects of the fall continue in Adam's descendants, the seduction and counterfeiting crop up not only in demonic voices but also in the voices of human beings who are subjects in Satan's kingdom (see John 8:44; Eph. 2:1–3; Col. 1:13). Human beings speak a mixture of truth and error. The fragments of truth mixed in with error make the error more seductive.

This mixed situation makes human communication problematic. We ourselves must undertake to sort out truth and error. And the most dangerous error is not innocent error, but desire for autonomy manifesting itself in distorted views of God, humanity, and the world. When we look at the products of counterfeiting, we simultaneously confront truth and error, truth and the antithesis of truth.

The writings of Cornelius Van Til are pertinent to the sorting process.[8] Van Til uses two terms, *antithesis* and *common grace*. Antithesis designates the radical difference in allegiance between those who serve God and those who are in rebellion against him. This difference in allegiance influences human relationships so that human relationships regularly contain the challenge of whether we will serve God or a substitute god—God or self. The antithesis between servants of God and enemies of God, or between Christians and non-Christians, manifests itself in differences in worldview, differences in conceptions of humanity, and differences in conceptions of the mind, rationality, and social relationships.

Van Til's second expression, *common grace*, expresses the fact that non-Christians are not as bad as they could be. They hold to fragments of truth, and they sometimes perform acts in external conformity with God's moral law. God is gracious even toward those in rebellion. Truth remains among human beings, in spite of the fall. And this remaining truth can be evaluated positively, as a gift from God. The gift remains among all people, not just those who consciously give their allegiance to God. But unfortunately the remaining truth can also function negatively, because fragments of truth, or half-truths, can be used to captivate people in the service of false gods and false allegiances.

---

[7]Poythress, *The Returning King*, 16–22.
[8]See especially Cornelius Van Til, *The Defense of the Faith*, 2nd ed. (Philadelphia: Presbyterian and Reformed, 1963).

14

Redemption through Christ

For the word of the cross is folly to those who are perishing,
but to us who are being saved it is the power of God. For it is written,
"I will destroy the wisdom of the wise,
and the discernment of the discerning I will thwart."

—1 Corinthians 1:18–19

How can we escape from the effects of the fall? In particular, how can we sort through the mixture of truth and error left by the effects of counterfeiting? We need repair both in our relationship to God and in our relationships with human beings. The fall alienated us from God. How do we return? The Bible directs us beyond the fall to a second crucial event within world history, the coming of Christ. Christ came to rescue us from the fall and from its effects—not only sin, but the corruption in our relationships. Christ renews our fundamental relationships:

> But now in Christ Jesus you who once were far off have been brought near by the blood of Christ. For he himself is our peace, who has made us both [Jews and Gentiles] one and has broken down in his flesh the dividing wall of hostility by abolishing the law of commandments expressed in ordinances, that he might create in himself one new man in place of the two, so making peace, and might reconcile us both to God in one body through the cross, thereby killing the hostility. (Eph. 2:13–16)

The fall had many effects. Naturally in this book we concentrate on the effects on relationships. The effects have penetrated every area of human life. The immediate effect of the fall into sin was alienation from God and spiritual death. That effect remains to this day unless Christ rescues people from their alienation. But effects multiply: physical death among human beings, disease, war, hatred, murder, oppression, sins of many kinds. In addition, the threat of judgment looms over us, because God is a just and holy God, and we have behaved unjustly both toward him and toward our fellow human beings.

Christ undertook to redeem people from both sin and its effects. The redemption that he accomplished is comprehensive, touching on every area infected by the fall. We cannot explore every aspect of the implications of redemption. We will concentrate on its effects on relationships.

Substitutionary Exchange

First, the crucifixion and the resurrection of Christ accomplished a substitutionary exchange. This exchange is expounded in the classic Protestant doctrines of penal atonement and justification. Christ bore the punishment for our sins on the cross (Isa. 53:5–6; 1 Pet. 2:24), in order that the penalty for our sins might be paid and we might be qualified with the righteousness of Christ, which makes us fit to stand in the presence of God the holy One and to receive the blessing of the eternal inheritance in Christ (Rom. 5:21; 2 Cor. 5:21). *Justification*, in the technical sense of the word, includes both forgiveness of sins and the positive pronouncement from God as Judge that we are accounted righteous on the basis of the righteousness of Christ. Justification is defined in juridical terms, against the background of God as Judge and the righteousness of God as the standard for judgment.[1] Justification implies reconciliation with God and therefore repair of our relationship with God (Rom. 5:5–11). But it has potential implications for our reconciliation to others. Peace with God includes peace with others who are included in the same body of reconciled persons (Eph. 2:13–17). It remains for this reconciliation to be worked out in practice.

Common Grace

Reconciliation is a benefit of Christ's atonement. So how can a non-Christian have any peaceful relationships at all? In fact, we can press the issue even further. If sin makes people liable to death and hell, why do not the sins of non-Christians lead to their immediate deaths? The doctrine of common grace addresses such questions. Common grace is an undeserved benefit from God given to a non-

---

[1] I am aware of the recent disputes about the meaning of justification in Paul's writings. I cannot enter into the discussion in detail at this point. We need an answer to the wrath of God against individual sinners, as well as a corporate and cosmic answer to corporate corruption of the world. That answer is found in the person and work of Christ, who delivers us from God's wrath and gives us a right standing before God on the basis of his righteousness.

Christian.[2] It is in contrast with special grace. Special grace means undeserved benefits given to people who are in union with Christ, and who are saved by him. And sometimes the term *special grace* is extended to include those who are chosen in Christ before the foundation of the world (Eph. 1:4), but who have not yet come to saving faith in Christ. These are people who will become Christians but are not yet Christians. Because they are already chosen in Christ, we can understand how they might receive benefits that they personally do not deserve but that Christ has deserved and has obtained on their behalf. But what about common grace to those who will never become Christians?

Genesis 8:20–22 can help. In Genesis 8 God makes a promise to Noah: "Neither will I ever again strike down every living creature as I have done. While the earth remains, seedtime and harvest, cold and heat, summer and winter, day and night, shall not cease" (Gen. 8:21–22). In Genesis 9 God goes on to bless Noah and his sons and gives a dominion mandate very like that given to Adam (Gen. 1:28–30). These promises apply to Noah and his descendants, and so they include all human beings now on earth. God promises blessings even to those who are not included in his special holy people. They are thus blessings of common grace.

The blessings and promises were given immediately after "the LORD smelled the pleasing aroma" of Noah's burnt offerings (Gen. 8:21). These burnt offerings, like all the other sacrificial offerings by God's people in the Old Testament, prefigure the self-offering of Christ (Heb. 10:1–14). God is pleased with Noah's offerings because the animal sacrifices prefigure the work of Christ. Thus the work of Christ is the ultimate basis for God's blessings to Noah. And if so, it is the ultimate basis for the blessings of common grace given to Noah's descendants. Christ's work accomplished the salvation of the elect, the ones chosen in Christ from the beginning. But it also gave a basis for lesser benefits, the benefits of common grace that come to unbelievers. As sinners against God, we all deserve to die immediately. But we still receive life and food and sunshine and other benefits:

> For he [God] makes his sun rise on the evil and on the good, and sends rain on the just and on the unjust. (Matt. 5:45)

> Yet he [God] did not leave himself without witness, for he did good by giving you rains from heaven and fruitful seasons, satisfying your hearts with food and gladness. (Acts 14:17)

These are among the benefits of common grace. Now we may apply these truths to the situation with respect to peaceful human relationships. Such relationships are a benefit that rebels do not deserve in and of themselves. They come as one of the benefits of Christ. Christ has not only obtained reconciliation with

---

[2]See chap. 13.

God for his chosen ones but has also obtained the blessing of "common grace" relationships given here and there to unbelievers. This is so despite the fact that many of the beneficiaries do not know Christ and might even be offended at the suggestion that he had anything to do with their relationships.

Dying and Rising with Christ

The work of Christ results not only in justification but also in sanctification. That is, we who are united to Christ not only enjoy freedom to stand before God on the basis of Christ's perfect righteousness (justification); we also experience progressive transformation into conformity with the image of Christ (2 Cor. 3:18). More and more, we obey and serve God in thought, word, and deed. This process of sanctification takes place through fellowship with the dying and rising of Christ. We are identified with the dying and rising of Christ once and for all at the beginning of the Christian life, as symbolized by baptism:

> We were buried therefore with him by baptism into death, in order that, just as Christ was raised from the dead by the glory of the Father, we too might walk in newness of life. (Rom. 6:4)

> We know that our old self was crucified with him in order that the body of sin might be brought to nothing, so that we would no longer be enslaved to sin. (Rom. 6:6)

> For the death he died he died to sin, once for all, but the life he lives he lives to God. So you also must consider yourselves dead to sin and alive to God in Christ Jesus. (Rom. 6:10–11)

We also experience fellowship with the death and resurrection of Jesus day by day:

> ... that I may know him and the power of his resurrection, and may share his sufferings, becoming like him in his death. (Phil. 3:10)

> ... always carrying in the body the death of Jesus, so that the life of Jesus may also be manifested in our bodies. For we who live are always being given over to death for Jesus' sake, so that the life of Jesus also may be manifested in our mortal flesh. So death is at work in us, but life in you. (2 Cor. 4:10–12)

Dying and rising with Christ includes renewal in our relationships:

> Put to death therefore what is earthly in you: sexual immorality, impurity, passion, evil desire, and covetousness, which is idolatry. On account of these the wrath of God is coming. In these you too once walked, when you were living in

them. But now you must put them all away: anger, wrath, malice, slander, and obscene talk from your mouth. Do not lie to one another, seeing that you have put off the old self with its practices and have put on the new self, which is being renewed in knowledge after the image of its creator. Here there is not Greek and Jew, circumcised and uncircumcised, barbarian, Scythian, slave, free; but Christ is all, and in all.

Put on then, as God's chosen ones, holy and beloved, compassionate hearts, kindness, humility, meekness, and patience, bearing with one another and, if one has a complaint against another, forgiving each other; as the Lord has forgiven you, so you also must forgive. And above all these put on love, which binds everything together in perfect harmony. And let the peace of Christ rule in your hearts, to which indeed you were called in one body. And be thankful. (Col. 3:5–15)

Giving up former ways of living may be painful. We not only must give something up but also must sort through truth and error, good and bad. We must resist temptations to cling to the bad and temptations to give up some bits of the good because we want to avoid the hard consequences of assimilating them into our lives. Giving up the old ways of living is a kind of crucifixion and death. Colossians 3:5 begins with the expression "Put to death," and is tied directly to a reference to the crucifixion and resurrection of Christ (Col. 2:12, 20; 3:1). Receiving a new way of life is part of what it means to benefit from Christ's resurrection.

One of the greater challenges is simply to have humility. Pride—pride in self—is among the root sins that infect us most deeply. In fact, we can say that Adam's fall was a matter of pride in thinking that he could manage a course independent of God. To submit to God, not just in one area but in every area, involves a crucifixion of self: "If anyone comes to me and does not hate his own father and mother and wife and children and brothers and sisters, yes, and even his own life, he cannot be my disciple. Whoever does not bear his own cross and come after me cannot be my disciple" (Luke 14:25–27).

Defeating Satan

A third benefit of the work of Christ is the defeat of Satan. The book of Hebrews indicates that Christ defeated Satan in his crucifixion and resurrection:

Since therefore the children share in flesh and blood, he himself likewise partook of the same things, that through death he might destroy the one who has the power of death, that is, the devil, and deliver all those who through fear of death were subject to lifelong slavery. (Heb. 2:14–15)

He has delivered us from the domain of darkness and transferred us to the kingdom of his beloved Son. (Col. 1:13)

Jesus won a victory against Satan in the resurrection, and that victory is fruitful in delivering people from the kingdom of Satan. The deliverance takes place at the beginning of the Christian life, when we first believe the gospel. And the deliverance is also progressive, as we come to know the truth more deeply and cast off enslavement to sin more thoroughly. The deliverance includes deliverance in thought, as our thinking moves from deceit to truth.

This change of heart affects our view of human relationships. In practice, we become more aware both of the positive power of our relationships to express love and of the negative power of relationships to cause alienation and suffering. Human relationships are not neutral but are battlegrounds in a spiritual war. And one key instrument in this battleground is the word of God:

> Stand therefore, having fastened on the belt of truth, and having put on the breastplate of righteousness, and, as shoes for your feet, having put on the readiness given by the gospel of peace. In all circumstances take up the shield of faith, with which you can extinguish all the flaming darts of the evil one; and take the helmet of salvation, and the sword of the Spirit, which is the word of God, praying at all times in the Spirit. (Eph. 6:14–18)

In sum, we need to rely on Christ and his word in order to transform our relationships.

15

Peoples and Cultures

Worthy are you to take the scroll
and to open its seals,
for you were slain, and by your blood you ransomed people for God
from every tribe and language and people and nation,
and you have made them a kingdom and priests to our God,
and they shall reign on the earth.

—Revelation 5:9–10

We have considered two great turning points within history, the fall and Christ's work of redemption. We look forward to a third, namely, the return of Christ and the establishment of the new heavens and the new earth (Rev. 21:1–22:5). Now we need to begin to look within world history at progressively smaller scales. We look at the packages within world history. Since human relationships develop within the context of a culture that shapes the relationships, we need to think about the diversity in peoples and in cultures.

Peoples

One of God's principal goals for world history is the salvation of many peoples through the work of Christ:

> Worthy are you [Christ] to take the scroll
>   and to open its seals,
> for you were slain, and by your blood you ransomed people for God
>   from every tribe and language and people and nation,

and you have made them a kingdom and priests to our God,
    and they shall reign on the earth. (Rev. 5:9–10)

> After this I looked, and behold, a great multitude that no one could number, from every nation, from all tribes and peoples and languages, standing before the throne and before the Lamb. (Rev. 7:9)

In the ancient world as well as in the modern world, political empires have sometimes governed a large area including many "people groups," that is, ethnic groups with distinct languages and customs. The book of Revelation invites us to think not simply about the largest political empires but about these distinct ethnic groups as well. In the consummation, all the distinct peoples will be integrated into a society and city of peace—the New Jerusalem (Rev. 21:2, 10). This is an appropriate context in which to consider the multiplicity of cultures, and the prejudices and separations and tensions that may arise from cultural differences.

Babel

The diversity of cultures arose in the world with the splitting apart of languages at the time of Babel:

> Now the whole earth had one language and the same words. And as people migrated from the east, they found a plain in the land of Shinar and settled there. And they said to one another, "Come, let us make bricks, and burn them thoroughly." And they had brick for stone, and bitumen for mortar. Then they said, "Come, let us build ourselves a city and a tower with its top in the heavens, and let us make a name for ourselves, lest we be dispersed over the face of the whole earth." And the LORD came down to see the city and the tower, which the children of man had built. And the LORD said, "Behold, they are one people, and they have all one language, and this is only the beginning of what they will do. And nothing that they propose to do will now be impossible for them. Come, let us go down and there confuse their language, so that they may not understand one another's speech." So the LORD dispersed them from there over the face of all the earth, and they left off building the city. Therefore its name was called Babel, because there the LORD confused the language of all the earth. And from there the LORD dispersed them over the face of all the earth. (Gen. 11:1–9)

The multiplication of languages went together with people being "dispersed." They were separated by language, geography, and culture. As a result they ceased to be able to cooperate in doing evil. But they also ceased to be able to cooperate in doing good. Redemption, then, includes a plan from God for overcoming the barriers that grew up as a result of Babel.

We see a beginning of the promise of redemption in Genesis 12:3. God says to Abram, "I will bless those who bless you, and him who dishonors you I will curse, and in you all the families of the earth shall be blessed." The mention of all the families of the earth reflects back on the division into people groups that took place at Babel and was cataloged in Genesis 10:1–32. All these "families" or groups, and not just Abram, will be able to receive God's blessing in connection with Abram. Later parts of the Old Testament explain more about God's purposes for the different peoples:

> May all kings fall down before him,
>   all nations serve him! (Ps. 72:11)

> Praise the LORD, all nations!
>   Extol him, all peoples! (Ps. 117:1; see Rom. 15:11)

> It shall come to pass in the latter days
>   that the mountain of the house of the LORD
> shall be established as the highest of the mountains,
>   and it shall be lifted up above the hills;
> and peoples shall flow to it,
>   and many nations shall come, and say:
> "Come, let us go up to the mountain of the LORD,
>   to the house of the God of Jacob,
> that he may teach us his ways
>   and that we may walk in his paths."
> For out of Zion shall go forth the law,
>   and the word of the LORD from Jerusalem. (Mic. 4:1–2)

"Many nations" will come to God. The result of submission to God will be universal peace:

> Nation shall not lift up sword against nation,
>   neither shall they learn war anymore;
> but they shall sit every man under his vine and under his fig tree,
>   and no one shall make them afraid. (Mic. 4:3–4)

Human relationships will be transformed as a result of the spreading of God's word.

Pentecost and Acts

Thus, in the Old Testament God gives promises about a future time when the nations will be blessed through Abraham. The New Testament indicates that the time has now come. The book of Acts describes the beginning of a process of bringing peace to the nations. In Acts 1:8 Jesus commissions the disciples to "be my witnesses in Jerusalem and in all Judea and Samaria, and to the end of the earth" (see also Luke 24:47). The commission begins to be fulfilled in Acts 2, when "the mighty works of God" (2:11) are proclaimed in the various languages of the Roman Empire (2:8–9). The Holy Spirit miraculously enables the apostles to overcome the language barriers. God through the disciples speaks his message of salvation to the language groups and people groups. Acts 2 thus offers a picture of a kind of reversal of Babel. People from different languages are able to understand one another.

This picture in Acts 2 is not complete, because the people groups still consist exclusively of "Jews" (Acts 2:5). But it anticipates the gathering of Gentiles as well. The rest of Acts records further expansions. Cornelius, the God-fearing centurion, comes to faith in Christ in Acts 10.[1] Cornelius and his friends are Gentiles, not Jews, as the subsequent narrative makes clear (10:28, 45; 11:3, 18). Cornelius, like other Gentiles who were called "God-fearers," has already come to acknowledge the God of Israel as the one true God (10:2). Later, the gospel comes to pagan polytheists as well, in Acts 14:8–18 and 17:22–34. Acts 2 describes the miraculous operation of the Holy Spirit's power. After Acts 2 the Holy Spirit continues to spread the gospel, but does so more by nonmiraculous means.

The spread of the gospel brings peace with God because it announces reconciliation between God and man through Christ:

> Therefore, since we have been justified by faith, we have peace with God through our Lord Jesus Christ. Through him we have also obtained access by faith into this grace in which we stand, and we rejoice in hope of the glory of God. (Rom. 5:1–2)

> All this is from God, who through Christ reconciled us to himself and gave us the ministry of reconciliation; that is, in Christ God was reconciling the world to himself, not counting their trespasses against them, and entrusting to us the message of reconciliation. Therefore, we are ambassadors for Christ, God making his appeal through us. We implore you on behalf of Christ, be reconciled to God. (2 Cor. 5:18–20)

Peace with God leads also to peace with one another: "For he himself is our peace, who has made us both [Jews and Gentiles] one and has broken down in his flesh the dividing wall of hostility" (Eph. 2:14). Peace between Jew and Gentile has

---

[1] We may add here the Ethiopian eunuch, who apparently was a God-fearer (Acts 8:26–40). There were also Gentile converts in Old Testament times, such as Rahab, Naaman, and the Queen of Sheba. But Cornelius represents the beginning of an era when larger numbers come to faith in the true God through the gospel of Christ.

fundamentally been achieved through the reconciling work of Christ. Human relationships have been healed. But peace must still be worked out in practice. The New Testament has numerous indications that struggles occurred between believers. To work out peace with one another, the people in the church had to receive both spiritual power through the Spirit of Christ and good theology concerning the implications of the work of Christ.

The distinction between Jew and Gentile is the most fundamental cultural division because it is not merely cultural, and not merely "religious" in the sense that pagan religions might differ from one another. A boundary was put in place by God himself, "the law of commandments expressed in ordinances" (Eph. 2:15), which separated the people of Israel from all the other peoples of the world, to be a unique people. At the time of the exodus from Egypt, God distinguished the people of Israel from all the other peoples: "Now therefore, if you will indeed obey my voice and keep my covenant, you shall be my treasured possession among all peoples, for all the earth is mine; and you shall be to me a kingdom of priests and a holy nation" (Ex. 19:5–6).

When Christ came, he removed this separation:

> For he himself [Christ] is our peace, who has made us both one and has broken down in his flesh the dividing wall of hostility by abolishing the law of command-ments expressed in ordinances, that he might create in himself one new man in place of the two, so making peace, and might reconcile us both to God in one body through the cross, thereby killing the hostility. (Eph. 2:14–16)

Thus the removal of the boundary described in Ephesians 2:14–16 is a unique step. But the reconciliation between Jew and Gentile also illustrates in specific form the broader reconciliation between nations of which Micah 4:3 speaks:

> Nation shall not lift up sword against nation,
>   neither shall they learn war anymore.

In the case of Jew and Gentile in the church, peace does not require that Gentiles become Jews. Cornelius and his Gentile friends are uncircumcised, that is, non-Jews. They are baptized with the Holy Spirit and then baptized with water signifying their incorporation into the church (Acts 10:44–48; 11:15–18). The apostle Peter appeals to this divinely ordained precedent when the Jerusalem council discusses the issue of Gentile converts (Acts 15). In Acts 15, the apostles and elders give a ruling that lays some requirements on Gentile believers (15:20, 28–29). Significantly, the ruling does not require the Gentiles to be circumcised and thus to become Jews—even though some people initially argued for such a rule (15:1, 5). Likewise, Jews are not required to become Gentiles or give up their customs (Acts 21:20–26). But neither are the customs sacrosanct. Compromises with respect to custom are sometimes appropriate in order to express and maintain the unity of the one people of God in Christ (Gal. 2:11–14).

The unity in the body of Christ is a unity in diversity. There is one body, but with many members, and the members have different functions (1 Corinthians 12). This unity and diversity applies not only to differences in gifts but also to differences in culture as well. Each individual and each culture make a contribution to the body of Christ. The biggest divisions among human beings are the divisions of language and culture. But even those who share a common culture can sometimes be divided by hatred and by marked differences in personality. Each individual is different from any other.

At an intermediate level, there can be divisions and misunderstandings among different subgroups within a larger culture. Thus, in modern Western countries, we can single out various youth subcultures, rural subcultures, medical subcultures, prison subcultures, theater subcultures, arts subcultures, immigrant subcultures, young-urban-professional subcultures, and so on. We can also distinguish subcultures by geography: New York City has a culture distinct from London or Sydney or Los Angeles. Within New York City there are subgroupings, such as the "culture" of Greenwich Village or Harlem or Wall Street. A particular business firm or sports team can have something of a distinct "culture" within it. Cultural classifications can cut across one another in various ways.[2] The picture of unity and diversity in the body of Christ, developed in 1 Corinthians 12, addresses in principle all these kinds of division.

---

[2]On culture, see D. A. Carson, *Christ and Culture Revisited* (Grand Rapids: Eerdmans, 2008); John M. Frame, *The Doctrine of the Christian Life* (Phillipsburg, NJ: P&R, 2009), part 5, 853–908. This material is also available as John M. Frame, *Christ and Culture: Lectures Given at the Pensacola Theological Institute, July 23–27, 2001*, accessed December 14, 2009, http://www.thirdmill.org/newfiles/joh_frame/Frame.Apologetics2004.ChristandCulture.pdf.

16

Principles for Cultural Reconciliation

And he came and preached peace to you who were far off
and peace to those who were near. For through him we both
have access in one Spirit to the Father.

—Ephesians 2:17–18

Peace among nations has already been achieved through the one sacrifice of Christ, who reconciles us to God and to one another. The peace and reconciliation of the gospel will be fully manifested in the new heaven and the new earth. Within this life, peace is to be progressively worked out in the context of the unity and diversity in the church, the body of Christ (Eph. 4:7–16; 1 Corinthians 12). Diversity includes cultural diversity. If we use the word *culture* in a broad way, it can include many kinds of differences between groups—ethnic differences, certainly, but also differences in subgroups according to geographical location, wealth, employment, and interests. For simplicity, we will focus primarily on the large-scale differences between major ethnic groups, such as Chinese, Japanese, Indian, Kenyan, German, and so on. Many of the principles can be applied eventually to more minor differences and divisions as well. Within the body of Christ, each people group retains its distinctiveness in language, customs, and culture, just as Jewish and Gentile Christians did. At the same time, each people group grows by interacting within the body of Christ.

The Progress of Peace

Growth requires the abandonment of some practices from the past. A people group must give up anything that is sinful itself, whether practices like prosti-

127

tution or false worship, or mistreatment or hostility or prejudice toward other cultures. In addition, in building relations with other groups, especially within the church, the people in various groups must practice loving their neighbors. This will involve cultural compromises in cases that involve cross-cultural friction (think, for example, of Jewish food laws, which were a source of friction in Gal. 2:11–14).

It is never easy to build a bridge between two distinct cultures. Frictions arise partly because of human pride and greed but also because of misunderstandings, frustrations, and the challenges of adjusting to what is initially strange and uncomfortable. The Christian who attempts to cross a cultural barrier out of love for others finds inevitably that it involves a painful dying to self. He dies as he surrenders the pride that he may have had in his native culture. And he experiences a kind of emotional "death" in the pain of repeatedly submitting to what is strange, and, in some cases, in the humiliation of finding himself inferior to children who are growing up in the new culture and therefore know more about that culture than he does.

The cultural neophyte not only has to learn new cultural practices; he also fights against the memory of what intuitively he feels things should be like according to his native culture. Instinctively, an American holds out his right hand to shake hands in order to greet someone. A Japanese man will bow instead. An American conducts events by the clock. A college class is over after exactly fifty minutes or whatever the schedule specifies. Many tribal cultures, by contrast, run by "social time," in which social events run not by the clock but by perceptions of social accomplishment. The event is over whenever the participants are satisfied with their experience together.[1]

Moreover, natives within the new culture can at times be quite pitiless: they may laugh at an adult who makes stupid, childlike mistakes in their cultural practices. The Christian finds here one instance where he experiences fellowship with the suffering and crucifixion of Christ. Christ crossed the biggest barrier of all, the barrier between God and man. Christians are called on to cross the subordinate barriers between cultures.

In a previous chapter we considered several aspects of Christ's work. He died and rose again for us. He also accomplished a substitutionary exchange in that he bore the penalty of our sins and gave his righteousness to us. His substitution is unique. But a faint echo of that unique exchange can nevertheless be found in acts of mercy that Christians do. A Christian may choose to undergo pain or inconvenience for someone else's benefit. In the case of learning another culture, a Christian dies to the comfort and familiarity of his own native culture in order

---

[1] See the discussion of clock time and social time in Vern S. Poythress, *Redeeming Science: A God-Centered Approach* (Wheaton, IL: Crossway, 2006), 138–43, 220–23.

that the benefit of hearing the gospel may come to people who belong to the other culture. Crossing language barriers with the gospel also leads to a defeat of Satan. Satan as lord of the "domain of darkness" (Col. 1:13) holds the nations captive through bondage not only to guilt but also to the worship of idols and spirits. The gospel, in coming to a new culture, opens the door to the people to receive deliverance.

Cultural Change

Deliverance in the long run includes change on many levels. A particular culture is not an unchangeable monolith. Cultures can and do develop and change (we have only to think of the impact of modernity on many traditional cultures). The question is how and in what direction? Do they develop under the power of the gospel, in a manner bringing progressive purification, light, peace, and blessing? For example, do marriages change over the decades as husbands and wives and children are empowered by the Spirit to obey God's pattern in Ephesians 5:22–6:4? Do governments change as Christians take a place in government and move it away from corruption and favoritism? Or does a culture develop or even disintegrate in a merely reactive manner, as has sometimes been the case when traditional cultures have clashed with modernity? The coming of the Christian faith to a particular culture changes people, and the people begin to change the larger culture.[2]

God has a universal plan that includes the spread of the gospel to all peoples and languages. But there are sometimes obstacles. The obstacles occur in the heart of the individual when he or she through spiritual blindness resists the gospel: "And even if our gospel is veiled, it is veiled only to those who are perishing. In their case the god of this world has blinded the minds of the unbelievers, to keep them from seeing the light of the gospel of the glory of Christ, who is the image of God" (2 Cor. 4:3–4).

In addition, sometimes whole cultures have a pattern of thinking that poses an obstacle. For example, ancient Greek philosophy and most of Greek religion were not receptive to the idea of resurrection from the dead, and so many Greeks balked when the resurrection appeared as a central part of the message of the apostle Paul in Acts 17:30–32.

A culture may *seem* unchangeable and sacrosanct to those living within it. They think that they *cannot* change. We find a clear instance in Acts 16. At Philippi the owners of a slave girl seize Paul and Silas and claim to the magistrates, "They [Paul and Silas] advocate customs that are not lawful for us *as Romans* to accept or practice" (Acts 16:21). The slave owners imply that Roman law forbids the

---

[2]On Christ and culture, and the issues of Christians as agents of cultural change, see John M. Frame, *The Doctrine of the Christian Life* (Phillipsburg, NJ: P&R, 2008), 853–908.

change that Paul and Silas advocate. In this case, their claim is not actually true. But human laws may sometimes stand in direct opposition to the demands of the gospel. For example, in some Islamic countries, laws are in place that forbid a Muslim to change religion. Even when human law forbids change, divine law has higher authority. Jesus criticized the Jewish leaders for elevating "human tradition" and thereby undermining God's law (Matt. 15:1–20). Human laws can be changed by those in authority. Change is possible, though it may be difficult, it may be resisted, and those who bring the gospel may be persecuted as a result.

The pattern of thinking within a particular culture may also contain subtle but deep barriers to the truth of the gospel. Jesus criticized the practices concerning washing hands and concerning dedicating to God what is owed to parents (Matt. 15:1–6). But these two practices were only the tip of the iceberg. They exemplified "the tradition of the elders," a larger body of tradition that became a barrier (Matt. 15:2).

Previous to contact with the gospel, a culture may not have a concept for "sin." In English, because of the preceding centuries of exposure to the gospel and to the contents of the Bible, we have developed an idea of sin that has theology built into it. Sin means falling short of God's righteousness, falling short of his moral standards. Without the idea of God, who is one universal God and is holy and righteous, the word *sin* would not mean quite the same thing as it does in a Christian context, which has been informed by the Bible.

In some cultures we may even have trouble explaining the idea of "human" or "humanity." A tribal culture with little exposure to the outside world may think of others outside its group as effectively subhuman. The tribe may not be prepared to think in terms of a basic commonality that they share with the outsiders.[3]

Struggle within the Church

When people within a particular culture become Christians, God changes their hearts and their direction in life. But they do not immediately become morally perfect in their thinking and in their behavior. It takes time. Sometimes their progress may be rapid. But sometimes the surrounding culture drags them back. And sometimes cultural ideas have so penetrated the church, the body of Christians, that the whole church in a particular culture makes culturally influenced excuses for its sins.

Even within the first-century church, James criticized people who were favoring the rich (James 2:1–7). Later on, as the church gained cultural power, the

---

[3]Paul had to make a point about the unity of mankind in a Greek context where the Greeks thought of themselves as superior to "barbarians": "And he [God] made from one man every nation of mankind to live on all the face of the earth, having determined allotted periods and the boundaries of their dwelling place" (Acts 17:26).

temptations to abuse power increased. Moreover, when it becomes culturally advantageous to join a church, the church runs the danger of welcoming into its membership people who join for social reasons rather than out of genuine love for Christ. These people then drag the church away from its true nature.

As a consequence, church authorities have sometimes endorsed practices that were in fact out of accord with biblical moral standards, such as ghettoization of the Jews and the persecution of those who held different religious views. The record is shameful.

Corporate Influences of Sin

Why do such difficulties arise? They are direct or indirect effects of sin on whole cultures and on the churches within the cultures. To put it another way, they are barriers, erected by sin and ultimately by Satan, to keep people in bondage and darkness. "In their case the god of this world [Satan] has blinded the minds of the unbelievers, to keep them from seeing the light of the gospel of the glory of Christ, who is the image of God" (2 Cor. 4:4).

But even in these cases God exercises sovereign control. According to his own purposes, he has not created each individual human being in total independence of his surroundings, but has made him part of a family and a culture. And his connections with family and culture can have bad as well as good effects.

God himself indicates a family connection with respect to the effects of sin: ". . . a God merciful and gracious, . . . keeping steadfast love for thousands, forgiving iniquity and transgression and sin, but who will by no means clear the guilty, visiting the iniquity of the fathers on the children and children's children, to the third and fourth generation" (Ex. 34:6–7). The effect on future generations is specifically tied to idolatry:

> You shall not make for yourself a carved image, or any likeness of anything that is in heaven above, or that is in the earth beneath, or that is in the water under the earth. You shall not bow down to them or serve them, for I the LORD your God am a jealous God, visiting the iniquity of the fathers on the children to the third and the fourth generation of those who hate me, but showing steadfast love to thousands of those who love me and keep my commandments. (Ex. 20:4–6)

Idolatry is a kind of spiritual darkness. It passes from fathers to children. This spiritual darkness is not only a natural effect of continuing in sin, but a judgment from God. We may conclude that one of the effects of idolatrous practices within a culture is to corrupt the thinking of that culture, to introduce confusion about the nature of the spirit world, and in the long run to corrupt the language as well. Suppose that a whole culture ceases to worship the true God and makes for itself idols (Rom. 1:18–25). It frequently talks about these idols as if they were gods; it stops talking about the true God. Then, over a period of generations, the culture still has a word *God*, but the cultural thinking has been corrupted by thinking about the "gods." In new generations, people grow up with this thinking.

In sum, after the fall of Adam, and after the division of cultures at Babel, we cannot assume that culture is simply a neutral environment that can be ignored as the gospel spreads. Many times missionaries must do some hard thinking about what cultural forms are acceptable and can be useful in the contextualization of the gospel, and what cultural forms are sin, from which people need deliverance. But the Bible still guarantees a basic commonality among human beings. All are made in the image of God, and no one escapes knowing God (Rom. 1:18–25). We also have the guarantee that God will save people from all nations. Through the power of the Holy Spirit, the gospel can overcome the barriers and be received with faith among all the peoples and cultures. Through the gospel the Holy Spirit works in transforming both individuals and churches. Churches can repent and break free of captivity to a cultural sin. But sometimes when a church has become captive to sin, it refuses to repent. God can judge it for its sins and remove it (Rev. 2:4–5). Then the work of the Holy Spirit begins again as a new church is raised up in the culture.

17

Good and Bad Kinds of Diversity

> . . . that there may be no division in the body, but that the members
> may have the same care for one another.
>
> —1 Corinthians 12:25

> Now you are the body of Christ and individually members of it.
>
> —1 Corinthians 12:27

Cultures do differ, sometimes in striking and in serious ways. But when the barriers of human sin are overcome, and people come to Christ, they are united in one body. The unity does not dissolve the diversity, but people are united in "one faith" and "one hope" as well as "one Lord" and "one God" (Eph. 4:4–6). The "one faith" indicates commonality in belief and in knowledge.

Kinds of Diversity

How do we approach cultural diversity? Thinking in terms of multiple perspectives can help. We have already at several points introduced multiple perspectives on the same subject matter.[1] In a sense, each person has his own "perspective"

---

[1] See for example, the triad of authority, control, and presence introduced in chap. 4. More about perspectives can be found in Vern S. Poythress, *Symphonic Theology: The Validity of Multiple Perspectives in Theology* (Grand Rapids: Zondervan, 1987; repr., Phillipsburg, NJ: P&R, 2001); John M. Frame, *Perspectives on the Word of God: An Introduction to Christian Ethics* (Phillipsburg, NJ: Presbyterian and Reformed, 1990); and the triad for lordship in Frame, *The Doctrine of the Knowledge of God* (Phillipsburg, NJ: Presbyterian and Reformed, 1987).

on life or on a particular issue. But people can be wrong; they can be in error with respect to facts and with respect to evaluations of the facts. They can misconstrue the meaning of their own life. So not all perspectives are valid. Nevertheless, *some* perspectives are valid. When multiple perspectives are legitimate, they are intrinsically harmonizable because there is only one God and one world that God has made. Diverse cultures are like perspectives through which people understand God and the world. The differences in culture are not merely to be homogenized, as if they were trivial. But neither are they in tension, at least if all the people involved are following the truth. This kind of diversity enriches the body of Christ.

What kind of diversity are we talking about? Within the body of Christ diversity does not mean a shallow "tolerance" of all kinds of differences. That is, we do not follow those skeptics who have given up because they think that no one can know the truth.[2] Rather, because God has blessed us through Christ and has given us his word and his Spirit, we do know truth, including truth about God and about his moral standards. At the same time, we can grow by adding more truths to what we know and by knowing truth more deeply. We grow partly through learning from others, as is described in Ephesians 4:11–16:

> And he [Christ] gave the apostles, the prophets, the evangelists, the shepherds and teachers, to equip the saints for the work of ministry, for building up the body of Christ, until we all attain to the unity of the faith and of the knowledge of the Son of God, to mature manhood, to the measure of the stature of the fullness of Christ, so that we may no longer be children, tossed to and fro by the waves and carried about by every wind of doctrine, by human cunning, by craftiness in deceitful schemes. Rather, speaking the truth in love, we are to grow up in every way into him who is the head, into Christ, from whom the whole body, joined and held together by every joint with which it is equipped, when each part is working properly, makes the body grow so that it builds itself up in love.

In addition, we grow in the truth partly through repudiating false teaching:

> Now the Spirit expressly says that in later times some will depart from the faith by devoting themselves to deceitful spirits and teachings of demons, through the insincerity of liars whose consciences are seared, who forbid marriage and require abstinence from foods that God created to be received with thanksgiving by those who believe and know the truth. . . .
>
> If you put these things before the brothers, you will be a good servant of Christ Jesus, being trained in the words of the faith and of the good doctrine that you have

---

[2] On postmodernism, see appendix G, and Vern S. Poythress, *In the Beginning Was the Word: Language—A God-Centered Approach* (Wheaton, IL: Crossway, 2009), appendices A and B.

followed. Have nothing to do with irreverent, silly myths. Rather train yourself for godliness. (1 Tim. 4:1–7)

Love is one of the bonds that creates enjoyment of diversity and unifies us in the midst of diversity. If we love, we exercise patience in listening to others and trying to understand them, and then we learn more of the truth that they have grasped. On the other hand, genuine love also implies being willing to protect others from false teaching, which corrupts people's minds and lives. In this process the Bible guides us, just as Paul gave inspired guidance to Timothy and expected that he would be able to tell the difference between true and false teaching.

The love in the body of Christ ultimately reflects the love between God the Father and God the Son. Hence, the unity in diversity in the body of Christ reflects Trinitarian unity in diversity. The enrichment of the body of Christ through the diversity of cultures is a positive reflection of the Trinitarian diversity of persons.

We can put the same point in another way. Consider first the principle of unity. The Father knows all things in his wisdom, who is the Son (Col. 2:3). God's unified knowledge is his eternal vision of truth. God reveals his knowledge to us in Christ and in the Bible, so that we come to a unified understanding of the truth. All the members of the body of Christ share in one faith, and in "the unity of the Spirit in the bond of peace" (Eph. 4:3), thereby expressing their unity. In the new heaven and the new earth, each of us will "know fully," "face to face" (1 Cor. 13:12); we will see God's face (Rev. 22:4). Human beings will enjoy profound unity and a depth of satisfaction that we cannot imagine. All ethnic groups will share in this unity.

Next, consider the principle of diversity. On the divine level there are three perspectives on knowledge: the perspectives of the Father, of the Son, and of the Holy Spirit.[3] Within the Bible, there are four Gospels, which offer four perspectives on the life and work of Christ. The four Gospels are a good example of the positive value of the right kind of diversity. Matthew emphasizes that Jesus fulfills the Old Testament promises about the coming Messiah in the line of David. John emphasizes that Jesus reveals God the Father. Since each Gospel is what God says, and God speaks truly, there is no contradiction between the different Gospels. They are all in harmony.[4] At the same time, they offer differences in emphasis and differences in what they choose to include.

On the human level, within this world there are many cultures. The gospel is spreading into each culture. As it spreads, the truth is being manifested in each

---

[3] See Poythress, *Symphonic Theology*, 47–51.
[4] But it may sometimes be hard for us as human readers to figure out just how they harmonize. See ibid.

language and culture. Behind the human communicators of the gospel is God, who empowers them. Through the gospel God himself addresses the hearers: "Therefore, we [bearers of the gospel] are ambassadors for Christ, God making his appeal through us. We implore you on behalf of Christ, be reconciled to God" (2 Cor. 5:20). In this way God is a speaker in each cultural community and makes himself known in each language.

The diversity of cultures, like other forms of diversity in the body of Christ, enriches the body. Each person grows in the truth through receiving truth from those with different perspectives, including different cultures. Since the church has multiple ethnic groups, human beings do not now have on earth one "final culture." All Christians have unity because they know Christ who is the truth. They share common convictions about who Christ is. But their unity does not eliminate all diversity.[5] Rather, the unity of one faith is compatible with the diversity among ethnic groups. That is analogous to the fact that the unity of one work of Christ is compatible with the diversity of the accounts in the four Gospels.

Culture as Barrier or Benefit?

Cultures as well as individuals are corrupted because of sin. Fortunately, cultures are capable of redemptive transformation. People can hear God speaking as the gospel comes even to the darkest dungeons of human depravity. Christ came to save sinners, not the righteous: "I have not come to call the righteous but sinners to repentance" (Luke 5:32; see Matt. 9:13). Thus, even though the fall has had its effects, the promise of God guarantees that the gospel can reach into any cultural situation, and that people within that culture can hear and be transformed.

Because the Bible is breathed out by God (2 Tim. 3:16) to address all nations (Luke 24:47), it is true and pertinent to every culture. God so designed it. We know it is universal in its reach, not by intellectual insight that has given us a godlike superiority, but simply because God has told us so, and we trust him. But that universal reach is not worked out in practice without missionaries and translators having to confront surprising knots, complexities, resistances, and rich perspectival diversities.

The Bible is not acultural. It does not owe its universality to rising above cultures into thin, disembodied universal philosophical platitudes (which would

---

[5]The unity and diversity among different people in the church is analogous to the archetypal unity and diversity among the persons of the Trinity. Within the church, a single monolithic vision of the truth, without diversity, would be analogous to Unitarianism, which believes in one God but no diversity in God (Unitarianism denies that there are three persons in God). The opposite extreme would be diversity without real unity: each person would have a distinct conception of truth, and the different conceptions would never be reconciled. That kind of diversity corresponds to polytheism. True unity in diversity within the church reflects the true unity and diversity in the Trinity. See Poythress, *In the Beginning*, appendix D.

actually falsify its very specific message). In the Bible God addresses immediate issues in the first century and in the Hebraic cultures of Old Testament times. Through the apostle Paul God warns the Corinthian church about divisions; he warns the Galatian churches to rely on Christ and not on circumcision.

God also speaks universally, by indicating to all nations how he accomplished worldwide salvation precisely in the once-for-all, culturally and historically specific events concerning the descendants of Abraham leading up to Christ. As part of its universal scope, the Bible also contains many general, universal statements: "All have sinned and fall short of the glory of God" (Rom. 3:23). "The LORD is one" (Deut. 6:4).

> Righteous are you, O LORD,
> and right are your rules. (Ps. 119:137)

God expects us to believe his universal claims and not to evaporate them by artificially restricting them to one culture. The missiologist does not need to "make" the Bible universal. It is already that (Acts 1:8).[6] Rather he needs to help people in each culture take their place as disciples in the Bible's universal world history.

The disciple of Christ does not slavishly duplicate the details of the wilderness wandering of the Israelites or the Davidic monarchy or the Corinthian church, but grows in understanding how God addresses both David and Corinth, each in his context, and how through them God also addresses a Manila grocer. The Manila grocer can grow, and needs to grow, in understanding the cultures of Bible times, in order for him to see the cross-cultural span of the Bible's vision and lose his cultural parochialism. (The same goes, of course, for American or Spanish parochialism.) The missionary anthropologist can be a facilitator, but he needs to beware of becoming a new intermediary, a new priest. The Manila grocer, in fellowship with a Manilan church, can see the relevance of the Bible to his cultural situation.

Counterfeits to Cross-Cultural Integration

Because of the magnitude of differences in culture, achieving peace between different people groups is not easy. It can come through the power of Christ and his gospel. But it comes at a price. The price is the shedding of "the precious

---

[6]Thus the idea of distilling a "supracultural" core to the Bible is reductionistic. We can of course summarize the gospel in a few words (e.g., 1 Cor. 15:1–4; also Acts 10:36–43; Rom. 1:2–6; 10:9–10)—but the summaries are many and each points to the larger whole. The whole Bible is both culturally specific and "supracultural" in that God speaks it to all nations. The two sides are perspectivally related. See the discussion of contrast (universality) and variation (particularity) in chap. 18, and the discussion of perspectives in chaps. 7, 34, and 35, and in Poythress, *Symphonic Theology*.

blood of Christ" (1 Pet. 1:19). Followers of Christ also pay a price in their own way because each one must give up his pride. On top of the challenges of translation comes the challenge of dealing with human pride in one's own culture. God created human diversity, and so there can be a proper way in which people may rejoice in the blessings and the human community that they have received through their native culture. But since sin has come in and contaminated human relations, human pride distorts our attitude toward our native culture. We have a protective pride, and with that comes a disdain or hatred for what is different. This is a sin, for which the gospel is the remedy.

Because all people are made in God's image, all people have desires to overcome the pain in the differences in culture. For some people, the desire to overcome pain may take hideous form. They are tempted by hatred to wipe out another ethnic group or forcibly to convert them to their own way of life. That is a counterfeit remedy for cultural pain. Among sophisticated Westerners, counterfeits come in more genteel forms. For example, counterfeit solutions to cultural differences appear in philosophy. Philosophy in many of its forms has claimed to arrive at godlike knowledge that would rise above the limitations of any one culture or any one language. Reason, which is assumed to be uniformly the same throughout all cultures, becomes the source that philosophy hopes will lead to universal agreement on truth and cultural reconciliation.

But a view of what is reasonable depends partly on culture. For example, it seems unreasonable to the modern secularist, within the cultural climate of secularism, to believe in demons. But has he ever looked seriously at the beliefs in other cultures and the reasons supporting those beliefs? The typical secularist is just going along with the crowd.

Postmodernism, in contrast to much of Western philosophy, wants to treat with utmost seriousness the diversity of cultures. But that diversity threatens the peace and unity of mankind. How do we deal with this threat? One form of postmodernism of a more relativist kind offers a reconciliation and a peace based on the principle of tolerance.[7] This kind of thinking might say that traditional religions have a place. They are one colorful aspect of culture. We learn to tolerate them by seeing them as expressing the commitments and customs belonging to their own particular culture. This kind of approach provides a place for religion. But it forbids religion from "getting out of hand" by making a universal or intolerant claim that would apply to other cultures. Religions are thereby tamed.

But they can be tamed only by a strong claim, namely, that religions are merely cultural preferences, since no one can know religious truth. That claim is itself a

---

[7] I am here focusing on a popular postmodernist attitude and not on any particular thinker. Postmodernism has many aspects, and here I am choosing only one. See also Poythress, *In the Beginning*, appendices A and B.

kind of religious claim, since it claims to see deeper than the adherents to any one religion. It is a godlike claim to godlike insight. So this kind of popular postmodernist recipe for cultural peace is a counterfeit for the peace and reconciliation offered in the Christian gospel.

Both the postmodernist recipe and Christian faith want to promote reconciliation among diverse cultures. One, the Christian form, finds reconciliation through the work of God in Christ, and the spiritual power to love and to crucify pride. The other, a postmodern recipe, finds reconciliation in a self-achieved godlike vision of the nature of religion and language and knowledge (see table 17.1).

Table 17.1

	Christian view	Rationalist Western philosophy	Popular postmodernist tolerance
basis for unity among human beings	man made in the image of God	common rationality	emphasis on diversity rather than unity
basic problem	sin	ignorance	fear of difference
solution	salvation in Christ	knowledge through reason	tolerance: affirm all differences as valid personal preferences
the message	the gospel	enlightenment through casting off tradition in favor of reason	understanding influence of culture
goal	unity in diversity in the body of Christ, displaying the glory of God	uniformity through reason	affirmation of diversity

Contextualization

Unity and diversity can take both good and bad forms. The difference between good and bad comes out when we consider the missionary challenge of contextualization. How do we communicate the gospel in a clear and winsome way to a new culture? The term *contextualization* describes a process in which a missionary adapts the gospel to a new cultural context. Is this a good or a bad thing?

A rigid, monolithic emphasis on unity might insist that contextual thinking is not necessary or important. Some nineteenth-century missions made the mistake of thinking that the task of missionary work was to "civilize the heathen" and make them Europeans; Christianizing was part of the total package of civilizing. That extreme view obviously does not respect the diversity of cultures and makes a mistake analogous to requiring Gentiles to become Jews. It does not recognize that God has ordained good kinds of diversity in cultures.

Reconciliation among Cultures and Languages

Less dramatically, a missionary may mistakenly think that issues from within one culture can be transported without any adaptation into all other cultures. Let us consider an example. Broadly speaking, the Reformation was concerned to address the universal problem of human guilt and the universal human tendency to seek salvation by works, accompanied by pride in human achievement. The human tendency to pride can take subtle as well as blatant forms. The blatant form is to base salvation directly on human achievement. One subtle form is to introduce pride into a framework where people give token acknowledgment to God's grace.

These problems, though universal, take different particular forms in different cultures. In the time of the Reformation the issue came to focus in the practice of indulgences. The Roman Catholic Church did affirm that salvation comes partly through grace offered in Christ. But the church's offer of an indulgence alleged that a monetary payment—a work—could buy someone's way out of purgatory. That practice based salvation partly on human work. In the first-century church, reliance on human work cropped up in the issue of circumcising the Gentiles. In an animist culture, reliance on human work may come to focus in the demand to propitiate the spirits in order to protect crops. In Hindu religion, reliance on work is expressed in the idea of karma, which says that you must pay for your misdeeds in future reincarnations. The particular temptations within a particular culture, and not just the general principle, need to be addressed.

The opposite mistake in contextualization is the mistake of uncritically celebrating every kind of diversity. In the name of contextualization, a missionary can make his version of the "gospel" fit in so well with the target culture that it accepts some of the false views and values in the culture: it becomes indistinguishable from the culture and does not challenge it at a fundamental level. The mistake also occurs in less obvious forms. People can talk about developing African or Latin American theologies as if these theologies had to start all over again in order to be authentic to their own cultures. But the truths that the Reformation uncovered in the Bible are indeed truths, and so they are true and applicable to all cultures everywhere.

Thinking through implications for a new context is quite different from despising the insights of the Reformation. Such despising of the fruits of Western theology is itself a kind of reverse ethnocentrism, in that it runs the danger of endorsing a false pride and isolation in Third World Christians. The unity in the body of Christ implies not isolation of various indigenous theologies but cross-cultural appropriation, Europe to Africa, Africa to Asia, Asia to Europe, and so on. Otherwise, we are denying the unity of the one faith (Eph. 4:5). Each truth found in each context, if it is indeed the truth at all, is universal truth.[8]

What does proper Christian unity look like? We can only begin to sketch it. In a culture that is in bondage to the fear of evil spirits, a missionary may easily start with announcing Christ's victory over Satan and over the evil spirits under him (Luke 10:18–19; Col. 2:15; Heb. 2:14–15). But deliverance from Satan must include deliverance from his accusations (Rev. 12:10), and therefore deliverance from guilt. That thought leads to acknowledging the importance of Christ's substitutionary atonement and justification from guilt. Conversely, suppose the missionary confronts a culture that is beset by guilt. He first proclaims Christ as the substitute who bears the penalty for guilt and wins justification for us. But one aspect of guilt is guilt for having abandoned service to God and given allegiance to false gods, behind which stand Satan and his demons (1 Cor. 10:20). So deliverance from guilt must include deliverance from demonic bondage. Each culture should, over time, grow in realizing that Christ's deliverance is deeper and richer than what they first imagined they needed.

Because of the dominant influence of the West in industry, trade, entertainment, and ideas, it may often seem to the struggling contextualizer that he has only two black-and-white choices: to accept the West or to repudiate it. In the first alternative, he accepts Westernization, including the Westernization of his theological thinking. Then he unilaterally imposes on every culture all the particularities that belong to the issues in their Western form. He paralyzes his ability to adapt to a non-Western culture. Or he chooses the second alternative. He rejects Westernization, ignores the ancient creeds and the Reformation, and starts fresh with so-called indigenous theology, constructed from the ground up.

But both routes are deeply wrong. In practice, they deny the unity and universality of the truth. And both avoid the cross of Christ by refusing the challenge to suffer in order to bring together diverse cultures at a deep level. We must work not merely to appropriate truth from other Christians in other cultures, but also to appropriate critically, testing truth claims in the light of Scripture and warning fellow Christians when we see dangers of syncretism and cultural compromise. Someone who is foreign to a particular culture runs the danger of premature, harsh judgment against cultural practices that he does not understand. But, conversely,

---

[8]On truth, see Vern S. Poythress, *Redeeming Science: A God-Centered Approach* (Wheaton, IL: Crossway, 2006), chap. 14.

the foreigner may sometimes be able to discern sins when the native is unaware, because the native's culture has hardened his conscience to some areas of sin.[9]

The Challenge to Christians

The challenge of cross-cultural reconciliation for Christians is not primarily intellectual. We who are Christians must avoid falling into the trap of seeking merely an intellectual solution, such as others have sometimes offered. The Bible offers an answer that does indeed address human intellectual capacities and that does give satisfaction in the long run. Christ has given us a Bible that includes within it not only spiritual nourishment but intellectual instruction, and a worldview in which cultural differences have a positive place. But the Bible's answer centers on Christ and on his suffering. And Christians must suffer in serving him.

Culture crossing and explaining the gospel are hard. Loving and reaching out to people who may be hostile to the gospel are hard jobs. To love, we have to suffer and thereby follow the pattern of the suffering of Christ. We are to strive through the gospel to bring genuine reconciliation to people groups through cultural unity in diversity and diversity in unity. We replicate in human beings the glory of the unity and diversity in the Godhead.

This unity in diversity offers an answer that differs from other common answers abroad today. Our answer differs from forced uniformity, which some people think they can attain through autonomous reason. That hope for uniformity is the answer associated with what has been called modernism. Our answer also differs from the popular recipe of tolerance, which celebrates diversity but gives up on universal truth (see table 17.1).

---

[9]Consider an example. In 2008, African Anglican bishops called on American Episcopalian clergy to repent of their abandonment of biblical authority and their endorsement of homosexual practice. This movement of theology and exhortation goes from Africa to the United States. Unfortunately, the Americans, when they are ethnocentrically confident about their own allegedly "progressive" culture, are not likely to listen. Their culture tempts them to harden their conscience and excuse their sin. Postmodernism in its popular relativist form does not help. It naturally wants to favor multicultural "tolerance," according to which each church and religion within a culture would develop, in its own way, in harmony with its culture. Almost automatically it sides against the Africans for trying to "impose" their patterns on Americans. But in so doing, it shows its European-American ethnocentricity: it is prejudiced against the belief found in other cultures—and, above all, within the Bible itself—that universal truth exists and matters and can be accessible to us.

18

Human Action

All things have been handed over to me by my Father,
and no one knows the Son except the Father,
and no one knows the Father except the Son
and anyone to whom the Son chooses to reveal him.

—Matthew 11:27

Human relationships always take place in a context of surrounding circumstances and cultures, and the context can have a decided influence on the relationships. So let us now consider human action in the context of culture. Cultures are many. We can speak of "Western culture" as a large whole. Or we can speak of "English-speaking culture," or within that "British culture," "Scottish culture," "Scottish Highlands culture." We can look at smaller and smaller groupings in culture.

Human action includes interaction between two or more ethnic groups with vast differences between them. Such interaction, as we saw in the previous chapters, can be both a great struggle and a challenge for reconciliation. Cross-cultural interaction has a very significant role in God's plan for drawing all nations to himself. But most human action takes place within the context of some degree of shared culture, whether it is only the broader umbrella of "Western culture" or the narrower confines of the "culture" of a particular city like Easton, Pennsylvania. Divine action superintends all of history. But God also interacts with each particular culture. So we now take another step in narrowing our focus. We focus not on world history and its many cultures, but on smaller-scale actions within a particular culture. Once again, we will be focusing primarily on culture associated with ethnic groups, but the principles apply to smaller-scale subcultural groupings of many kinds.

Insiders and Outsiders

Meaning is always meaning in context.[1] The same physical action may not have the same cultural meaning when seen within the context of two distinct cultures. That difference can generate misunderstanding, anger, and pain. For example, an American may cross his legs when as a guest he is enjoying a conversation in his host's living room. In traditional Chinese culture, showing the sole of your shoe to another person is a way of insulting the person. So people keep their feet on the floor and do not lift up their feet to cross legs.

The person who travels from one culture to another may not be aware of the differences and may as a result generate misunderstanding. In addition, a particular culture may have ceremonies and customs with no real equivalent outside the culture. The people have special dances, or festivals, or architectural styles, or gestures, or a regular order for meals. All these have meaning within that culture, but they may be difficult for the foreigner to decipher.

The native and the foreigner have different perspectives on a culture. The native grasps the inside meaning. The foreigner starts with only vague ideas or possibilities for meaning. For example, Americans know the meaning of a credit card. But a member of a tribal culture that has never previously seen a credit card can only guess at its significance.

Insiders' and Outsiders' Perspectives

In general, an insider and an outsider differ in their awareness of all kinds of elements that belong to language and culture.[2] They have two different perspectives. In addition, we can distinguish two different kinds of outsiders. The first kind is the foreigner trying to learn a particular language or culture for the first time. He has the learner's perspective. The second is the theorist who tries to generalize about many languages or cultures, and who classifies the phenomena of one culture into a larger taxonomy. He has the classifier's perspective. Both

---

[1] See chap. 7.

[2] In technical terms, the insider's perspective is called *emic*, while the outsider's perspective is called *etic*. These terms need explanation. The study of the sounds used in languages is called phonetics. Phonetics takes an outsider's or foreigner's point of view. It studies the sounds as a machine might record them. Linguists can also study sound from the insider's point of view, by asking which sounds are perceived as making a difference. This study is called phonemics. Kenneth L. Pike, *Language in Relation to a Unified Theory of the Structure of Human Behavior*, 2nd ed. (Paris: Mouton, 1967), 37–72, generalized and codified this difference with the pair of distinctive terms *emic* and *etic*, which apply to language analysis and cultural analysis in their broadest forms.

are "outsiders" in a sense. But the latter may in fact also be an insider who is temporarily standing back from his involvement in one culture in order to conduct multicultural analysis.

This existence of inside and outside perspectives derives from the diversity among human beings, which also makes its way into the diversity of the body of Christ. The diversity is designed by God. It does not make any of the perspectives "unreal." In particular, the insider is experiencing exactly what God designed him to experience. It is all real, including the cultural meanings that attach to the festivals and the meals and the gestures. These are all specified by God, who has the Mastery over every culture in every detail. The classifier's outsider perspective can open the door to the temptation to think that only an outsider's universal, "scientific," "objective" analysis shows what is real. But that would be to reduce to one perspective the fullness of what God creates and sustains.[3] The classifier's perspective, insightful though it may be in certain respects, does not dissolve the realities of other perspectives.

The reality of the insider's perspective is particularly worth emphasizing because some people have claimed that a culture or language group "constructs" the world of human meaning. There is a grain of truth in this claim. It is true that any one human being can have innovative thoughts and speeches and in that sense introduce a new idea into his culture. Even such innovations, of course, do not take God by surprise but are eternally known by him and are under his control. But in addition, cultures and languages are passed on to the next generation. No generation literally "constructs" its culture from scratch. More important, no generation ceases to live in the presence of God, under the control and authority of God. By contrast to this situation involving God, the word *construct* can tend to suggest autonomy in human action. And it can suggest that the cultural meaning is illusory, because it is "mere" construction rather than a reality appreciated by God even if every human being should disappear or forget.

Behavioremes

We now turn to consider the insider's perspective. Kenneth L. Pike invented a general term to describe any unified human action within a particular culture: the *behavioreme*. A behavioreme is a unit of human action that has human purpose and is recognized as a meaningful unified whole within the culture in which it occurs.[4] It is recognized by insiders.

---

[3] For an analogous problem that crops up in the natural sciences, see the discussion in Vern S. Poythress, *Redeeming Science: A God-Centered Approach* (Wheaton, IL: Crossway, 2006), chap. 16.
[4] Pike, *Language*, 73–149. Technically, "a behavioreme is an emic segment or component of purposive human activity, hierarchically and trimodally structured, having closure signaled by overt objective cultural clues within the verbal or nonverbal behavior of the domestic participants or

A behavioreme may consist in the unified action of a single human being: in America, brushing one's teeth is a behavioreme. But other behavioremes may consist in a whole series of actions by a number of human beings acting in a coordinated way. A credit card purchase, a party, a workday at a business, a basketball game, a family breakfast, and a church service are all behavioremes. The insider recognizes the action as a whole, and he shares that recognition with others within his culture. His perspective on the action may differ markedly from that of an outsider. The outsider sees the human action but does not know its cultural significance.

Behavioremes include acts of verbal communication; verbal utterances are one kind of behavioreme. But the term applies more broadly. It applies to any culturally significant activity. A behavioreme is characterized both by particular instances and by a general, somewhat regular pattern common to its instances. Any particular credit card purchase is a behavioreme. But we may also think in general terms of the purchase behavioreme, the common pattern apparent in many individual purchases.[5]

Why is this significant? Any particular human interaction, and any particular human relationship, exists in a context. The context includes patterns of relationships. Our expectations for a relationship are influenced by what *kind* of relationship we think it is. If Bob thinks it is a romantic relationship, and Linda thinks it is only a friendship, they will sometimes act at cross-purposes.

Interlocking Aspects: Contrast, Variation, and Context ("Distribution")

We can now briefly explore some of the characteristics belonging to behavioremes in general. As we do so, we are preparing the way to use the results when we later

---

domestic observers, and occurring through its free or conditioned, simple or complex variants within a behavioral system (or composite of systems) and a physical setting which are also emically, hierarchically and trimodally structured" (ibid., 121). The "trimodal" structuring is closely related to the interlocking of (1) contrastive-identificational features, (2) variation, and (3) distribution, as discussed below. The ending -*eme* indicates that we are treating the unity of behavior as perceived by an insider. The insider's perspective is called an *emic* perspective (cf. note 2, above).

[5]Philosophers and students of language have spoken of the "type-token" distinction. A "token" is any particular instance—any one credit card purchase or any one basketball game. A "type" is the generality—the class of all purchases or the class of all basketball games. Kenneth Pike's theory differs subtly from many analyses at this point because it acknowledges that, in practice, type and token, though distinguishable in principle, are never isolated from one another. We grasp the general class through its instances, and we grasp the instances as instances of one or more classes. The classes are closely related to the contrastive-identificational features; the instances are variations in the class (see below). Both occur in ways qualified by context. See Pike's discussion of the related issue of form-meaning composites (Pike, *Language*, 62–63), and coinherent modes (ibid., 84–94; Pike, *Linguistic Concepts: An Introduction to Tagmemics* [Lincoln: University of Nebraska Press, 1982], 41–65). Thus there are no "pure" universals that we know apart from particulars, and no "pure" particulars known apart from universals. This coinherence of universal and particular is ultimately founded in the unity and diversity in the persons of the Trinity in their coinherence.

focus on specific kinds of personal relationships. Behavioremes can be described in terms of three interlocking aspects, which are related to three perspectives: the particle, wave, and field perspectives (chap. 7). Consider a situation where a father and a son are working together to solve a jigsaw puzzle. The action of putting the puzzle together is a behavioreme. It has a definite purpose, recognized by the participants and by onlookers as well.

First, consider puzzle solving from the standpoint of the particle perspective. The activity is a distinct whole. It is not a board game, or a baseball game, or a game of hopscotch, or a family breakfast. It is identifiable by a distinct structure of human interaction and a distinct set of rules. It has an identity, and it contrasts with other kinds of behavioremes. This first aspect may be called *contrastive-identificational features*.[6]

Second, we use the wave perspective. Puzzle solving takes place in time and is spread out in time. But this by itself is not what we are going to focus on. The awareness of development is closely connected to awareness of the specificness of this particular case of puzzle solving. This puzzle, along with the sequence of moves by which it is gradually put together, is not quite like any other puzzle. Moreover, if the father and son put the same puzzle together a second time, the details will still differ. The sequence of additions of pieces will differ in its details, and the times when they may take breaks or enjoy a snack will differ. One instance of puzzle solving is a particular instance, never to be repeated. Other activities of puzzle solving at other times and places will show considerable variation, without ceasing to be instances of the jigsaw-puzzle behavioreme. Each instance is part of the variation possible for this behavioreme. The second aspect is therefore called *variation*.[7]

For the sake of simplicity, analysts of culture often treat a particular culture as uniform. But a more refined analysis always shows up variations among subcultures. Each individual is never exhaustively assimilated into a particular culture or subculture but remains unique and different. He is still able to interact with those around him and to share in commonly identified behavioremes because the behavioremes allow variation in subcultures and in individuals. The father and son both know what it is to go about putting together a jigsaw puzzle. If the son is a young child just learning about jigsaw puzzles, he needs time and a few instances of the experience, and then he is assimilated to the jigsaw-puzzle subculture. The father and son may nevertheless vary in the way that they go about it. Some families may have the custom of completely separating and mixing all

---

[6]In Pike, *Language*, this aspect is closely associated with the "feature mode." See also Pike, *Linguistic Concepts*, 42–51.

[7]In Pike, *Language*, this aspect is closely associated with the "manifestation mode." See also Pike, *Linguistic Concepts*, 52–59.

the pieces before starting. Others may consider two or three pieces stuck together as a benefit that they take advantage of.

Third, we use the field perspective. From this perspective we see puzzle solving as embedded in a larger human context. The father and son may have set themselves to do several puzzles, one per week. Other members of the family, or even acquaintances outside the family, may be asked to join in the puzzle for a time. Some people like jigsaw solving only when the puzzles are reasonably easy. Others like jigsaws only if they have a beautiful landscape when the puzzle is done. Or for a father and son, they may enjoy spending the time together and talking about this and that. The goal is not so much the puzzle itself as the time spent together. Their puzzle solving belongs with the other things that they do together. And it also belongs with puzzle solving activities that other people in the culture practice—not only jigsaws but word puzzles, number puzzles, logic puzzles, and so on.

In sum, the activity of solving a jigsaw occurs within particular human contexts, and in Kenneth Pike's terminology we say that we are then describing the distribution of the behavioreme in its larger contexts. This third aspect is called *distribution*.

Why not just call it context? The word *distribution* is intended to be a little more specific. For a jigsaw-solving behavioreme, we are not just interested in any context whatsoever. We focus on the characteristic patterns that belong to just those contexts in which jigsaw solving is expected to occur. The patterns that characterize the typical contexts of jigsaw solving help to define what jigsaw solving means within the culture. Jigsaw solving is "distributed" in various places in the culture.[8]

---

[8]See Pike, *Language*, 85–86; Pike, *Linguistic Concepts*, 60–65. A more fine-grained analysis of distribution can distinguish three dimensions or aspects to distribution. The first dimension is distribution "as a member of a substitution class." Here is Pike's explanation: "A unit, whether a person or word, is in part characterized by its membership in a class of replaceable units which may appropriately occur in the same place(s) in a particular kind of structure. The set comprises a distribution class of units. For example, *kitten, dog, bicycle* are members of a (sub)class of nouns which can appropriately substitute one for another as head of a noun phrase; compare the phrase *a large kitten* with *a large dog, a large train, a large bicycle*" (ibid., 62). A jigsaw-solving behavioreme is a member of the "distribution class" of puzzle activities, games, and other leisure activities that occur among families and friends.

The second dimension of distribution is distribution "as part of a structural sequence." Pike explains: "A unit is in part defined by the constructions in which it occurs, in addition to the class of items of which it is an appropriate substitute member within such structured sequences. The nouns just listed are in part recognized by the fact that they can occur in a noun phrase, preceded in that phrase by an article (*the kitten*), or an adjective (*the lovely kitten*), or followed by a modifying phrase (*the kitten I used to own*)" (ibid.). Jigsaw solving occurs within a sequence of activities of the family, spread throughout the day (or several days). In addition, it may sometimes occur within a sequence of puzzle-solving activities of other kinds, or with other jigsaw puzzles.

All behavioremes are characterized by contrast-identity, by variation, and by context ("distribution"). And these interlock. They are "coinherent." For example, one of the features that makes jigsaw solving a case of puzzle solving is not merely human movements that look like they might be part of a solving process, but an understanding on the part of the participants. Such understanding comes from context, where they have already agreed to work to solve the puzzle. Thus the contrastive features identifying the activity of puzzle solving cohere with actions before the puzzle solving, that is, actions in context ("distribution"). And if other people watch the process of puzzle solving, they too have a cultural context in which they already have an idea of the meaning of puzzle solving and of jigsaw puzzles in particular. Their understanding belongs to the distributional aspect of puzzle solving.

There can be variations in the distributional aspects. Some activities of jigsaw solving may belong to a sequence of activities of puzzle solving or other kinds of game playing. Some activities may take place in a leisurely way within a family, while other activities may be timed, competitive activities where different participants or teams of participants try to solve the puzzle in a minimum time. The variations also help to define in the average person's mind what puzzle solving means. Variations in tempo, variations in the number of pieces, variations in the scenes in the puzzles, do not make one particular instance of jigsaw solving anything other than puzzle solving. But some variations would: for example, if we put monkeys in a cage with the pieces and then observed whether they ever put two or more pieces together.

Behavioremes also involve God's action in an inextricable way. God is always involved as primary cause in addition to the secondary causes in human action. God has authority over the standards and the meanings expressed in behavioremes; he controls the action and development in behavioremes; he is present in the entire development and present with each individual in the action.

These three aspects of God's lordship are expressed in the three perspectives particle, wave, and field. To put it another way, God by his authority specifies the contrastive-identificational features; he controls the variations; and he is present both in the action itself and in its distributional context. God's authority, and with it his meaning, is the foundation for human meaning and human intentionality

---

The third dimension of distribution is distribution "as a point in a system." Pike explains, "One can in part define a unit by the place it fills in a matrix of units (an n-dimensional system of units)" (ibid., 65). A jigsaw-solving behavioreme fits into a multidimensional classification of various types of individual, team, and group puzzle solving and other kinds of leisure activities.

These three aspects of distribution correspond to particle, wave, and field perspectives on distribution, respectively. These perspectives are rooted in the Trinity (chap. 7). The character of distribution shows one area where Trinitarian coinherence is reflected in more microscopic as well as a macroscopic analysis.

in the individual and corporate actions. God's power, and with it his control, is the foundation for human power to influence the course of action. God's goal, and with it his presence in blessing at the end of history, is the foundation for the goals involved in human action.

Solving the puzzle is a little echo of the winning of the eternal reward toward which the whole of history travels.[9] To put it another way, human action is purposeful. Human beings have plans and hopes that animate their actions, though sometimes these hopes are inchoate. Human beings work at a project, using the powers of action and control that God through creation has given to them. Human beings arrive at some goal, either the hoped-for goal or something else, that gives them satisfaction or disappointment as the fruit of their action. That fruit depends for meaning on its beginning, when the participants had hopes that are now compared with the result.

Behavioremes are unified wholes at least partly because they are meaningful in terms of an intention (beginning), a work (middle), and a culmination (end), the last of which is tied to the originating intention. Human action has built into it both imitation of and empowering by divine action.

The Holy Spirit brings to us the power of God animating human action. He gives life, not only at the supernatural level of regeneration, but also at the natural level of human action, as we can see by comparing the following verses:

> The Spirit of God has made me,
>> and the breath of the Almighty gives me life. (Job 33:4) (natural human
>> action)

> As long as my breath is in me,
>> and the spirit of God is in my nostrils, . . . (Job 27:3) (natural human
>> action)

> If he should set his heart to it
>> and gather to himself his spirit and his breath,
> all flesh would perish together,
>> and man would return to dust. (Job 34:14–15) (natural human action)

Truly, truly, I say to you, unless one is born of water and the Spirit, he cannot enter the kingdom of God. (John 3:5) (supernaturally renewed, eternal life)

It is the Spirit who gives life; the flesh is no help at all. (John 6:63) (supernaturally renewed, eternal life)

---

[9] See J. R. R. Tolkien, "On Fairy-Stories," *Essays Presented to Charles Williams*, ed. C. S. Lewis (repr., Grand Rapids: Eerdmans, 1966), on "eucatastrophe," 82–84.

Some of the passages about natural human action may have in mind partly the role of a person's human spirit within him. But even these suggest that God's Spirit is the ultimate source and sustainer of the life of the human spirit.

Communicative Action in Language

All behavioremes have meaning in a broad sense. Members of the culture identify them as distinct (contrastive-identificational aspect) and as having a purpose and "fit" within the culture (distribution). In a broad sense, all behavioremes "communicate" something both to those participating in them and to those who are part of the larger culture. The principle applies then in particular to behavioremes involving language as well as other communicative media like music, painting, sculpture, and film (including silent film). Conversations are behavioremes where language is dominant. They may also include gestures, facial expressions, and postures that serve the communication. We are not disembodied, and communication in language occurs in context (distribution).

Behavioremes, in fact, occur in many different sizes. Smaller pieces are embedded in larger ones. A sermon is a behavioreme that is one piece of the larger behavioreme, the church worship service. And this behavioreme may be included in a still larger behavioreme, the Sunday morning program, which includes two worship services with Sunday school sessions sandwiched between, and maybe space for coffee drinking and casual conversation. The sermon contains within it paragraphs, sentences, and words, all of which are themselves embedded behavioremes.[10]

God's wisdom and God's control are reflected in the complex structures that we find in behavioremes, and in the interlocking of their various aspects. We rely on God whenever we undertake coherent action.

---

[10]Monologues can also be termed *utteremes*. See Pike, *Language*, 121, 133–49, on the uttereme and utteretics. For further discussion of language, see Vern S. Poythress, *In the Beginning Was the Word: Language—A God-Centered Approach* (Wheaton, IL: Crossway, 2009).

PART 3

Interpreting Human Relationships

19

Meanings in Personal Action

The purpose in a man's heart is like deep water,
but a man of understanding will draw it out.

—Proverbs 20:5

We now turn from human actions and relationships to focus on the *meanings* of those actions and relationships. What meanings belong to personal action? Even to describe an activity as "putting together a jigsaw puzzle" involves ascribing meaning to the activity. Any behavioreme, by definition, involves meaning that the participants see in it. Whole behavioremes have a unity in meaning that an insider can recognize. That unity is related to human purposes. The participants have intentions in what they do. The father and the son intend to put the puzzle together.

Unified Meaning

It is natural in many ways to assume that we will find a unified meaning. In order to work on the puzzle together, the father and the son have to share in understanding the meaning of what they are doing. They will only be frustrated if one is putting together the puzzle while the other is tearing it apart.

But sometimes unity of meaning is incomplete. If the son is just starting with his first experience of jigsaw puzzles, he may think at first that the point is merely to enjoy the shapes and colors. The father has a more definite goal, namely, to put the puzzle together. But he is doing it with several larger purposes in view: he wants the challenge of the process, the satisfaction of the endpoint, and the sharing of both the process and the endpoint with his son. He may consciously desire to train his son in eye and hand coordination; or he may just vaguely want to spend time with his son.

For a father, who is a mature adult, we expect definite plans. But in the informal setting of a family, he may even as an adult have only vaguely formulated plans.

Disharmony from the Fall

We must also reckon with the effects of the fall. Human beings contaminated by sin are never in perfect harmony with themselves. On the one hand, they are made in the image of God, with the built-in impulse to be in fellowship with God and to worship him. On the other hand, they are in rebellion. They are not only in rebellion against God but also in a sense in rebellion against themselves, against what they were created to be. The result is double-mindedness. At a deep level, they are not of one mind. And so they cannot have one perfectly unified intention in interpersonal action.

We may illustrate with the example from Acts 17:28, "In him we live and move and have our being." The apostle Paul here quotes from a Greek poet, probably Epimenides of Crete. There is some uncertainty about the poet's views, but he probably meant the sentence in a pantheistic sense. That is, he meant that we are a part of a god or identical with a god. This view misrepresents our relation to God. But it also distorts a more original knowledge of God that we cannot escape. On the one hand, in opposition to the true knowledge of God, the poet affirms pantheism. On the other hand, in harmony with true knowledge of God, he affirms the presence of God and his dependence on God. The poet is in conflict between two possible meanings of God's immanence, namely, a Christian and a non-Christian view.[1]

This instance is only one possible way in which a person may be in conflict with himself. Everyone has a sense of right and wrong (Rom. 1:32). But people rebel against what they know. That rebellion can take the form of breaking moral rules that they know. A person may steal even though he knows that stealing is wrong. But he may also make excuses for himself, and he may become confused about what is right and wrong—particularly if the culture in which he participates is confused in the same way.

The father knows that he should care responsibly for his son. And partly, he may want to do it. He is motivated partly by love. But he may also not want to do it. He may wish that he could just work longer hours, or just be on the golf course while his son raises himself. His motives are conflicted. And the conflict may come out in action, if he is interacting with his son in an absentminded fashion because his mind is on his work. Or he may be devoting himself intensely to his

---

[1]See the discussion of Christian and non-Christian views of immanence in John M. Frame, *The Doctrine of the Knowledge of God* (Phillipsburg, NJ: Presbyterian and Reformed, 1987), 13–15.

son so that he can feel good about himself for having done it. He is nursing his own pride, and again his motives are divided.

Not only individuals but also social relationships are corrupted by sin. Sin in the form of selfishness sets us at odds with one another. So we have disharmony between the intentions of different people.

When a person comes to faith in Christ, he is renewed and transformed. He has a renewed mind: "Do not lie to one another, seeing that you have put off the old self with its practices and have put on the new self, which is being renewed in knowledge after the image of its creator" (Col. 3:9–10; see 1 Cor. 2:16). But the renewal is progressive (Rom. 12:1–2). Consequently, insofar as the believer is not yet perfected in his heart, he too is double-minded. That is, he still has indwelling sin, and sin corrupts his motives. As a result, no action of merely human origin represents fully unified meaning.

The difficulties occur as well with observers and analysts of human interaction. An observer may analyze a situation with love for the participants; he genuinely wants to understand. At the same time, he may observe with imperfect love, and in selfishness may also want to twist the meaning of an activity for his own benefit. He wants fame or praise. Or he wants the meaning he finds to match his own prejudices. He obtains a result that is a mixture of good and bad. We once again confront the importance of redemption and of receiving wisdom from God. The observations that we made earlier concerning the work of Christ apply in the sphere of analyzing human interaction as well as every other area of life.

God's Meanings

God himself is holy, pure, and unified in his own mind. He has complete harmony in himself. And so he produces harmonious action. When Christ became incarnate as man, he acted with complete integrity and with harmony not only with respect to his divine nature but also with respect to his human nature. But there is disharmony in the confrontation between God's holiness and the human unholiness of sin. Christ had severe words to say concerning the seriousness of sin. He confronted human sinful reactions when he broke with human traditions concerning Sabbath observance and concerning his association with "sinners."

We should note one other truth. The unity of the mind of God is a unity of one God with one plan. It is also the unity of the Father, the Son, and the Holy Spirit in the diversity of persons. Unity of meaning within God himself is not unitarian, but Trinitarian. Each person in the Trinity knows all truth and all meaning in knowing the other persons. Among the persons of the Trinity, each person's understanding is unique to that person, as well as in total harmony with the understanding of the other persons.

God's unity is the model or archetype for the unity in diversity that is to be achieved by many cultures and many peoples coming together in the body of Christ. But this analogy is limited. God is infinite, and we are finite. And as long as we are in this life, our minds are not entirely free from sin. So within the church we have to sort good from bad. Scripture, by contrast, is perfectly pure (Ps. 12:6; Prov. 30:5).

Diversity within Unity

We can look at several instances of diversity within unity. Consider first what happens with actions in the Bible that are empowered by the Holy Spirit. A person who acts in the power of the Holy Spirit is acting not just with his own intentions and his own meanings, but also with the mind of the Spirit. The Spirit as well as the human person acts. The Spirit knows his meaning perfectly. The human being agrees with the Spirit, and so there is unity of meaning. But the human actor remains finite and does not plumb all the depths of the implications of what he does. And so his understanding is not exactly the same as the understanding by the Holy Spirit. This is a diversity in understanding. And so there is both unity and diversity in meaning when a human being acts by the power of the Spirit. This is true for the writings of Old Testament prophets, New Testament apostles, and other divinely authorized spokesmen for God.[2] It is true also of divinely empowered miraculous actions such as healings and exorcisms.

Spokesmen for God in the Bible have a unique, unrepeatable role. But we can see analogies between their roles and the actions of ordinary Christians. Christians can be filled with the Spirit, and the Spirit can use what they do even though their actions are not absolutely pure. Spirit-filled activities may include not only speaking in a way that blesses the hearer (Eph. 4:29; Col. 4:6), but also administering, helping, and any other activities coming from gifts of the Spirit (1 Cor. 12:28). The father doing a jigsaw puzzle with his son can be empowered by the Spirit to bless his son with his presence and his love. The Spirit may empower gracious actions in situations not only where benefit comes to fellow Christians, but also where it comes to non-Christians. The potential scope is as wide as human action as a whole.

The Holy Spirit has his intentions even in this kind of case. In this case also there is a unity between the Spirit's meaning and the human actor's meaning. But there is also diversity, because the Holy Spirit understands more, and understands more deeply, than the human actor. And what the Holy Spirit means is completely pure, while what a Christian believer intends may be contaminated by his remaining sinfulness.

---

[2]See Vern S. Poythress, "Divine Meaning of Scripture," *Westminster Theological Journal* 48 (1986): 241–79.

The goal of human action, the goal that will be climactically fulfilled in the new heaven and the new earth, is not autonomous, independent action on the part of human beings, but action arising from a heart in deep fellowship with God and empowered by the Spirit of God. Such action has both unity and diversity in meaning. It is not human action in isolation from God but action that makes manifest the wisdom of God and the power of God, action that surpasses the capacity of "independent" humanity. We aim for harmony in fellowship with God. We aim to express God's meanings through our own.

Meaning under Control

Let us continue to reflect on some of the limitations in noninspired activities. Even if an actor could enjoy full unity as an individual, he would still experience limitations in his actions. If the father and son undertake the challenge of a more difficult jigsaw puzzle, they may find that they do not have the time to complete it. Or, halfway through the project, they may realize that they could complete it but still judge that the time spent would not be worth it. They show the limitations of being creatures with only so much time and energy. Because human actors are made in the image of God, they do have powers for action—they have dominion and control—but they are not God, and so their control is not exhaustive.

As illustrated in figure 19.1, they do not completely master the culture in which they live; they do not exhaustively control the meanings of its customs; they do not know their own thoughts perfectly; they do not plan completely what they do; when engaging in a longer work they do not remain completely the same over the time during which they are working; they are not conscious of all the implications that they may want others to draw from what they do. When the

Figure 19.1. Partial Mastery

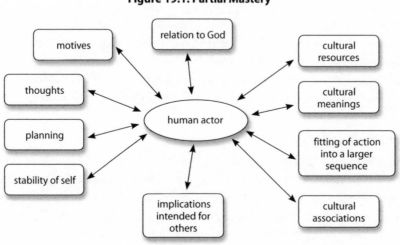

content of an activity is simple, these limitations may not make much difference. But with more complex activity they have their effects.

We can see some of these limitations more clearly when we consider a small child learning cultural customs, or an adult learning a second culture. Neither is master of the culture. So when does a child become master? At ten years of age, or fifteen, or twenty, or fifty? In fact, through continued interaction or through formal instruction, people can always develop greater skill in their culture. No one is a perfect master.

Moreover, because of the presence of variation in cultural meanings, in behavioremes, and in actors' contexts, meaning is not fixed with infinite precision. There are different varieties of jigsaw puzzles. There are different ways in which a father and a son may devote themselves to jigsaw solving, with intensity and concentration or else with leisurely playfulness. Human actors do not have the godlike control to attain infinite precision. They have only partial control in their thoughts, in their previous experience of culture, and in their participation in relationships. They may find themselves expressing things about themselves that they hoped to conceal—a hot temper, for example. They may fail to express some aspects of what they wanted to express—a father's genuine affection for his son.

The father's tone of voice or a physical tension in his body may tell his son that he is frustrated, even though he undertook to work the jigsaw as an occasion for expressing and building a loving relationship with the son. He may disclose a resentment for the time taken away from other activities of his own, even though he did not want that information to be revealed. Moreover, even in his own mind a father does not define with perfect precision what he intends. He undertakes to work with his son on the jigsaw. He intends that they solve it together. But what further intentions does he have with respect to building a relationship, or improving his son's skills, or showing his own skill? Many times he does not consciously formulate them to himself. The sinful aspects of intentions are often buried down beneath conscious awareness because we are uncomfortable with them, and we make excuses for ourselves.

Thus the ideal of perfectly precise intention in human action is indeed only an ideal. Human beings do not have the depth of control that only God possesses.

Limitations with Interpreters

Similar limitations affect those who interpret human action. How does the son interpret his father's intentions? The son may misread as well as understand. Human beings do not perfectly master their culture or the cultural meanings that they observe; they do not know their own thoughts perfectly as they go through the experience of interpreting the meanings of human action in a culture; they do not remain completely the same as they go through the process of interpreting; they do not plumb all the implications of what they interpret. A son who grasps his father's meaning does "control" it in some sense. But for human beings the grasp of meaning is partial, and the control is partial. Each interpreter is different from each actor and from every other interpreter, and even subtle differences are instances of variation that affect understanding in subtle ways.

Effective Understanding

We have been focusing on limitations. But many times culture sharing and communication still succeed. We rightly pay attention to human actors because we assume that they have a purpose in what they are doing and that they are capable of carrying it out. We assume that they show us a stable intention because in many easy cases we can discern what their intention is, and we can reexpress their intention either in words or in imitative action. We have real understanding, understanding that is sufficient and effective for practical goals. For example, the father and the son can, in the end, complete the jigsaw puzzle and may have a common sense of satisfaction in having done it. So it is with human action in general. The presence of imprecision and of the possibility of variation does not destroy all stability.[3] Stability is still there, and we express that stability when we describe or imitate someone's action. We can rightly say that two distinct actions in solving jigsaw puzzles have basically the same cultural meaning. We can say that two actors have the same intention of solving a jigsaw puzzle.

What difference does all this make? People who try to understand society without God can be tempted to fly off to extremes. They sometimes think that either we must be God and know everything, or we know nothing. Either we must have completely unified and coherent intentions, or the intentions must be totally unstable. God has made us in a different way. We are finite, but in communion with God we can have genuine knowledge and real intentions.

---

[3]Stability is the focus of contrastive-identificational features, which express the unity of meaning. Stability is enhanced, rather than destroyed, by recognition that the meaning of a particular action depends also on distributional context. See the previous chapter for discussion of contrastive-identification features, variation, and distribution.

20

Social and Cultural Analysis

It is the glory of God to conceal things,
but the glory of kings is to search things out.

—Proverbs 25:2

Human action includes instances where human beings undertake methodical analysis of human action. Human beings study themselves, and that shows our ability to stand back and "transcend" the immediacy of our situation. For example, how would we go about studying the meaning of a father and son working on a jigsaw puzzle?

Analysis as Human Action

In the West, especially, we have developed a complex tradition of scientific analysis that includes not only natural sciences but social sciences as well. The social sciences in one sense have an advantage over the natural sciences in that the subject of study is always close at hand. We are studying ourselves, human beings, or at least some aspect of human beings. But the advantage is also a disadvantage, because our own preconceptions about ourselves and others threaten to have an influential role in the actual work. The problem is the problem of transcendence. How do we obtain a grasp of a whole of which we ourselves are a part? In fact, as one aspect of being made in the image of God, human beings can "stand back" from their involvement in some sense (chap. 11). This standing back can take place with great self-conscious attention to establishing and maintaining methodological controls, often in imitation of the natural sciences.

Some investigators want the rigor that comes from quantifying and statistically analyzing data (appendix C). But quantification is itself a choice to leave out aspects that are not easily captured by quantity. There are many ways of "standing back" and thinking about what we are doing or have done. Each of these many ways has its own unity of human purpose.

We can have the purpose of focusing on and understanding consciously a particular aspect or form of human action. This unity of analytical purpose is a purposeful unity, recognized in Western culture.[1] It is recognized by insiders. It has an identity distinct from other kinds of human action. Variation permits us to say that there are many subtypes, some more scientific and some less. Various kinds of analysis are more or less extensive in length and may be focused in more than one direction—analysis can be sociological, anthropological, linguistic, psychological, cognitive, logical, and so on. The writing of this book is one instance of this kind of analysis. And so is the reading of this book. Sociology and cultural anthropology are built up by sociologists and anthropologists who engage in analysis focusing on human interaction in society.

Analysis can bring to our attention many interesting facts and interesting structures in human behavior. But the very nature of analysis is to be selective. We focus on one thing or one aspect while simultaneously leaving others in the background. Finite consciousness does not focus simultaneously on everything. As a result, we can always ask what is being left out.[2]

Interpretation as Reflective

Some discussions of interpretation like to say that almost all human interaction is interpretation. We "interpret" the meaning of a green light or a stop sign. We may even "interpret" the beauty of a sunset. This kind of description has a reasonable basis. We bring to our current experience the fund of knowledge, attitudes, and expectations from our previous experience, as well as the uniqueness of our own personalities. One person's reaction to a sunset may differ from another's.

The illustration with the green light is even more pertinent because the meaning of the green light depends on a system of signification within a given culture. In the context of modern traffic, the green light signifies that traffic can go forward. A person coming from another culture with no knowledge of vehicles and traffic would not know that the green light means "go." Its meaning must be interpreted to him. Similarly, the meaning of a jigsaw puzzle can be interpreted to someone who has never seen one and does not understand the goal of puzzle solving.

---

[1]To make plain that this analysis constitutes a behavioreme (chap. 18), we can even give it a name: the analytical behavioreme.

[2]See appendices A–G for discussions about what may be left out in various kinds of analysis relating to social interaction.

But in many common situations people do not talk about "interpreting" the green light. They react automatically to a light. They do not have to pause to think it out. Nor would people commonly talk about "interpreting" the purpose of the activity of solving a jigsaw puzzle. Why not? They do not usually stand back and reflect on what they have seen. They do not need to. They already understand—automatically, as it were. They just go on to the next thing. Of course the process of understanding has become automatic only because a long record of experiences, language learning, and enculturation preceded their perception of a particular cultural act. But in the end it does become automatic. Similar observations can be made about verbal interpretation.[3]

Goals of Interpretation

So what is the goal for this kind of reflective study and interpretation? There might be many goals. Suppose an interpreter is interpreting for the benefit of someone else who is inquiring about the meaning of a credit card. Then the path of the interpreter depends on what the inquirer's difficulties are and what his interests are. Is the inquirer a foreigner who does not understand the meaning of credit cards? Is he a teenager who is getting a credit card for the first time? Is he familiar with credit cards and wondering why his latest transaction was rejected by the credit card company?

Study can focus on the actors, on the action, or on the larger effects of the action. A particular activity (a behavioreme) like a basketball game or a session for jigsaw puzzle solving can be used as a resource for research into the culture in which it takes place, rather than primarily as a source concerning the actors' individual or corporate intentions. Or an activity could be used primarily as a source for entertainment for those who observe it. Consider the case of "reality" TV shows, where the cameras constantly watch people who have volunteered to try to survive on an island or to live together in a house or to attempt to accomplish some physical challenge.

Using the earlier categories of authority, control, and presence,[4] we can distinguish three foci for interpretation. We can focus on what the actors express and reveal about themselves (presence); we can focus on action and interaction, asking what is its meaning within its cultural context (authority, especially of the actors in their intentionality); we can focus on the purposes and possible effects on the actors and their situation (control). As usual, these three categories interlock.[5]

---

[3]See Vern S. Poythress, *In the Beginning Was the Word: Language—A God-Centered Approach* (Wheaton, IL: Crossway, 2009), chap. 21.

[4]See chap. 4.

[5]As usual, the triad for human action analogically reflects the triad for God's action. See chaps. 3–4 and the further discussion of the expressive (actor-focused), informational (action-focused), and

Reflective interpretation involves standing back and consciously analyzing, rather than just immersing oneself in the process of human action. Often, the analysis takes place on behalf of other potential observers and interpreters, in which case the interpreter stands between the actors and the observers. Analysis may interrupt or put to one side the actors' self-expression and its effects on observers. The analysis then focuses almost wholly on stable cultural meaning content. Thus many forms of analysis naturally focus on meaning content. That is one possible choice, but only one.

The goal is a worthy one, from the standpoint of biblical ethical standards. The Bible proclaims, "You shall love your neighbor as yourself" (Gal. 5:14; Lev. 19:18). A living actor is my neighbor; so out of love I should respect the actor and try to understand what he means by what he does.

Just how we ought to pay attention depends on the situation and the purposes of a particular action. If the particular action involves technical work, or precisely defined rituals, or detailed specifications for a building or a map of a terrain, the human purpose in the situation may require very close attention to detail in an actor's purposes. If unclarity remains, the people involved work together until all the significant sources of unclarity are eliminated.

In other situations, an actor has as a main purpose stimulating the creativity of others. Then it is not so important to try to clear up all imprecision. In fact, an actor may use imprecision positively in order to leave open to respondents a spectrum of opportunities for creativity. For example, if a father and son are working together on a jigsaw puzzle, the father may suggest that the son work on putting together the part of the puzzle that pictures a house, while the father concentrates on the part that pictures the sky. But the father may also just leave it open to the son which part he works on, or whether he hops around between different parts, or whether he works mostly by color rather than mostly by shape. Those choices are part of creativity. The father's own intentions are imprecise in order to open space for creativity.

Similarly, more than one kind of creative response can be appropriate in analysis. Is only one kind of social analysis "right"? It depends on the circumstances and on who is responding.

Actor intention is supremely important if we are dealing with the Bible and with God as its main actor. Then, if we are to submit to God, we must understand what he intends in his actions, both verbal (speaking to human beings) and nonverbal (acts of providence, and acts of deliverance and judgment). We must meditate on his meanings.

---

productive (effect-focused) perspectives in Vern S. Poythress, *God-Centered Biblical Interpretation* (Phillipsburg, NJ: P&R, 1999), 102–3.

But we also meet God; we experience his presence. Meaning coheres with presence. And God's meanings cohere with control. God transforms us by what he does: "You have been born again, not of perishable seed but of imperishable, through the living and abiding word of God" (1 Pet. 1:23). For human action in general, we can say similar things.

The Limits of Time and Energy

We should be aware of several other aspects of the situation. First, any one person's time and energy are limited. If other matters are calling for his attention, he may legitimately stop worrying about an actor's meaning in order to go on to those other things. It depends on the calling of the interpreter. Is he a student to whom the teacher has given an assignment to understand jigsaw-puzzle solving? Or is he just an ordinary observer looking for entertainment or stimulating ideas? Going on to other things may mean just walking away from the situation being analyzed. But it may also mean asking whether we can learn from interacting with a social situation in ways that other participants probably did not intend. For example, someone may choose to use a particular social interaction merely as the springboard for his imagination. Is that all right?

It depends on the situation. If we have a specific obligation to an actor, to obey a command, to finish a job he has appointed, to follow a map he made, or to explain his purposes accurately to someone else, we need to meet our obligation. We must not twist the actor's intentions to escape. On the other hand, if we are merely interacting with a situation in which we have no immediate obligations to an actor, our choices open up. We may exercise our imagination. Christ has set us free to love others in many ways (John 8:32). "You were bought with a price; do not become slaves of men" (1 Cor. 7:23). Freedom in the imagination is one dimension of freedom, and it is important to exercise this freedom in order that through discoveries of the imagination we may bless other people, as well as praise God more deeply.

Corrupt Content

Second, we must reckon with the fall as well as creation in the image of God. Actors are fallen, and observers and interpreters are fallen. And that contaminates human interaction; it introduces satanic ideas and satanic motivations into human action. Respondents and observers cannot always trust actors. Sometimes the respondent should refuse to go along in a common purpose with his fellow. Sometimes he should just walk out because the situation is producing garbage. True love does not mean accepting anything whatsoever. In fact, loving another person includes being hardy enough to resist the evil in what he is saying or doing and to figure out something of what is wrong. Depending on the opportunity, it may include rebuking the other person. "Understanding" the other person or deciphering his meaning is not an absolute ethical requirement, from a biblical point of view. In a sense we are not supposed to "understand" morally evil actions, but reject them. The counsel of the apostle Paul is relevant:

> Finally, brothers, whatever is true, whatever is honorable, whatever is just, whatever is pure, whatever is lovely, whatever is commendable, if there is any excellence, if there is anything worthy of praise, think about these things. (Phil. 4:8)

> I want you to be wise as to what is good and innocent as to what is evil. (Rom. 16:19)

Love involves paying attention to another person long enough and with enough sympathy to be able to try to interact with him in an apt way. Even when we are paying attention to someone engaged in evil, we may sometimes obtain useful insights, by virtue of common grace, or by contrasting what is good with the evil that we are observing.[6] Or we may find that our own habits and ways need to be corrected. We are to observe respectfully those whose practice differs from ours:

> The way of a fool is wise in his own eyes,
>   but a wise man listens to advice. (Prov. 12:15)

But there are limits to our intimacy with others. Some Christians, according to their callings, will have greater ability to interact without moral compromise with anti-Christian thinking and practices. Others will have lesser ability in this area, and they must accordingly draw back from practices that tempt them into sin. Jesus associated with tax collectors and "sinners," in order to bless them. But a person tempted to drunkenness may have to step back from too close association with the bars in which his drinking buddies gather.

All of us are always to respect the limits indicated in God's own biblical instructions about moral purity. When a neighbor is engaging in moral evil, we must out of love for the neighbor search for ways of helping him out of the evil. But the help of another human being is always limited. Only God has unlimited ability to bring people out of evil. We must believe that he can do so even when we find that we ourselves can do nothing except pray. Engaging in moral compromise in the hopes that it will help others never really does good within God's world.

It is worthwhile for academics, in particular, to reflect on this principle. We, along with all other human beings, are flesh and blood, subject to temptation,

---

[6]On common grace, see chap. 14.

and obligated to moral purity, including purity of thought and purity in human associations. Some types of association are not good for us because they are too tempting or too deceitful. The world of scholarship can sometimes generate the pretense that purity can be ignored and that we have an infinite and absolute obligation to pursue objective "understanding," whether it be understanding of an evil philosophy or understanding of a social problem such as pornography or prostitution. But the desire to understand may include a satanic distortion—and a prideful one—of the real obligation to love and to serve the glory of God.

But, says the exploring mind, *how can I know which ideas and practices are right, without first participating in all of them?* No one has the time to look at everything in human cultures. When we do look, we must still respect the fact that God's way of wisdom for mankind is to be nourished and purified spiritually through one pure source, his own word. He invites us into fellowship with Christ through the Holy Spirit, in order to renew us. When we are renewed and given "the mind of Christ" (1 Cor. 2:16), we may effectively sort through the pretended wisdom from other sources. Once we have fellowship with Christ, we have spiritual solidity, and we are then able more and more to discern in other areas.[7]

Crossing into Another Person's Viewpoint

Suppose, then, that in a particular case we are morally able to pursue the quest for interacting with an actor's intentions. Can we understand? The actor is a different person. His thoughts are not necessarily the same as ours. It is easy for an observer to impose his own meaning, too quickly assimilating an actor to his own viewpoint. The challenges are especially great when the actor belongs to a different culture. We could easily repeat here what we have already observed about the diversity of cultures and the challenge that Christians face in crossing cultural barriers.

---

[7]To the world, particularly to the postmodern world, such confidence based on God's word looks like "dogmatism" or fanaticism or cultural prejudice. The world detests such dogmatism. This disapproval of dogmatism does have some good motives behind it. People are looking at the damage done by fanatics with their false claims of certainty and their lack of sympathy for others. Fanaticism of a dangerous kind can arise within Christian circles as well as elsewhere. Those who have come to know the truth through Christ may still pridefully overestimate the depth and thoroughness of their grasp of truth. They may ungraciously attack those who disagree and are a threat to their pride. They may deceive themselves about their motives by labeling their attitude "righteous zeal." And then through their pride they bring disgrace on the name of Christ. Nevertheless, people who humbly devote themselves to Christ can legitimately have confidence about what God has shown them. The world is skeptical about such confidence. But why? Can we for a moment be skeptical about the skeptics? Modernism dogmatically thinks that in its autonomous rationalism it is superior to the humble Christian. Postmodernism dogmatically claims that God cannot speak clearly to us. Both reject confidence in God's instruction because they have a counterfeit conception of God.

Even when the actor belongs to the same larger culture, there remain differences in subcultures and differences in individuals. In a broad sense, deeply understanding another person always requires a step analogous to culture crossing. No mechanical recipe automatically makes the crossing succeed. We need Christian love. We need the power of Christ. We need willingness to sacrifice our own selfish interests for the sake of respect for another: "Let each of you look not only to his own interests, but also to the interests of others. Have this mind among yourselves, which is yours in Christ Jesus . . ." (Phil. 2:4–5).

Trying to understand another person and his meanings is a form of love. Loving another person deeply comes through the power of Christ, and takes place in imitation of Christ, as Philippians 2:4–11 indicates. "We love because he first loved us" (1 John 4:19). In this respect as well, crossing into another person's world is like a small version of crossing into another culture or another language. When done rightly it includes, figuratively speaking, a pattern of death and resurrection. The observer surrenders the security of his own point of view and his own desire to enforce his point of view on the other person. He thereby dies to himself and his pride and his selfishness. In reaching out, he grows in love, and God thereby enriches his life. That enrichment is a figurative resurrection. It is an enrichment even if, in the end, he fails to understand the other person. At least he has tried. The Lord sees that and rewards it.

Love also involves a kind of substitutionary exchange. The observer gives up the exclusive concentration on his own point of view, in order that another person's point of view may prosper and momentarily have preeminence in his mind. This exchange imitates the climactic exchange when Christ gave his life for us (Matt. 20:28).

Finally, love includes victory over Satan. It is always a victory over Satan to resist the temptation to selfishness and to treat another person respectfully. So it is a victory when it takes place in the area of interpretation. Increased understanding of a person is a small victory over the lies and confusion in Satan's dominion (John 8:44).

Three Perspectives on Interpretation

Let us now use the particle, wave, and field perspectives to look at interpretation.

The Particle Perspective on Interpretation

In the particle perspective, we naturally focus on the stability of intention and meaning. God is stable and faithful to himself. And so all his actions have stability of meaning. Human beings, created in the image of God, also carry out actions with stable intention. The father and son intend to solve the jigsaw puzzle, and an analyst can figure out that this is indeed their intention. In this area, as in others, the fall and sin lead to corruption but do not completely destroy human ability to have intentions and to carry them out.

We can grasp the intention for either an act of God or an act of man. We can then proceed to express the intention and explain it. We can imagine an indefinite number of expressions of intention, by different people in different cultures, explaining a jigsaw puzzle. This potential for cross-cultural explanation exhibits the stability of intention across cultural boundaries.

The Wave Perspective on Interpretation

We may also use the wave perspective. Acts by God or by human beings are meant to go somewhere. Acts have intentions that go beyond the moment. Long sequences of coordinated actions often show real dynamic development of intentionality. Any particular action within a sequence is not meant (note the intention!) to be a complete endpoint, but is to be taken in the context of what precedes and follows. Putting one piece into a jigsaw puzzle goes together with putting in other pieces. The intention with one piece makes sense in the context of the intention with other pieces.

Suppose two people together are drawing up plans for a wilderness hike or for building a building. Their interaction is moving toward a unified plan. But there may be comparison or competition of alternative plans along the way. Any one stage must be understood in the light of a goal. If the goal is achieved, then they may look back and say that such and such a stage in the process was not very helpful, and that an earlier partial plan turned out to be a dead end, or that the moment of insight into a promising way forward came at one particular point. They experience a dynamic development of their plans.

Even a completed artistic work like a painting or a film can function in this way. Do analysts examine an artistic work only in order to try to recover the artist's intent? Perhaps some do. But for others there is interest in the whole train of secondary reactions that have sprung up in the wake of an important work. We can ask what Elvis Presley has come to mean in American culture, as well as asking what his intentions were in his own lifetime. In fact, different groups, and different persons within a group, grow in slightly different ways as they interact with a particular artistic work. The artist may even have intended his work to have many diverse benefits for many diverse people. These effects are a process, a wave.

Remember the model of the unity and diversity in the body of Christ. There is health, not merely danger, in diversity. For each of us human beings, our understanding is finite and human, not divine. It is not absolutely comprehensive. So also, our reexpressions of cultural meaning in moments of analysis are not comprehensive. Good interpretations of cultural phenomena do share many of the contrastive-identificational features with the cultural product that they interpret. They do all express one meaning. But they express it with variation. They show differences as well as common features.

In a wave perspective, meaning is not quite the easy thing that either popular modernist or postmodernist thinking may sometimes take it to be.[8] There is much complexity in both modernism and postmodernism. So in summarizing them we will simplify and deal with stereotyped forms of both.

Modernist thinking tends in its analysis of cultural issues to want unity without diversity, through the complete domination of pure, autonomous reason. As a result, in modernist thinking, the meaning of a particular act or a particular artistic work is what it is, namely, a pure, isolated essence, and we must all submit to it by wiping out, suppressing, and destroying all differences.

By contrast, postmodernist thinking is prone to want diversity without unity. Each person in his diversity produces whatever meaning seems right in his own eyes. Since many modern people believe that God is nonexistent or inaccessible, there is no way to adjudicate among interpretations, and no confidence that the Holy Spirit will bring the humility and love that lead to genuine understanding of God or of any other actor, for that matter. So, for the sake of peace, people may celebrate diversity of all kinds, sometimes including error and aberration.[9]

The Field Perspective on Interpretation

We may also use a field perspective on cultural meaning. People understand the relations of what they are doing to a larger social interaction. At office parties an employee may be expected to interact with others not merely for the sake of business information but also for general socialization. He cements the social atmosphere of the office. The speech making at a political rally is one focal point within a total experience that is intended to promote the morale, the dedication, and the fund-raising for the political cause. The total experience is important, and the "meaning" of a political speech is found not merely in its obvious content but also in its social contribution in relation to the rally as a whole. The jigsaw solving by a father and son has meaning as a contribution to many pleasant leisure interactions between the two of them. One session of puzzle solving has a good deal of value and significance because it contributes to an ongoing intimate relationship. The puzzle solving coheres with the larger relationship.

---

[8]On modernism and postmodernism, see Poythress, *In the Beginning*, appendix A.

[9]How we deal with unity and diversity on earth among human beings tends to reflect what we believe about unity and diversity in God. If people promote diversity without enough unity, it is akin to polytheism (many gods, with little or no unity). By contrast, promoting unity without diversity is like Unitarianism, which affirms one God, but not three persons in the Godhead.

To focus in isolation on one act of putting one piece in place would be possible, but it would miss other dimensions, because meaning in a broad sense belongs to the relations of one act to the whole process of solving the puzzle. And solving the one puzzle relates to the many other actions that father and son do together. The "meaning" of any particular human interaction is integrally related to other meanings, including cultural meanings in the surrounding cultural contexts. We would subtly falsify the richness of human interaction if we pretended that meaning could be precisely cordoned off, delineated with infinite precision, and confined to a single act now treated in isolation.

21

Interpreting God's Actions

And he gave the apostles, the prophets, the evangelists,
the shepherds and teachers, to equip the saints
for the work of ministry, for building up the body of Christ,
until we all attain to the unity of the faith
and of the knowledge of the Son of God, to mature manhood,
to the measure of the stature of the fullness of Christ.

—Ephesians 4:11–13

We can also reflect on what it means to interpret God's actions. With God's actions we confront added richness, because God may act as primary cause alongside secondary causes, including human agents (chap. 5).[1]

Knowing God

How can we begin to understand the meaning of God's actions? Is not God beyond our understanding? God is *incomprehensible* in a technical sense. He knows himself completely, but we as finite human beings know finitely. God is the standard for who he is and what we know about him; we are not.[2] That is the meaning of God's

---

[1] As a key example of dual agency, see the discussion of dual authorship in Vern S. Poythress, "Divine Meaning of Scripture," *Westminster Theological Journal* 48 (1986): 241–79; Poythress, "The Presence of God Qualifying Our Notions of Grammatical-Historical Interpretation: Genesis 3:15 as a Test Case," *Journal of the Evangelical Theological Society* 50, no. 1 (2007): 87–103; and Poythress, *In the Beginning Was the Word: Language—A God-Centered Approach* (Wheaton, IL: Crossway, 2009), appendix J.

[2] See the important discussion of transcendence and immanence, and the implications for knowledge

transcendence. God's incomprehensibility applies to the meaning of his actions. He knows completely the meaning of all his actions. We never do.

God is also *immanent.* He is present to us and we can know him. God's own omnipotence makes it possible for him to make himself known to us, whom he made in his image. It is important that we affirm the reality of human knowledge. Even unbelievers know God, according to Romans 1:21. The notion that God is unknowable is really a non-Christian corruption of the biblical idea of God's transcendence.

As a consequence of God's immanence, we can and do know the meaning of many of his actions; we know truly, but we know in part, finitely. As people created in the image of God, with minds analogically related to the mind of God, we are naturally "in tune" with the meaning of God's actions. In many cases, God's actions are analogous to our own, and his intentions are analogous to our own.

We can illustrate even with the spectacular actions of God in creating the world. He created a whole universe and different kinds of creatures within it. We cannot do that. But God has made us "sub-creators" who can make stories about made-up worlds. And he has given us the capability of forming and shaping and remaking things—taming or breeding animals; making pencils and houses and cars; engaging in creative work. God planned to create the animals and then executed his plan. We plan to rearrange the living room furniture or plant a garden, and then we execute our plan. We are in this respect "in tune" with God's intentionality and his powers of execution (chaps. 3–4).

Of course, since the fall, it is also true that we corrupt and distort our knowledge of God. We make ourselves idols. Idolatrous conceptions concerning God result in idolatrous conceptions about God's actions—or about the alleged actions of an alleged plurality of gods, because that is one form of distortion. So God provides us with the Bible, with redemptive acts, with the presence of the Holy Spirit—all as part of a process leading us back into true knowledge of him.

Multiple Causation

When God created the world, he was the main actor. In one respect the situation is simpler in that case than when secondary causes are also at work. How do we discern the meaning of God's action in the midst of secondary action from human beings or animals or physical causes?

The book of Job in chapters 1–2 provides us with a key example of multiple action. God as primary cause brought the calamities on Job, as Job affirms (1:21). Human raiders, the Sabeans and the Chaldeans, took away Job's flocks (1:15, 17). Satan instigated the whole series of disasters (1:12; 2:7). We can

---

of God, in John M. Frame, *The Doctrine of the Knowledge of God* (Phillipsburg, NJ: Presbyterian and Reformed, 1987), especially 13–15.

see clearly three different intentionalities: of God, of the raiders, and of Satan. God intended to test Job but in the end to enable him to grow; the Sabeans and the Chaldeans intended to seize Job's property and kill his servants for their own selfish benefit; and Satan intended to overthrow Job, discredit his piety, and undermine God's glory. The intentions are different, and accordingly the actions of the actors are different from one another. But there is only one series of physical effects.

The situation here may at first look impossibly complex, but in the end it is not. We are persons, knowing God, and so we can interpret other persons. Because we are persons, we can understand to a degree the intentionality of other persons, even a divine person or an angelic person. We interpret action based on the information that we have about the action itself, but also on the basis of what we know about the person.

The extra difficulty with the events in Job arises from our incomplete knowledge of God and of Satan. But we also have incomplete knowledge of ourselves, as well as incomplete knowledge of other human beings. So we must avoid exaggerating the difficulties belonging to this particular case. On the other hand, there *are* difficulties, because God often does not tell us his reasons. How many people have agonized about reasons after a loved one has died an untimely death or some other tragedy has befallen them? Job himself agonized over why the calamities had fallen on him. The challenges here can go very deep.

In the book of Job we have a privilege Job himself did not have, because we receive further information by God's special revelation in chapters 1–2. We know about Satan's accusation and God's response. Without that knowledge, we would find it more difficult to interpret the meaning of the disasters and the meaning of God's action in them. We would be more in the position of Job and his three friends. And that is indeed a difficulty. Job's three friends do know things about God, true things, such as his justice and his zeal to bring consequences for sin. But Job's friends presume to know too much in the way that they interpret the meaning of the disasters. They think Job must have sinned in some particular way, and that is the reason why God brought the disasters. In this respect they have an oversimple view of God's providential action, his purposes, and the meaning of his purposes.

The same temptation to overestimate our understanding of God confronts us as modern interpreters. On the one hand, we do know things about God, especially on the basis of his special revelation in the Bible. We know he is just. We also know, or ought to know, just as Job and his friends did, that God is in control of disasters as well as pleasant events. None of the disputants in the book of Job has any doubt about that. And God himself, when he appears to Job, affirms his universal sovereignty rather than suggesting that Job and his friends overestimated it. Denial of God's control over disasters is an unbiblical way out, despite its attractiveness to some modern interpreters.[3]

So God is in control of a modern disaster like a hurricane. If God is just, should not we conclude that the hurricane must have been sent to destroy people who were especially wicked? No, the book of Job says that it does not work that way in every case. Jesus confirms this principle:

> There were some present at that very time who told him [Jesus] about the Galileans whose blood Pilate had mingled with their sacrifices. And he answered them, "Do you think that these Galileans were worse sinners than all the other Galileans, because they suffered in this way? No, I tell you; but unless you repent, you will all likewise perish. Or those eighteen on whom the tower in Siloam fell and killed them: do you think that they were worse offenders than all the others who lived in Jerusalem? No, I tell you; but unless you repent, you will all likewise perish." (Luke 13:1–5)

Jesus rejects the simplistic inference that the Galileans were worse sinners. At the same time, he does encourage people to draw some inferences: death is a judgment from God, and we are all liable to his judgment. The incidents with the Galileans and the tower of Siloam remind us of truths about God's character and therefore about his actions.

When God's providential actions are not accompanied by specific words from God explaining them, we must be cautious. But in the Bible he gives explanations for some events, and then we can be confident on the basis of his explanations. We are confident about the meaning of the great events in which God acts to create and to redeem. And God invites us to apply the lessons of these great events to our present circumstances. God is redemptively at work as primary cause in our present circumstances. But we trust in him even when his actions remain mysterious.

Three Perspectives on God's Actions

Now let us concentrate on insights that can come from using the three perspectives—particle, wave, and field (from chap. 7).

A Particle Perspective on Interpreting God's Action

First, let us apply the particle perspective to understanding God's actions. God knows beforehand all of the ways in which he desires people to understand and appropriate an action of his—whether one of the great acts of redemption, such as the exodus from Egypt, or an "ordinary" providential action, such as causing

---

[3]See also Gen. 50:20; Lam. 3:37–38; Rom. 8:28; Acts 4:27–28; Eph. 1:11.

the opening of a flower bud into a blossom or empowering a father to move a puzzle piece into place. God's knowledge encompasses all the reactions to what he has done throughout history. All the approved reactions are part of his intention. Even reactions that God does not approve of are still within his sovereign control. In fact, in a larger sense God's intention for the exodus would include hypothetical approved reactions that do not happen to occur in the actual historical process. God knows the possibilities as well as the actualities (see, e.g., 1 Sam. 23:9–12).

The knowledge of God is complete and does not change. So his total intention for the exodus, the total meaning of the exodus, does not change with time. The same is true for his total intention for the moving of a jigsaw piece. In the particle perspective, we would focus on this unchanging total intention. If we equate God's meaning with his intention, we can say that the meaning is unchanging. "Heaven and earth will pass away, but my words will not pass away," Jesus says (Matt. 24:35). The same kind of unchanging meaning belongs to an act like the exodus.

A Wave Perspective on Interpreting God's Actions

Now let us consider the wave perspective on God's actions. Individuals and communities grow gradually in the knowledge of God's actions and their implications. Growth is a wave; it is a process. Within this life it does not come to an end. The process includes moments of careful, exacting analysis of past events. The careful, exacting analysis has come to be described as "historical interpretation"—or "grammatical-historical interpretation" if we are dealing with an event of verbal communication.[4]

Historical scholars and cultural analysts endeavor to discipline themselves so as not merely to read in what they want. They try to see what meanings belong to people within another time or another culture than their own. Even within a modern situation where they have greater familiarity, they try to ask lots of questions, to query many people's viewpoints, and not to leap to conclusions that just confirm their initial prejudices. Potentially such analysis can offer a valuable contribution, because whole groups of people—Christians included—may collectively develop a subculture and a tradition that finds ways to "tame" the meaning of what has happened. A community tradition may end up distorting meaning in order to avoid the pain of confronting the community's corporate sins. The scholarly investigation is a process, but its goal is stable meaning, often

---

[4]I have written elsewhere concerning the benefits and limitations of this mode of interpretation. See Vern S. Poythress, *God-Centered Biblical Interpretation* (Phillipsburg, NJ: P&R, 1999), especially chaps. 9–10; Poythress, "Presence of God."

the meaning that would have been experienced by the people who actually went through the events being investigated.

Now, we should note a difficulty. Where in the process does the scholar reckon with God's presence and his action as primary cause? Modern scholarship typically leaves God out, whether it looks at the exodus from Egypt or at a father and son working a jigsaw puzzle. The process falsifies the events by leaving out one of the actors, and the most important one at that. Why? Because God is uncontrollable? Does his presence make analysis too difficult? But that is like refusing to work on a hard math problem or a hard ethical problem, substituting an easy one instead, and then putting forth the answer to the easy problem as if it were the answer to the hard problem. The whole world of events is falsified by this kind of procedure. Scholarship like this asks us to live in an imaginary world where it postulates that God either does not exist or is inactive or is unknowable.

We can see a little more what is happening. It is the same story described in Romans 1:18–23, where the living God governing the universe is replaced by a system of impersonal laws, in this case impersonal laws or regularities about history and human action and human societies (chap. 9). The substitute of impersonal for personal is a kind of idolatry. And with the substitution come changes in judgment all along the line. The regularities are differently understood, and so the events being investigated are differently understood. In particular, the final reference point for meaning is no longer the meaning in God's mind, but meaning from human reason or from human "construction."[5]

Human Creativity in Interpretation

Both for scholars and for ordinary participants, the total process of interpretation also includes creative insights. The creativity can take the form of envisioning a new way of construing the meaning of an event like the exodus. Or it could be insight into an application to the modern life—a moral or spiritual or political "lesson." Or it could be a sense that God is showing me here and now something about my own life, in a way that may not derive from my best discernment of the meaning that earlier participants saw in the events of long ago. Or it may be a thought or an inspiration, seemingly out of nowhere, only loosely associated with the events I have investigated, but seeming to be a thought given by God's blessing.

Not all such thoughts and meanings are approved by God. We need to remember that the Devil tempted Christ by quoting Scripture and giving it his own spin, his own evil application:

---

[5]For further discussion and illustration, particularly with respect to modern sociology, see appendices A–G.

Then the devil took him to the holy city and set him on the pinnacle of the temple and said to him, "If you are the Son of God, throw yourself down, for it is written,

> "'He will command his angels concerning you,'

and

> "'On their hands they will bear you up,
>   lest you strike your foot against a stone.'"

Jesus said to him, "Again it is written, 'You shall not put the Lord your God to the test.'" (Matt. 4:5–7)

So how do we distinguish between creative ideas that are a positive gift from God and ideas that ought to be rejected? As the Reformers recognized, the Bible is our only infallible guide; and within that guidebook, what is clear in Scripture interprets what is unclear.[6] Creativity that gets into tension with what is clear is out of bounds. But creativity in harmony with Scripture is in bounds. Even creative thoughts "out of nowhere" can sometimes be valuable gifts from God. But we must avoid confusing them with the central, clear meanings from the Bible. In addition, we need to do what is normal for Christians in the body of Christ: test new ideas in the light of Scripture and talk to other Christians to see what they think. In particular, we must not pressure other Christians to receive an idea that is not clearly supported by particular texts in the Bible.

God is the sole Creator of the world. But human beings made in his image are derivatively creative, in analogy with his archetypal creativity. Those in fellowship with God should find that their creativity is stimulated and sharpened over time, rather than stifled. Many rebels have imagined that submission to God, because it gives definite moral boundaries and definite boundaries for our thinking about God (no false gods), must stifle creativity. But God is the source of all fruitful human creativity. Knowing him richly expands our minds, expands our horizons, and lets the light in.

---

[6] Some postmodernists delight in showing that no meaning is "clear," because we can always see it in a new context. Yes, contexts vary, and rebellious people often cleverly invent new contexts that suit them. But God controls all contexts. He calls on us to trust him and to believe that through the work of the Holy Spirit he moves those who trust in him more and more into righteous paths. They begin to think God's thoughts after him, and their new thoughts and new life provide the contexts for clarity:

> But the path of the righteous is like the light of dawn,
>   which shines brighter and brighter until full day.
> The way of the wicked is like deep darkness;
>   they do not know over what they stumble. (Prov. 4:18–19)

Modernism wants a firm, final, clear answer to social meaning through mechanical application of the right method. That squelches creativity and personal fellowship. Relativism wants creativity, but without God's presence creativity can degenerate into arbitrariness, which is next door to meaninglessness.

God's answer is different from both. We grow, as God has designed us to grow, in the body of Christ; we grow both in unity and in diversity, in stability and in creativity. Rightly used, creativity contributes to stability, because creative ideas from one believer can later be checked out more methodically and rationally by another believer. If they do check out, they add to stable knowledge. Conversely, stability contributes to creativity, because stability from one member of the body provides direction for another member's creativity: it points the way to the most promising new avenues that the creative member explores.

When the church is functioning in the way in which it was designed, the Holy Spirit is present among the members, and the Spirit himself empowers them to serve one another within the body of Christ (1 Corinthians 12). We can use an analogy from work in science. The creative scientist does new explorations in Antarctica or in the Andes. The stable scientist provides a body of knowledge that instructs the creative scientist as to what kind of questions might be most fruitful when he travels to the Andes. So likewise in the body of Christ. So likewise when we are thinking about society rather than about geology or biology.

A Field Perspective on Interpreting God's Actions

In view of God's design for the body of Christ, individual interpreters of history and social action need to interact with other members of the body. The principle of diversity in the body of Christ extends to interpretation of history and society. Different members may notice different things, and their observations then supplement one another. They may also correct one another.

The Bible has a central role, not only because God gives us there his infallible word, but also because we need it to correct sinful distortions in our thinking and in our social life. The Bible itself indicates that its principles have to be applied in our lives.[7] So we can benefit from people who have keen insight into various aspects of our lives, including their social dimensions.

Growth comes not only through the sharing of different observations about the positive message of Scriptures and its implications, but also from correction and rebuke when someone begins to distort the Bible.

---

[7]The attention to our situation for the sake of application constitutes what John Frame calls the "situational perspective," in contrast to the "normative perspective," which concentrates on God's norm (found in Scripture). See John M. Frame, *The Doctrine of the Christian Life* (Phillipsburg, NJ: P&R, 2008). For a shorter introduction to Frame's three perspectives on ethics, see Frame, *Perspectives on the Word of God: An Introduction to Christian Ethics* (Phillipsburg, NJ: Presbyterian and Reformed, 1990).

Thus any one person's work in interpreting social action has a complex inter-action with the body of Christ. No one person on earth has already arrived at a comprehension of all the implications of God's meanings. One person supple-ments another and corrects the other when the other is astray. We pay attention to the relationships between different people's views and to relationships between the Bible's instruction and the social contexts that we investigate.

Paying attention to relationships can also foster the creativity that we discussed under the heading of the wave perspective. In particular, I intend in this book to exercise creativity in thinking about human action and social relationships. Of course we must first pay attention to the clear and direct things that the Bible has to say about God's action, about man's creation, about Satan, and about redemp-tion. But then we also go out and look at society. We use the insights from those who have studied societies intensively. We endeavor to sift through good and bad, and creatively to relate the Bible's more explicit teaching to what we are learning about social relationships. I invite others to go beyond what I say and to explore further. That is part of the wave perspective, which acknowledges continuing creativity.

We have now looked at particle, wave, and field perspectives on interpreting social relationships. We can apply each of these perspectives in interpreting any one culture, or any one event within the culture. Each of these perspectives is given to us from God, on the basis of his Trinitarian character. And from each of these perspectives we explore riches that God knows perfectly and has provided for our exploration and delight.

22

Cultural Learning

Hear, my son, your father's instruction,
and forsake not your mother's teaching,
for they are a graceful garland for your head
and pendants for your neck.
My son, if sinners entice you,
do not consent.

—Proverbs 1:8–10

Why does it seem natural to people who live in China to eat with chopsticks, while chopsticks seem unnatural to Americans? One part of the answer comes from distinguishing insiders and outsiders in a culture. The Chinese, as insiders to Chinese culture, view the use of chopsticks from inside. They know and practice the custom of using chopsticks in eating. From their inside viewpoint, it seems natural. By contrast, an American, when he first sees chopsticks, sees them from outside. They are just thin sticks. He does not even realize that they are eating implements until he is told.

Origin of Cultural Understanding

How does the difference arise between insiders and outsiders in a culture? Where does "naturalness" come from? Some people naively think that there is something racial here. They might say that chopsticks are in the genes of the Chinese. But that is not true. The large-scale immigration to the United States and subsequent adoption of American culture by the descendants of immigrants show the flexibility of cultural practices. People who come to the United States from China or Vietnam or Poland or Germany have children and then grandchildren and great-grandchildren who, after a few generations, show few differences from the practices of other Americans. Or consider the situation where an American family adopts and raises a Chinese baby. The baby grows up with American rather than Chinese cultural habits.

We can therefore infer that cultural practices are learned rather than biological. All of us have to eat; that is a biological reality built into the physiological processes in our bodies. But how we eat is another matter. Will it be with chopsticks or with fork and spoon or with the fingers? As children we learn how to eat "politely," that is, in conformity with practices of the culture around us. Students of society call this learning "socialization." Children learn from their parents primarily, but also from others with whom they have close contact, whether siblings or relatives or teachers or playground friends or TV. Children assimilate much without consciously realizing it. By the time children are grown, many cultural practices are completely natural to them. The practices of the culture affect not only eating implements, but also the kinds of foods served, the preparation of the food, and the social interaction during the meal. The same is true for other cultural practices.

The Presence of God in Learning

Children learn from their parents and friends. Does this learning process exclude God? Modern secularized thinking tempts us to assume that God is absent from the process. But it is God who himself designed the process. When God created human beings, he did not begin with a billion people all at once. He designed that one couple, Adam and Eve, should have descendants over a period of generations. Children would learn from their parents according to the process described in Proverbs:

> Hear, my son, your father's instruction,
>   and forsake not your mother's teaching. (Prov. 1:8)

> Whoever spares the rod hates his son,
>   but he who loves him is diligent to discipline him. (Prov. 13:24)

The Bible specifically instructs parents to teach their children about God and his law: "And these words that I command you today shall be on your heart. You shall teach them diligently to your children, and shall talk of them when you sit in your house, and when you walk by the way, and when you lie down, and when you rise" (Deut. 6:6–7).

God is present as parents raise their children. He is teaching the children through the parents. And he may teach them in other ways as well. The Bible specifically compares God's discipline to the discipline of an earthly father:

> My son, do not despise the LORD's discipline
>   or be weary of his reproof,
> for the LORD reproves him whom he loves,
>   as a father the son in whom he delights. (Prov. 3:11–12)

Effects of Sin

But now what about cases where the parents are not following God? Parents may never even mention the word *God*, and some children may never hear the word until they are older. And then they would need to have it explained to them. Or, if they were to grow up in ancient pagan Greece, they would hear of "gods" but never hear about the true God of the Bible. Do such children grow up without knowing God?

This kind of effect is not surprising to God. In fact, God designed the human race with parent-child relations. He did not make each person to be merely an individual, in total isolation from other people. He designed us to be in relation-ships. And he does not create each new human being immediately as a mature adult, but brings infants into the world in a context where they have to be raised and trained and nurtured, either by their biological parents or by others who function in a parental role.

In a world with human relationships, sins and righteous acts both have con-sequences on other people—particularly on those who are being nurtured. The drunk who wastes his property has no property to pass on to his children. Worse, the children may imitate the pattern of their parents and become alcoholics themselves. The lying parent may raise children prone to lying. The parent who values truth may hope to raise children who value truth.

God talks about generational effects of sin right in the middle of the Ten Commandments:

> You shall not make for yourself a carved image, or any likeness of anything that is in heaven above, or that is in the earth beneath, or that is in the water under the earth. You shall not bow down to them or serve them, for I the LORD your God am a jealous God, visiting the iniquity of the fathers on the children to the third and the fourth generation of those who hate me, but showing steadfast love to thousands of those who love me and keep my commandments. (Ex. 20:4–6)

This instruction comes from the second commandment, which discusses idolatry. If the parents are idolaters, they encourage their children to worship in the same way. Idolatry and its effects are passed from one generation to another.

It is clear that God condemns idolatry. But in this very context he also indicates that he is the one who has ordained the connection between parents and children. Parents are the most important people in shaping the lives and practices of children. But others also have an influence, and the same principle extends to them. The Bible discusses the possibility that a relative ("your brother") or a friend or a whole city can entice a person to idolatry (Deut. 13:6, 12–13). A peer group can have its effect:

> My son, if *sinners entice you,*
> > do not consent. (Prov. 1:10; see 1:14)

We know that all cultures are contaminated by sin. So how can we escape the sins of the culture within which we live? It is not easy. Pervasive cultural sins, like prostitution or slavery within some cultures, represent a strong temptation, because those around us within the culture are not condemning them. If we are brought up within the culture, we have probably been propagandized with arguments and justifications that excuse sins.

Does Our Culture Excuse Us?

So is a child merely the victim of his environment? Does he have no choice? God holds individuals responsible, and that shows that indeed they have responsibility (see Ezekiel 18; 33). They go in one direction when other directions are open to them.

The life of Jesus on earth shows that human beings are never merely prisoners of their culture; they are never forced into sin by cultural circumstances.[1] Jesus was fully human. As a man, he grew up (Luke 2:40, 52) and lived in the Palestinian culture of the first century, a culture that was not morally flawless. It had its strengths, among which was a devotion to the Law of Moses. It had its weaknesses, both from the corruption of the Roman overlords and from the more subtle moral and religious corruption of the Jewish religious leaders. Jesus lived in this compromised culture and did so without sin. He criticized the leaders where they were wrong in their teaching or their practice. A mere prisoner to culture could not have done such criticism. The same is true of the prophets who criticized sins that were popular in Israel. The same is true of modern people when they

---

[1] Sin is personal rebellion against God's standards and involves personal consent. If Tim physically compels Charlie, the sin belongs to Tim, not Charlie.

make a moral complaint about how cultures hem people in! Sin is never morally compelled by the "prison" of circumstances or of culture.

None of us is sinless. We inherit corruption from Adam's initial rebellion. But there is no excuse for the sins we do commit. Why not? We all live in the presence of God. The law of God, written on the heart, is known even if in sin we try to suppress it (Rom. 1:32). Second, our hearts are not prisoners to the culture in a way that removes our responsibility when we go along with the culture. We make choices. We do not have to go along with the crowd, though we may lose prestige if we are different. Moreover, we have alternatives in the situation. God always ensures that there is some alternative route of action: "No temptation has overtaken you that is not common to man. God is faithful, and he will not let you be tempted beyond your ability, but with the temptation he will also provide *the way of escape*, that you may be able to endure it" (1 Cor. 10:13).

We must remember that God is present in the world through general revelation. According to the Bible, everyone knows God inescapably (Rom. 1:18–25). As part of this knowledge, everyone also knows God's moral standards (Rom. 1:32). The children who grow up in an atheist or pagan home know God. They suppress the knowledge, and their parents of course promote and aid that suppression. Children grow up with the effects of this atmosphere.

God understands these atmospheric effects. He takes notice of them. He knows that people raised in one environment do not have the same privileges as others. He takes this into account in a principle: "Everyone to whom much was given, of him much will be required, and from him to whom they entrusted much, they will demand the more" (Luke 12:48). The child raised in a Christian home is more deeply guilty if he rebels against that privileged upbringing. But the child raised in a dysfunctional home or on the streets is still responsible for his conduct, day by day, because he still lives in the presence of God.

The Presence of God in Simple Activity

Consider an example. A child watches an older boy hitting a ball. That activity is possible only because God is continually present. God created the boy with the ability to hit the ball. He gave the boy the ability to have purposes, in particular, the purpose of hitting the ball. He created the ball in such a way that it could receive the hit. He created the atmosphere and the force of gravity that influence the path of the ball. He ordained the structures of cause and effect, and he himself is continually at work as primary cause. He specifies the structures in such a way that the boy's action enjoys an analogy with God's action. Analogy comes with the very possibility of human personal action.

The child who watches the boy with the ball understands the purposes and the causes because he himself is a person with purposes and with abilities to act.

He is able to think about purposes because his mind is made in the image of God, who has purposes. The child cannot escape God, and part of the reason why he cannot escape is that he cannot escape personhood. The child experiences the presence of God and the presence of God's action in each activity. He does not merely watch a boy's action in isolation from God. The Father expresses his love for the Son in making a world that imitates the intra-Trinitarian love. This imitation includes the humble relation between agent, action, and recipient that God sustains in the boy's activity.[2]

Consider the boy's action from the perspective of God's involvement. God empowers the boy with the ability to have purposes and to intend as an agent to hit the ball. Even in the process of having purposes and making plans, the boy imitates the fact that God has purposes and plans. The boy's planning illustrates the fact that he is made in the image of God. God empowers the boy in the action of hitting, and God as primary cause brings about the hitting. The boy, of course, is active on his level, and that too is significant; he is the secondary cause. God empowers the relations of secondary causes and effects so that the ball gets hit—it becomes a recipient. God's control goes together with his authority and his presence; they are inseparable. In particular, God is present when the boy hits the ball. The boy's hitting the ball has meaning in relation to God's plan. And God's plan has meaning in relation to his character, which is preeminently expressed in God's loving his Son. The plan concerning the world is an expression of the Father's love.

The child who is learning skills in personal action has before him in the activity of the older boy the manifestation of the authority, control, and presence of God. The activity cannot do anything other than reveal God because it has meaning only in relation to the mind of God.

Wrath and Redemption

Children always grow up knowing God. But such knowledge just makes them guilty, rather than rescuing them. The situation is described in Romans 1:18–32. Redemption through Christ includes not only redemption of individuals, but also redemption from the social dimensions of sin. Sin does get passed from one person to another and from one generation to another. Escape is in fact impossible unless God acts (Luke 18:27). God's redemptive activity does not destroy social relations and just start over. Rather, beginning with the human heart, he removes "the old self" and has us put on the "new self," after the new pattern of

---

[2]On agent and other roles, see Vern S. Poythress, *In the Beginning Was the Word: Language— A God-Centered Approach* (Wheaton, IL: Crossway, 2009), chaps. 24, 30–31. On general revelation, see also Cornelius Van Til, *An Introduction to Systematic Theology: Prolegomena and the Doctrines of Revelation, Scripture, and God*, 2nd ed. (Phillipsburg, NJ: P&R, 2007), especially chaps. 6–9.

Christ's holiness (Col. 3:9–10). This fundamental transformation leads to the transformation and reconfiguration of human relationships such as marriage, family, and work (Eph. 5:22–6:9; Col. 3:18–4:1).

The transformation takes time because sin is deep and subtle, twisting human society as well as the individuals within it. But transformation is possible because Christ has triumphed over sin universally and completely. Even during his earthly life he effected transformations in social life, as he associated with tax collectors and sinners (Luke 15:1; see 5:29–31).

The Significance of Variation

We can see one possibility for escape from cultural bondage in the fact of *variation*. Cultural institutions and cultural behavior have fixed patterns and stabilities, that is, contrastive-identificational features. But they also—always—display variation. There are always possibilities for doing things a little differently. Jesus reclined at table when he ate because reclining was the custom in first-century Palestine. But he ate with tax collectors and sinners, which was different from what the religious leaders expected. People can also act in unprecedented ways that break out of the existing patterns. Jesus drove out the money changers from the temple. The apostles spoke out about the gospel even though they had been forbidden to do so by the religious leaders (Acts 4:18–20; 5:25).

When the Holy Spirit works in people, as he did in the apostles, they become creative in doing good. Existing cultural patterns begin to change, either subtly or violently. The Holy Spirit, who is God, ordained the cultural patterns in the first place. He is free to change them. It is especially appropriate for him to change them when the change is part of the process of delivering people from cultural bondage to sinful ways of thinking and acting.

If a father and a son are constantly bickering while they put together a jigsaw puzzle, they can stop the bickering and still continue with the jigsaw. Solving the jigsaw (a behavioreme) is still "the same" socially significant action even though it now varies through the elimination of bickering. A family can change and still be identifiable as a family.

We can also consider the possibility of large-scale change in a society through smaller incremental changes. A government in which bribery is widespread can become an impartial government either by a sudden "clean sweep" that replaces large numbers of officials or by a gradual change in practices. Certain basic functions of government in law enforcement nevertheless remain in place, and we can still in a broad way identify the government as a government.

Institutions can also change their functions over time. For example, the YMCA, founded as a specifically *religious* organization, has evolved into a general service organization.[3] In a period of anarchy a particular family could begin to serve a local area by helping to settle disputes. In time, the family could take over more functions of government and begin to be perceived as the governor in that area. We can see here a kind of social analogue to literary metaphors. A literary metaphor creatively extends words and sentences to new meanings. Similarly, the order of a family can be creatively extended to serve as the foundation for the order of a civil government. The creativity that God has given to human beings allows us not merely to perpetuate a cultural practice, but also to extend it or alter it into an analogous practice.

This creativity has implications for ethical evaluation. No cultural practice is ethically acceptable just because it happens to exist. Cultures can change, and sometimes they need to change. Even before the culture changes, individuals within it are responsible to God. They always have before them the possibility of change, even when in fact they are just "going with the flow" and conforming to long-standing cultural practices. God is present to them, and his ethical standards confront them, even though they may evade and suppress the implications of his presence.

On the other hand, no cultural practice is unethical just because it belongs to people who are in rebellion against God. By common grace (chap. 13) people in rebellion may still preserve many outward practices that conform to God's standards.

Sinful Influence on Culture

Now, what happens if we belong to a culture some of whose practices are sinful? For example, what if the government or leadership structures are full of bribery? And is a practice properly called bribery if it is the accepted thing? Is it still wrong?

We must always apply biblical principles in evaluation. It is not wrong for a government official to get pay in some way for his work. That pay could in principle be arranged by a legal rule that said that the person requesting a building permit or a shipping permit should pay a standard fee, and that part (or all) of the fee should go to the official who issues the permit. Moral evil enters in the form of injustice where the official is prejudicial toward his family or his friends or those who promise special favors in return. A situation must be analyzed against the background of its cultural context in order to understand whether we are looking at a legitimate fee or a prejudicial favor.

---

[3]The religious origin is visible in the original name, Young Men's *Christian* Association.

23

Human Knowledge within Culture

The Jews were entrusted with the oracles of God.

—Romans 3:2

The learning process with children leads not only to cultural skills but also to knowledge of many different kinds. We need to consider the influence of culture on knowledge.

How do we know what we know? We learn some things by self-conscious observation. We learn others by being taught. We learn still others without realizing that we are learning. How did you learn your mother tongue? You must have had a large number of experiences in hearing and using language. But it happened when you were a child, in the dim past; so you have no clear memory of such learning.

Similarly, within a monocultural environment, children learn much cultural knowledge without self-consciously realizing it. We learn what kind of clothes are appropriate both for the culture in general and for special occasions within it. We learn views of time and money. In some cultures punctuality and clock time are important. In others there may be no clocks. In some cultures passing on or accumulating wealth may rate highly; other cultures may value giving and sharing more than accumulating.

Religious Tradition

We also learn religion or its absence. Children with religiously committed parents learn the religion of their parents. Children with indifferent parents learn religious indifference. Children with parents vigorously advocating atheism learn vigorous

190

atheism. If a whole culture has predominantly one religion, children may not be aware of alternatives. On the other hand, if the culture is religiously pluralistic, the children grow up with knowledge of several alternatives. They may nevertheless be firmly committed to one religion, or they may serve several (as can happen in a polytheistic environment), or they may find it difficult to decide and end up with little commitment to any particular religion.

Evaluating "Knowledge"

A surrounding culture has an influence on what a child grows up knowing. And the influence can be negative as well as positive. A child is prone to practice the religion of his parents and close associates even if that religion has falsehoods in it. The same holds in principle for knowledge in other areas. Many times we think we know some truth because that truth is widely acknowledged within our subculture. Confrontation with ideas from some other culture or subculture then raises questions.

What do we do with these questions? How do we obtain the real truth? Is truth impossible because cultural influence can never be completely overcome? As we observed, God has designed us to come into the world as infants, to be raised in families, and to receive instruction not only from parents but also from others in the community. But in a fallen world this situation passes on sinful ideas as well as truth.

God's redemption includes redemption in knowledge: "If you abide in my word [Jesus's word], you are truly my disciples, and you will know the truth, and the truth will set you free" (John 8:31–32). The good news ("gospel") about God's redemption through Christ is now going out into the world, destined for every culture (Matt. 28:18–20). Through the good news, people come to know Christ, who sends his Spirit and instructs them in the truth. The truth gradually straightens out the false conceptions within a particular culture.

Desire for Autonomy

One major competitor to the biblical gospel is autonomy. Ever since the fall, people have desired to be their own savior. One form of saving oneself would be to determine truth for oneself, without reference to any human or divine author-ity (see appendix A). But such an idea is in fact a socially shared idea, passed on within human societies. Why should we believe this idea more than any other? The claim for autonomy is in fact just one more claim for authority, this time the authority deriving from the alleged total competence of the individual thinker.

There is, in fact, no escape from authority. Many religions claim to have contact with a god or gods or spirits or the world-soul or some source who knows more than we do and who, it is alleged, can be trusted. But not all these religions can be right. A religion is more plausible when everyone around us, or everyone who has cultural prestige, gives allegiance to the religion. Similarly, the claim for the autonomous individual is a claim for authority *over against* other claims, including religious claims. It has notable difficulties: (1) an individual would have to know a lot, and know deeply, to be sure that he is more competent than any religion of the world; (2) confidence in individual autonomous thinking becomes plausible mainly in an environment (like the contemporary United States and Europe) where it has cultural prestige; and (3) it is at odds with the fundamental dependence that we have on others. We cannot operate in practice in the world without shared knowledge of insiders' understanding of social structures.

Once individual autonomy is seen as just one more ultimate allegiance, alongside traditional religions, it loses some of its modern sheen.

In sum, by God's own design all of us are dependent on others for knowledge. And human knowledge is corrupted, corporately as well as individually, by sin. God's redemption in Christ comes to deliver us from this corruption. The deliverance comes partly through instruction in pure truth, which is found in Christ: "If you abide in my word, you are truly my disciples, and you will know the truth, and the truth will set you free" (John 8:31–32).

Does Culture Imprison or Reveal the Real Person?

As we have seen, culture has a monumental influence on children. Children raised in Thailand grow up with Thai culture, Thai religion, and Thai ways of thinking. So also with children who grow up in the United States or in Mexico or in Algeria. If we think that culture is a merely human product and not governed by God, cultural influence can seem to be a prison to the human spirit. According to individualistic thinking, the real person is the person apart from any influence from others. The influence of a particular culture "bends" the person strongly and forces him into the cultural mold. This forcing is innately oppressive and confining to the person. The real person never has a chance for self-expression of freedom because the culture tells him how to behave, how to relate to others, how to eat, how to marry, how to think.[1]

According to this kind of thinking, real "freedom" is freedom to escape all culture whatsoever. But such "freedom" does not match what God made us to be. A freedom with no boundaries, a freedom in which an individual can do whatever he pleases for whatever reasons he pleases, has no value for human beings, because if we reject socialization, we have to reject knowledge, reasoning, and

---

[1] Egalitarian ideology, which we will address in chap. 27, often builds on the assumption that the real individual is what he is apart from culture. According to this logic, culture forces inequality on an original idyllically free individual, and so culture is oppressive.

opportunities. Part of the excitement about a modern industrial society lies in the sheer volume and diversity of opportunities and choices, which are available only because of complex social relationships. Apart from participation in society, the opportunities are inaccessible and ultimately meaningless to an individual.

The longing for an absolute freedom is akin to the longing to be God. God has absolute freedom. But even with God, his freedom goes together with the stability of his character. God never acts contrary to who he is. And his character is "fully developed," if we may speak in such a way in order to contrast him with human development from infancy to childhood to maturity. The persons of the Trinity have loving relations to one another, and they never act in disharmony with one another.

For human beings, who are finite, God himself has designed social environments. If you grew up in an American or a Chinese environment, the "molding" you received took place according to God's design, in order to make you who you are and who you will be in the future. Even now you are not complete. The constraints from your culture are not a prison, but God's means to the goal.

Our frustration derives not from our finiteness, and not from the fact of culture as such, but from sin within and without. All cultures of this present world are in some ways oppressive when they contain thinking and practices that are sinful or unwise. God made us as social creatures, and sin has these kinds of effects. God sends a remedy not by making us able to be completely independent, with no corrupting relationships with others, but by redeeming us both individually and corporately. The church as a new society shows how this takes place. It shows how, that is, when it is functioning as it should. But within this world the church too is subject to corruption by sins, corporate and individual. Christ's redemption is full and complete, and has power to heal us in all aspects, including social aspects. But the working out of that redemption in our lives is still in process.

PART 4

Smaller Wholes within Society

24

Varieties in Society

For everything there is a season,
and a time for every matter under heaven:
a time to be born, and a time to die;
a time to plant, and a time to pluck up what is planted;
a time to kill, and a time to heal;
a time to break down, and a time to build up;
a time to weep, and a time to laugh;
a time to mourn, and a time to dance;
a time to cast away stones, and a time to gather stones together;
a time to embrace, and a time to refrain from embracing.

—Ecclesiastes 3:1–5

The different kinds of purposes that human beings have in their actions give rise to differences in kinds of action and kinds of results. Modern societies offer a bewildering variety of institutions and activities. The variety, in fact, is so extensive that it would be overwhelming if we were unable to understand some larger groupings and commonalities.

Kenneth Pike's concept of behavioreme (chap. 18) offers us a beginning. All basketball games belong together under the single category of the basketball behavioreme. All activities of solving jigsaw puzzles are instances of the jigsaw-solving behavioreme. How do we further classify the many kinds of human action?[1]

---

[1]Verbal action is excruciatingly complex and deserves separate discussion, such as in Vern S. Poythress, *In the Beginning Was the Word: Language—A God-Centered Approach* (Wheaton, IL: Crossway, 2009).

Behavior in Context

The particle, wave, and field perspectives (chap. 7) can come to our aid. Human action is composed of "units" of action, behavioremes. Units have a particle-like character. But we can also use the particle, wave, and field perspectives in a more general or more fundamental way by noticing a difference between focus on action and focus on stable pieces that play stable roles in the action.

Creatures as Particles

The world, according to God's design worked out in Genesis 1, is composed of *creatures*. God prepared spaces, the sea and the dry land, and then plants, animals, and human beings inhabiting the spaces. He made the sun, the moon, and the stars. As we learn later in the Bible, he created angels, some of whom rebelled and are now called demons. He made the mountains. The activity of any of these creatures and the activity of God presuppose the existence of the actor who is a stable center for the activity. The actor is, if you will, stable or particle-like in comparison with the activity, which is wave-like. But actors interlock with their actions. The same is true with respect to God. God is a God who acts. The Father necessarily loves the Son, so God is necessarily characterized by action even before the acts of creation. And the creatures he made were made with capabilities of acting.

As a result, society includes organized, structured, purposeful action by God and by creatures. But it also includes God and creatures as the actors. Finally, it includes relationships among the actors. Human beings interact with one another, according to God's design (Gen. 2:18, 24), and their interaction brings about and expresses relationships. They also interact with animals, plants, and nonliving things (the mountains, the water, the soil). These interactions also express relationships. I am here treating animals, plants, and nonliving things as "actors" in a broad sense. Human action, as personal action, has a distinctive sense of intention and purpose and consciousness; but in the broadest sense of "action," the ground "acts" on the farmer when it produces or fails to produce a crop.

So our three perspectives lead to three foci in examining the world. The particle perspective focuses on actors. The wave perspective focuses on actions. The field perspective focuses on relationships. The world has all three—actors (God and creatures), actions, and relationships. God made it that way.

Artifacts

Human beings made in the image of God have the capability of being "sub-creators," who make objects like houses, chairs, tables, lyres, and swords. They make these objects only because they receive power and capability from God.

God is the Maker as primary cause; a human artisan is the maker as secondary cause. Particularly within an industrial culture where we are often surrounded by man-made objects, it is important to remember that God is their Maker. Each chair has exactly the structure, shape, and artistry that God planned. Man-made items, which we may call "artifacts," stand alongside all the living creatures. All these participants, as stable particles, can play roles in dynamic processes, processes that are the natural focus of a wave perspective.[2]

As usual, both the participants and their processes can be viewed either from an insider's ("emic") cultural viewpoint or an outsider's ("etic") viewpoint.[3] The participants matter; but people's *views* of the participants also matter. It matters, for instance, whether we view our neighbor as made in the image of God and therefore necessarily a person to respect and to protect, or whether we view him as an ultimately random collection of molecules in motion, such as a materialist worldview postulates.

Behavior as Waves

Now let us focus on the processes, the activities. Individual actors engage in purposeful actions that have structure and unity determined by purpose and capable of being recognized within a culture. These actions are one kind of behavioreme. Social structure includes a large number of different kinds of behavior, which need further classification. To this subject we will later return.

Relationships as Field

The field view focuses on relations. Within a society the actors and the activities relate to one another in many complex ways. Are relationships prominent in some structures in society? Yes, they are. We find friendships, kinship relationships, bureaucratic relationships, romantic relationships, and so on.

Institutions

In some cases the relationships hold together in a way that gives the members of a culture the sense of a semipermanent larger social whole. What do we have in mind? Think of a marriage. Two people make up a larger social unit, their marriage. A father and mother and children make up a family unit. We can have larger groupings: the family may be part of a recognized clan (e.g., the Shaw clan in Scotland), and the clan a part of a larger ethnic group (the Scots). We also have schools, sports teams, colleges, businesses, governments, churches, chari-

---

[2]Compare the discussion of "things" in Kenneth L. Pike, *Language in Relation to a Unified Theory of the Structure of Human Behavior*, 2nd ed. (Paris: Mouton, 1967), chap. 17.
[3]See chap. 18, note 2.

ties, museums, newspaper organizations, and so on. We may call these things *institutions*, in contrast to individual creatures.

Marriage is undoubtedly the most intimate of these institutions. God intends it to be permanent within this life (Matt. 19:6). "They [the man and the woman] shall become one flesh" (Gen. 2:24). Even though they are one "flesh," as expressed by their physical union, they remain two distinct individuals as well, with distinct responsibilities, as can be seen in the discussion over the guilt for the fall (Gen. 3:6–19). It is all the more true in other kinds of relationships that humans are both individual and social creatures. We are distinct from one another and at the same time related to one another, including relations as members of stable institutions.

Both individuals and institutions are emic units, recognized by the culture. They can be analyzed for contrast, variation, and distribution (chap. 18). The activities (behavioremes) of both individuals and institutions can also be so analyzed.

Noninstitutional Relationships

We can also observe that the sense of wholeness belonging to a number of individuals in relationship can vary. The individuals belonging to a single family have relationships that manifest a larger social whole, namely, the family as a whole. But some relationships, like a friendship, seem to me within my social context not to have the same character. Sue is friends with Linda. But we do not usually think of their relationship of friendship as constituting a larger social whole, an institution that we would call "the social whole or social group of the friendship of Sue and Linda." Friendship seems to be different from a clique, which is indeed a social whole, and thus is an "institution," according to my definition. It is an institution even though it may be shorter lived than a business or a government.

From an insider's (emic) point of view, the family is an institution. The relationship between the father and the son within the family is not, though it is still a long-term relationship. My relationship with the clerk who checks out my purchase at the grocery store is a social relationship, but not an institution. The grocery store is an institution. An institution is a social whole that we as insiders treat *as a larger, integrated whole*, with some degree of stability and permanence.

Multiple Social Types

In sum, careful use of the particle, wave, and field perspectives draws our attention to the variety in social structures. From an insider's point of view, we have, most fundamentally, actors, actions, and relationships. And relationships of complex structure sometimes involve social complexes with a semipermanent identity and wholeness, namely institutions.

All these are designed by God. In fact, as our use of trimodal perspectives suggests, they are designed by the Trinitarian God, who coheres with himself. The coherence of particle, wave, and field reflects in a shadowy form the ultimate ontological coinherence of the persons of the Trinity. The unity in diversity appears in a single, unified social institution with several individuals within it. This unity in diversity reflects the final unity in diversity of the Trinity. We depend on God in profound, basic ways of which we are not normally conscious.[4]

Reality

Institutions are in a sense more abstract. So the question naturally arises as to whether they are really "there," or whether they are just in our imagination. What is a business? For example, what is the grocery store where I bought my apples? Is it just the physical property, the building, and the food stuffs within the building? If we are intent on reducing everything to the material level and ignoring any other kind of meaning, we may begin to think in that direction. But such thinking would be a reduction. It goes together with a materialist worldview, which ignores God.[5]

In fact, God designed human beings to be rich in their personality and multidimensional in their activities and their relationships. A business like a grocery store is more than the physical property. It is indeed a "social" institution, designed by God. It was designed in general terms by God's act of creating human beings with the capabilities that have now developed and blossomed in the business world. But, since God is also involved in the details, we can affirm that as primary cause God designed all the details of this particular business, with these particular managers and clerks and accountants and cleaners and stockers, and with all the regular business practices that they follow. God also designed us humans so that we can understand and appreciate what goes on in a grocery store. What we see is *real*, a social rather than merely a physical reality. The father and the son working on the jigsaw experience a real, personal relation, not just physical sensations of sound, color, and touch.

Influence of Social Contexts on Meaning

The principle of meaning in relationships implies that the meaning of any particular action within an institutional setting or within a larger series of actions will be

---

[4]For an earlier trimodal approach to analyzing society, see Pike, *Language*, chap. 17.
[5]See the analogous discussion of reality and reductionisms in Vern S. Poythress, *Redeeming Science: A God-Centered Approach* (Wheaton, IL: Crossway, 2006), chaps. 15–16.

colored by the setting in which it occurs. The differences may be subtle, or they may be dramatic. In a family setting, the family may have a pot of cash that can be dipped into for an emergency if one person runs out. In the grocery store, the clerk had better not try to dip into the pot of cash in his or her cash register!

The same principle holds for whole cultures. Theft means what it means against the background of cultural understandings of property. If within a given tribal culture much of the property is held in common among the whole tribe, any tribal member may use it. If in a second culture that property belongs to an individual or to one family, appropriation to oneself amounts to theft.

God gives us a command not to steal. He also gives us the cultures in which we live. The exact application of his command depends on the cultural setting. That is all right because he has authority over both the command and the setting. And, we should add, he is present to instruct us through his Spirit, giving insight in our hearts concerning the relation between the command and the social setting.

Specialized Institutions, Activities, and Relationships

Since God created human beings in his image, they have richness in their purposes, imitating the original richness in his purposes. This richness and variety gets expressed in the multiple types of institutions and activities and relationships.

We discussed earlier (chap. 12) the three offices of prophet, king, and priest. These, when generalized, correspond to three major kinds of divine and human activity: (1) thinking and speaking (prophetic); (2) ruling and controlling and making (kingly); and (3) sharing and blessing and cursing (priestly). The diversity in God's activity derives ultimately from the diversity in the persons of the Trinity, a diversity in unity that harmonizes with the coherence of one God. Human activities reflect this diversity. Human institutions do too, to some extent.

Activities like conversation and thinking through difficulties are prominently prophetic (though not completely without kingly and priestly aspects, by perspectival coinherence). Activities like managing, directing, and making things are prominently kingly. Activities like celebration, sharing to meet needs, and exclusion are prominently priestly. Institutions can also show prominence in their purposes. Educational institutions prominently follow prophetic purposes. Manufacturing and farming institutions prominently follow kingly purposes, as do governmental institutions. Charities and hospitals prominently follow priestly purposes. A research hospital follows the priestly purpose of serving the sick. But in addition, it has a prophetic purpose of gaining knowledge about medicine and passing on that knowledge to the next generation.

We can observe further kinds of specialization and see that these find their ultimate roots in how God made us.

Markets for trade, buying, and selling are dominated by economic concerns; and these economic concerns go back to the concepts of ownership and lawful change of ownership. Lawfulness goes back to God, who is the author of law, including the law, "You shall not steal" (Ex. 20:15). Ownership goes back to God, who owns the whole world (Ps. 50:12; 1 Cor. 10:26), and who makes us subordinate owners or stewards (Lev. 25:23).

Marriage imitates the love of God for Israel and the love of Christ for his church (Ezek. 16:8; Eph. 5:25–28). The family should be dominated by love and care, particularly the love and care of the father. In this the father imitates the love of Christ (Eph. 5:25–28) and the love of God the Father for God the Son (John 3:35). Governments are supposed to follow justice, and justice derives from the God who is just (Ps. 119:137).

Educational institutions should be dominated by concern for wisdom. In this they depend ultimately on the wisdom of God. They imitate on a larger scale the passing on of wisdom from father to son, as described in Proverbs (1:8; 3:1–2; 4:1). Proverbs indicates that the Lord is the final source of wisdom (Prov. 1:7; 2:6–8). The ultimate font of wisdom is Christ, who is the wisdom of God (1 Cor. 1:30; see Col. 2:3). God the Father shares his wisdom with his Son through the Holy Spirit. The intimate sharing of wisdom between God the Father and God the Son is thus the ultimate foundation for the sharing from a human father, who should seek the power of the Holy Spirit in sharing with his son. And that in turn is a model for educational transmission of wisdom.

Human speech goes back to God's speech. God spoke to create the world itself, and God the Son is the Word, the archetypal speech of God (John 1:1).

Human farming echoes God, who planted the garden of Eden.

Human giving echoes divine giving.

Human manufacturing and creating imitate God's acts of making the world. This imitation includes practical products like furniture and electronic devices, or artistic products like paintings and musical compositions and films, or combination products like architecturally beautiful buildings or stylishly enhanced MP3 players.

Human artistry imitates the artistry of God, whose beauty is reflected in the beauties of creation.[6]

These potentialities for human action have blossomed remarkably in industrial societies, with their enormous variety. The potentialities were already there, as if in seed form, when God made Adam and Eve. He made them in his image, which implies their potential to imitate him and to be creative in a host of ways. And he put them in fundamental relationship, namely marriage. Marriage led to children,

---

[6]On beauty, see ibid., 23, 285–86, 318; Frank E. Gaebelein, *The Christian, The Arts, and Truth*, ed. D. Bruce Lockerbie (Portland, OR: Multnomah, 1985).

and children to family. The family contains multidimensional relationships and activities, and so is capable of branching out into specializations. A family farm becomes a larger, industrial farm. Craft work within a family becomes industrial manufacture. Teaching from father to son becomes an educational institution. Kindness to a sick or grieving family member, or to a neighbor of the family, develops into institutions specifically geared toward practicing kindness to the needy. Discipline of a wayward child becomes a government-directed penalty for a social wrongdoing. Division of the family inheritance develops into larger-scale social guidelines for recognizing property rights.

Specialized relationships may focus on prophetic, kingly, or priestly characteristics in action. For example, a chat over the fence focuses on communication, information, and language expression. It exercises human prophetic gifts, which echo God's prophetic speech ability. But these gifts can be exercised either righteously or unrighteously. The chat over the fence may become an occasion either for sharing a blessing or for gossip. Acts of aggression, anger, or submission express power relations, and so exercise human kingly gifts. They echo God's kingly ability to rule. Again, they may be exercised rightly or wrongly. Expressions of love or celebrations of togetherness in play or leisure may be multidimensional, but they may frequently include an aspect of sharing that exercises human priestly gifts. They echo God's priestly ability to bless and to share his personal presence.

Any of the human gifts can be abused in sinful directions. These abusive exercises still partially reflect God's gifts to human beings, but they echo the goodness of God's abilities in a distorted way.

Commonality

Because of the commonality among human beings across cultures, outsiders who observe human activity from a particular culture can often achieve a good approximation in their assessment of a particular activity. We are all made in the image of God. Fathers and mothers and children have roles in all societies because of the way that God made us. We all have a sense of justice, and so we can see commonalities among human governments in different cultures.

But cultures do differ. The success of outside observers in understanding does depend on which activities and institutions they confront, and the obviousness with which they can be associated with broader human purposes, in distinction from purposes that may be narrowly defined in the context of some culturally specific practice.

For example, modern Westerners understand marriage in the Bible because marriage exists both in the ancient biblical contexts and in modern contexts. Marriage is virtually a universal institution, and so we can cross over cultural boundaries. But Westerners are less apt to understand the details in arranged marriages, betrothal, and the "bride-price" (Ex. 22:16–17; 1 Sam. 18:25), because in the details, contemporary Western society does not do things the same way. An arranged marriage may seem to us stupid, arbitrary, or "primitive," because we have grown up in a society that (usually) tells us that good marriages always come from two individuals who fall romantically in love, more or less independently of any parental influence. But the visceral reaction of rejecting any alternative is a cultural product. People who take enough time to become acquainted in detail with cultures with different marriage practices can come gradually to appreciate that those practices make a good deal of sense within their cultural context.

God has made us with a common humanity. We can understand one another, even across our individual differences, and even across our cultural differences. But the degree of understanding varies and may in some cases take a lot of effort. And, within a sinful world, it may sometimes fail.

This basis for understanding is important for understanding the Bible as well. The Bible was written in the context of ancient cultures—thousands of years ago for various Near Eastern cultures mentioned in the Old Testament. The New Testament came into being within the context of the diverse pluralism of the cultures of the Roman Empire. Our own contemporary culture does not exactly match any of the ancient cultures. Understanding the Bible involves making adjustments to see how it addresses people in cultures different from ours. But the differences should not be exaggerated. By God's design, and because of commonalities between cultures, it is possible to understand the Bible sufficiently well and to receive the spiritual nourishment and direction that come from fellowship with God in Christ. God is the universal God of all cultures and all times, and so the principles of his rectitude hold for all cultures.

25

Authorities

The LORD has established his throne in the heavens,
and his kingdom rules over all.

—Psalm 103:19

If you see in a province the oppression of the poor
and the violation of justice and righteousness,
do not be amazed at the matter, for the high official is watched
by a higher, and there are yet higher ones over them.

—Ecclesiastes 5:8

The fallow ground of the poor would yield much food,
but it is swept away through injustice.

—Proverbs 13:23

S ome of our relationships include *ruling* or *governing* functions. We need to look at the issue of authority and government, which is both complex and controversial.

Controversy

Controversy arises partly because people care about who rules and how. Rulers can do appalling damage to those under them. In a sinful world, the sins of people in power, even subtle sins that they excuse, can have massive effects. And sins of those in power have not always been subtle. People in power can get big egos, and they may be susceptible to flattery by those around them. They may cease to listen to the voice of conscience. Nahash the leader of the Ammonites demanded the right to gouge out the right eyes of the inhabitants of Jabesh-gilead, even if they were willing to submit to him (1 Sam. 11:1–2). Nebuchadnezzar threw Daniel's three friends into the furnace when they would not bow down to his idol (Daniel 3).

People can see these effects. They want to do something. Sometimes we have opportunities to help a person here and there. But it is not so clear how to solve the general problem. People produce ideas for reform. But these reforms do not get to the root. The Bible instructs us that sin is deep. It is not easily uprooted. In fact, it ultimately took the death of the Son of God on a cross to do it. He won the decisive victory. But now we are still trying to apply that victory in our lives, and it is shockingly hard to do. We long for the complete victory that will come in the new heavens and the new earth (Rev. 22:1–4).

Corruption in Thinking about Sin

Sin infects the mind as well. Our thinking about government, as well as government itself, gets corrupted. If we have a shallow view of our sin, we easily get a shallow view of how to root out sin in society, and we produce shallow ideas of reform. In fact, we produce counterfeits of the Christian way of salvation. The counterfeits feed our own pride. And pride corrupts the reformers.

Is this a real problem? It is. Karl Marx tried to analyze the woes of society around him and figured out a remedy in the form of the communist revolution. Many of the woes were real, but the remedy was inadequate. Marx's thinking became the foundation for communist revolutions that led to the Soviet Union and communist China. Many people adopted communism as their philosophy, and they were motivated partly by a sense of indignation over the plight of poor people. But the result was tragic. According to Stéphane Courtois, about 65 million people died in China in the cultural revolution, 20 million in the Soviet Union under Stalin, 2 million in North Korea. The statistics go on. Jay Richards comments: "Never has an idea had such catastrophic consequences. It illustrated a grim, simple equation: extreme moral passion minus reality equals mass death."[1]

Because the problems are so deep, and because our own thinking is distorted by sin, people have different ideas about reforming government, and they become suspicious of authority. We have to consider these controversies and these sus-

---

[1] Jay W. Richards, *Money, Greed, and God: Why Capitalism Is the Solution and Not the Problem* (New York: HarperCollins, 2009), 21; numbers for deaths are taken from Stéphane Courtois, *The Black Book of Communism* (Cambridge: Harvard University Press, 1999), 4.

picions, though in this book we have room only to consider some more general principles. Extended discussion of government would require a book.

God's Authority

God governs the whole universe:

> The LORD has established his throne in the heavens,
>   and his kingdom rules over all. (Ps. 103:19)

As Lord, he governs human beings as well as animals and plants:

> All the inhabitants of the earth are accounted as nothing,
>   and he does according to his will among the host of heaven
>   and among the inhabitants of the earth;
> and none can stay his hand
>   or say to him, "What have you done?" (Dan. 4:35)

His lordship includes authority, control, and presence (chap. 4). He has the moral *right* to govern (authority). He controls those under his governance (control). He is personally present with them (presence).

God Delegating Authority

God also delegates authority to people who are made in his image so that they exercise governance in some of their relationships. They exercise authority, control, and presence in a derivative manner. Parents have God-given governing authority over their children (Eph. 6:1–3). Officials in civil government (the state) have authority over their subjects:

> Let every person be subject to the governing authorities. For there is no authority except from God, and those that exist have been instituted by God. Therefore whoever resists the authorities resists what God has appointed, and those who resist will incur judgment. For rulers are not a terror to good conduct, but to bad. Would you have no fear of the one who is in authority? Then do what is good, and you will receive his approval. (Rom. 13:1–3)

Employers have authority over those who work for them (Matt. 20:15). Teachers have authority over their students (John 13:13; see Gal. 6:6). Elders in the church have authority over the church and its members (1 Pet. 5:1–5). Military leaders have authority over the soldiers under them (Matt. 8:9).

All of these different kinds of authority reflect God's authority. Not only does God *delegate* the authority, but the human authority imitates or reflects God's authority. God is the archetypal Father, whom human fatherhood reflects. God is the King, whom civil government reflects. God is the owner and Master of the universe, whom human ownership and supervision reflect. God is the ultimate teacher, whom human teachers reflect (Matt. 23:8, 10). God is the Shepherd, whom human elders in the church reflect (Ezek. 34:22–24, 31; 1 Pet. 5:1–5). God is the warrior-King in battle (Ex. 15:3), whom human military leaders reflect.

Each of these human authorities has its own distinctive focus and its limitations. Different *kinds* of authority are not interchangeable. Elders in the church have authority over the church, but not over the civil government. And their authority is limited to what Christ gives them as "undershepherds" (1 Pet. 5:2, 4). They are not supposed to invent new rules or impose new requirements of their own making, beyond what the Bible says (see Mark 7:1–13). They are themselves under biblical authority.

Analogously, teachers have authority over students with respect to their teaching responsibilities and their subject matter. Employers have authority over their employees with respect to the work for which they have been hired. And so on. Only God has unlimited authority. The delegated authority of human beings is always limited, not only by being under God's authority, but also by being focused on some sphere of responsibility.

We should recall that God establishes relations with people in prophetic, kingly, and priestly ways. The exercise of his *authority* is most closely related to his rule, his kingship. Human governance in any sphere takes place because a human being has become a delegated "king," reflecting and expressing the ultimate kingship of God.

Concerns about Authority

The key passage in Romans 13 describes the authorities as doing good, and that is their moral obligation. But sin corrupts human authorities along with everything else. Sometimes they do not live up to their obligation, and the apostle Paul, the author of Romans 13, was aware of it (Acts 16:37; 25:11; 28:18–19). God normally requires that those under authority obey the authority. But there is an important exception when an authority wants us to do something against God's commandments. "We must obey God rather than men" (Acts 5:29). Many people look with suspicion on authorities because they have seen how sin corrupts the workings of human authority and turns it into a destructive and oppressive menace.

Some kinds of human authorities are easier for us to accept than others. Many contemporary Westerners have widespread suspicion of authority, and sometimes outright rebellion against it. This Western attitude contrasts with some traditional hierarchical cultures (e.g., traditional Chinese culture) that have been more accepting. Both attitudes have their advantages. Suspicions help us to recognize and fight against abuse of authority. Tradition helped the Chinese to accept legitimate authority. But how do we discern the difference between abuse and legitimacy? How do we do so when we have examples from communism of well-meaning people gone astray?

The moral evaluation of human struggles poses a deep challenge. Where do we get standards for evaluation, since societies differ, and societies can be corrupted by ideologies?

Fuller answers about ethics as a whole need whole books.[2] The most basic answer is that we need God's instruction. And we need redemption in our own hearts, to enable us to understand and follow his instruction rather than to corrupt it. Otherwise, we are just following the prejudices of our society or of our own minds. And then we are in deep difficulty. If we do not have access to God, who is to say whether we or the Chinese are right? For that matter, who is to say whether right and wrong are anything more than mere personal and social preferences?

We are made in the image of God, and we know that abusive authority is wrong. But if there is no God, if we are just a random collection of molecules, if we are the product of mindless evolution, one person's inclination to kill or torture is just as much a product of evolution and random molecules as is your inclination to protect and nurture a fellow human being.

Critique of Pragmatism

So we need God to transform our views.

We can begin with one difficulty among many: the Western tendency toward pragmatism. Most people in contemporary Western societies are willing to recognize authority to a limited extent when they can see a pragmatic benefit. Children need to respect their parents, and parents exercise authority over their children because the children are immature. Similarly, teachers have authority because they know more about their subject areas, and we hope that they have thought through how others can learn it more effectively. But is authority *merely* an invention for pragmatic benefit?

To answer the question, we have to go back to God as the origin for authority. God's authority is both absolute and pragmatically beneficial. God is good and full of beneficence. His character is such that he desires to bless his creatures. Hence, we *do* reap practical benefits when we follow his ways (e.g., Prov. 10:3,

---

[2]I would recommend John M. Frame, *The Doctrine of the Christian Life* (Phillipsburg, NJ: P&R, 2008).

27). But the practical benefits do not *establish* God's authority. It is not up to us to decide, by our own alleged self-sufficiency, whether or not God's benefits are rich enough for us to *grant* him authority that he supposedly does not already have. He already has authority from all eternity. Rightly understood, God's authority is an aspect of the whole of his character, not an extra bonus or attachment that we give him if we deem it practical.

Source of Human Authority

Analogously, even human authority does not arise merely as a human invention or agreement or concession for our pragmatic benefit. Authority arises from God's design and appointment. The parents you have, you have because God appointed them for you (Ex. 20:12; Ps. 139:13). "Those [authorities] that exist have been *instituted* by God" (Rom. 13:1).

God's institution of an authority can take place in connection with more than one human means or sequence of secondary causes. People come to be parents through the biological processes of conception and birth. These processes are secondary causes. God is still the primary cause (Ps. 139:13). Similarly, civil governments arise through secondary causes. Governmental authorities can be elected by a large populace or by a smaller group of nobles. Or a king can appoint his successor. A large empire like Nebuchadnezzar's can be established by conquest. God nevertheless told the Jews to submit to it (Jer. 27:8; 29:5–7).

Thinking about Civil Government

We may be willing to accept the authority of the state when we see that it is beneficial for us. But we should remember that its authority does not arise merely from our consent.

We need to interact in particular with American thinking about government because such thinking has affected many parts of the world. Americans like to think of the language of Lincoln's Gettysburg Address, which talks about government "of the people, by the people, for the people." That phraseology, taken in isolation, can become totally man-centered. According to a man-centered picture, the authority of civil government allegedly derives from the people. The people *create* governmental authority.

Such an understanding is not quite fair to the original context of President Lincoln's Gettysburg Address. Lincoln mentions that the United States was founded on the principle that "all men are created equal," and he uses the expression "this nation, under God." His language acknowledges God as the more ultimate authority to which human civil governments are answerable. Nevertheless, the language "of the people, by the people, for the people" can be seductive, especially in a more secular age than Lincoln addressed. Within a secular context it suggests that authority *derives* wholly from "the people" and not from God.

We may also remember the American Declaration of Independence, which says that governments derive "their just powers from the consent of the governed." It sounds as if the Declaration asserts that governmental authority comes from the people ("the governed") and *not* from God. Again, that is not quite fair to the context of the Declaration of Independence. The Declaration begins by laying the foundation for government in God: "We hold these truths to be self-evident, that all men are created equal, that they are endowed by their Creator with certain unalienable Rights." The "Rights," given by "their Creator," then become the basis for inferring government: "That to secure these rights, Governments are instituted among Men, deriving their just powers from the consent of the governed."

The Declaration says that "Governments are instituted among Men." The word "instituted" has a remaining ambiguity. Does it mean "instituted by the people," or "instituted by God"? It is difficult to say. The immediately following phraseology, "the consent of the governed," suggests that "the governed," that is, the people, by their consent, institute their government. And that reading is confirmed by the subsequent clauses, which say that "it is the Right of the People to alter or to abolish it [Government that has become destructive of the Rights], and to institute new Government." Here "the people" is the subject of the verb "institute." The people institute new government. The previous references to the Creator, however, prevent this language from becoming completely one-sided. The Declaration seems to me to focus mostly on the role of secondary causes, namely, the people and governmental authorities, but nevertheless to allow the idea that God is still the primary cause of government.

The drift of much secular thinking, however, tends to detach government from any reference to God, lest religious thinking perturb a secular "public square." In a secular atmosphere, then, government can be seen as *wholly* and exclusively the construction of human beings, with God being either absent or irrelevant. The biggest difficulty with this picture is that, without God, authority itself, authority of any kind, becomes emptied of meaning.

How? Suppose we begin with the idea that the people, quite independently of God, establish a government and its authorities. They do so by consenting to the form of government that they establish. The expression "the people" is nice-sounding rhetoric, but the people do not agree with one another. Even at the time of the American Revolution, "the people" logically included both patriots in favor of independence from England and loyalists in favor of continued sub-mission to England. Why should the majority dictate to a minority, or to you or to me, or to any single individual? Who says, and how does he have the right to say it? That is the question of authority, and it arises whenever even one person does not consent. What if a person grows up in the United States but at some point decides that he does not "consent" to its form of government? In fact, he observes, he never did consent, because the form of government was put in place before he was born.

The Declaration of Independence avoids this dilemma by appealing to an unassailable ultimate authority, namely God. Without this higher appeal, it could not have risen above the human disagreements. Authority threatens to disintegrate, either into a multiplicity of human opinions and preferences, or into the power of the strongest. The criminal says, "Obey and don't ask questions, or else I will kill you." Are all governments merely criminals with greater power and legitimizing rhetoric? The Bible says no. In a fallen world, governments can degenerate into criminality. But a legitimate government owes its authority to God. The Bible points back to God as the ultimate authority who gives legitimacy (moral standing) to the civil government as a lesser authority under him.

The Limits of Civil Government

All human authorities are limited. Teachers have authority in their subject areas. Elders have authority in the church where they serve. So what about civil government? What is its sphere of authority?

Here there are serious differences. People differ in their views, and governments across the world differ in their practices. Once again, let me take the United States as one case. In the United States, on the average, political liberals want civil government involved in more areas of life; conservatives in fewer areas. The more and the fewer represent not merely two options, but a spectrum. On the liberal side, liberalism goes over into forms of socialism, where government controls many spheres of life: health care, retirement, transportation, education, care for the poor, and maybe major industries (but the industries may simply be heavily regulated rather than directly owned by the civil government). The conservative side goes over into libertarianism, where civil government is restricted almost wholly to defending against foreign invasion and settling cases of injury and dispute.

Again we have to be careful. Many of our ideas in these areas are influenced by what we have learned from others, and by the kind of governments with which we have become familiar. We have to submit our thinking to God and not be carried away by prejudices from our own desires, our parents, or any other part of modern society.

I may be wrong, but it seems to me that some socialists need more rethinking than do libertarians. Libertarians are often well aware of the good intentions of socialist programs, because these good intentions are prominently discussed in prestigious circles. Socialists, on the other hand, may think that conservative and libertarian views are generated merely by selfishness and lack of compassion.

That may be true in some cases. But socialists and liberals are often not aware that the libertarian reservations are based on the principle that government itself can generate injustices even with the best of intentions. Good intentions for the poor drove the moral passion of communism, but the results were disastrous. There are other, lesser examples. Socialist government control of large segments of society is meant to help the poor, but it has led to economic stagnation. The modern prison system was originally invented with the desire to help criminals reform their ways, but all too often it has become a corrosive environment where change is for the worse. Welfare is intended to help the needy, but the story of the welfare system in the United States shows that it has frequently generated unintended consequences that harm the poor.[3]

In addition, socialists do not often ask themselves about the limits of government. If there is a big need (poverty, racism, poor education), the government seems to them the biggest and most obvious resource of power, and the government is enlisted to "solve the problem." This reasoning seems plausible to many people, but it relies on questionable assumptions: (1) people see no limits to government authority; (2) people are confident that they have seen the full depth of the problem, and (3) they think there are no unintended consequences.

Coercion

By contrast, the libertarian side is concerned about the limits of government. Enforcement of government power involves coercion. The government agent "does not bear the sword in vain," as the Bible aptly says (Rom. 13:4). The reference to the sword reminds us that the government has authority from God to take away life. It can also command lesser penalties, such as taxation or confiscation of property. If a property owner uses bodily force to resist confiscation, the soldiers or police or agents of government will respond with bodily force. That is coercion. It is the bottom end of government. And given that we live in a fallen world, where people disagree with one another and where they are tempted to resist even legitimate actions of government, coercion is a necessary last resort.

Of course civil government operates more smoothly when people under it participate willingly. Many modern democratically elected governments have cooperative citizenry. The cooperation may lull us to sleep and make us think that coercion is no longer significant. But the *disagreements* among citizens, including disagreements about governmental actions, may lie just beneath the surface. We should ask *why* citizens are cooperating with government mandates. Perhaps they are cooperating because they actually agree with a particular government policy, whether it is a tax or a speed law or a school regulation. That is reassuring. But they

---

[3]Marvin N. Olasky, *The Tragedy of American Compassion* (Wheaton, IL: Crossway, 1992); Richards, *Money, Greed, and God*, 48–49.

also may be cooperating when they disagree. They may be cooperating because they have a community spirit. Or they may do so because they have given up on the possibility of change. Or it may be because for religious reasons they know they ought to respect authorities even when authorities are wrong. Or it may be because they know that the effects of not cooperating are severe.

In this last case, people are aware of the threat of coercion, but literal bodily force never actually appears because people are too sensible to force a confrontation. And when cooperation arises from religious motivations, or from despair about the possibility of change, it says nothing commendable about the government that receives cooperation. The government may be exceedingly oppressive and unjust, and yet receive "cooperation." We cannot assume that the government is not abusing power just because we see no overt rebellion. Coercion is at the back of civil government, even when coercion does not appear in overt form.

So the question remains: How often and in what circumstances is the threat of coercion from civil government legitimate? To ask about legitimacy is to ask about authority and its limits. The limits derive from the fact that God has given civil authorities whatever authority they have, and this authority is bounded. The state is not God. If we think that the state can solve all our problems, we are making it an idol, a substitute for God.[4] No doubt a really tyrannical government has the physical *power* to confiscate private property and to imprison or execute people for purely arbitrary reasons. But are such actions approved by God? Clearly not. When governments overstep their limits, they become unjust according to God's standards, which always remain in place.

Now, the libertarian position makes considerable sense. Libertarians are convinced that government authority is narrowly circumscribed. They may have compassion on the poor and on drug addicts and even on criminals, but they think their compassion ought to be exercised by them and by charitable institutions rather than by the government as an agent that takes these responsibilities for compassion on itself.

Limited Government according to the United States Constitution

The US Constitution provides an example of principles of limited government. The Constitution divided up governmental powers between the federal government (the US government, now centered in Washington, DC) and the states (Maryland, Pennsylvania, Virginia, etc.), and expected the states to limit their powers in relation to counties, cities, and neighborhoods. The cities would in turn

---

[4]On the Beast of Revelation as a symbol for making power into an idol, see Vern S. Poythress, *The Returning King* (Phillipsburg, NJ: P&R, 2000).

leave a wide space for the activities of individual citizens and civic organizations, including charities, schools (privately run), businesses, families, and churches.

The Tenth Amendment to the Constitution spells out a fundamental limitation: "The powers not delegated to the United States by the Constitution, nor prohibited by it to the States, are reserved to the States respectively, or to the people." "Delegation" means that the Constitution expressly grants power (such as the power of declaring war) to the federal government. Powers not explicitly enumerated in the Constitution are "reserved to the States"; they are outside the limits of the federal government.

In addition, the Constitution divides up the powers of the federal government into three "branches": legislative (Congress), executive (the president and his assistants), and judicial (the US courts). A system of "checks and balances" for this distribution of power was supposed to protect against tyranny arising from the concentration of power at only one point.

A large number of activities conducted by the US federal government today are not "delegated" to it by being enumerated in the Constitution and so are beyond its bounds, beyond the limits that it sets. Technically, these activities are unconstitutional and therefore unlawful. But the Tenth Amendment and its meaning have been largely forgotten, and has been reinterpreted by US courts. So, few people today understand what the Constitution's authors intended, and fewer understand why they intended it. The founders thought that government itself can be a source of injustice, when it deprives citizens of their liberties. By contrast, many today assure us that we need government action to meet this or that pressing need. No doubt, needs abound. But the concerns of the Constitution have disappeared from discussion.[5]

---

[5] In the United States all three branches of the federal government have failed. Congress passes laws in areas for which it is not authorized by the Constitution; the executive enforces those laws and proposes further laws without attending to constitutional limits; and the courts do not recognize that the laws are unconstitutional. In addition, the states of the United States do not protest the unauthorized extension of power. Why not? Partly because too few people care for the principles any more. Partly because the federal government has gradually enlarged its powers over decades, beginning with Roosevelt's New Deal, if not before. People have gotten used to it.

But in the United States widespread custom, even custom stemming from court interpretations of the Constitution, does not dissolve the fact that the Constitution and its amendments have authority superior to the courts and the Congress. We are corporately in rebellion against that authority. And this rebellion means that we are illegitimately using governmental coercion against whoever agrees with the Tenth Amendment.

Most people are not worried because most people approve. Or at least it appears they approve because dissenting voices are marginalized. If "we, the people" are the source of law, how can "we, the people" be in rebellion against the law? Well, there is a minority of people that popular opinion is ignoring. But, more importantly, God, not the people, is the ultimate authority. Under God, the Constitution and its amendments are the next highest authority. We, the people, are under the Constitution, not under the majority's idea of what would be a good government.

The US Constitution is not an ultimate authority—God is. The Constitution can be amended, and has been amended.[6] Other nations have their own constitutions and systems of law. But the general principle still holds: we should not be quick to use civil government, and therefore coercion, beyond limits that the Bible clearly authorizes, such as defensive war[7] and punishment for crimes and settling of legal disputes.

A Spectrum of Issues

Limited government is only one issue among many. Different nations have somewhat different challenges because their needs are different. Sometimes a weak or divided or poorly supported government has too little power to curb criminals. And when it has sufficient power, the exercise of power may be more or less corrupted by sin—sometimes in one direction, sometimes in another. Think, for example, of worldwide issues such as slavery (still practiced in some countries), state restrictions on religious freedom, corruption of government officials by bribery, government-sponsored or government-permitted genocide, laws favoring one ethnic group, use of government funds for lavish lifestyles of a ruling elite, government barriers to private property—the list is long.

In the midst of all these abuses of power, it remains true that God can use imperfect governments for his own purposes. A wise human king, and not merely a democratically organized political system, can be an agent for justice. We can thank God when we enjoy a measure of justice. But we will not have utopia within this life, and many injustices cannot be remedied within this life. We look forward to "new heavens and a new earth in which righteousness dwells" (2 Pet. 3:13).

Husbands' Authority in Marriage

Finally, husbands have authority over their wives. I have left this principle until now because it is controversial. Husbands' authority appears in Ephesians 5, where women are instructed to "*submit* to [their] own husbands, as to the Lord" (5:22). Unlike the submission of children to parents, this principle is highly disputed, partly because in the anti-authoritarian context of modern societies it does not appear to have obvious pragmatic benefit. Are not men and women equal?

We cannot enter into an extensive discussion in this book. Objectors have tried a number of routes to tame the force of the passage in Ephesians, and readers are

---

[6]The Sixteenth Amendment gave Congress the power to collect an income tax, and the Eighteenth Amendment prohibited alcoholic beverages. Both these amendments extended the power of the federal government. The Twenty-First Amendment repealed prohibition and thereby restricted federal power.

[7]I do not wish to ignore the Christian pacifist position, but neither can it receive extended discussion. See Frame, *Doctrine of the Christian Life*, on war.

of course free to explore their objections. For a defense of husbands' authority, I must refer readers to the extensive discussion in other books.[8] It must suffice here to make several observations.

First, *service* is not the same as *submission*. All Christians are called by God to *serve* one another in various ways. Our service imitates the service of Jesus Christ, who "came not to be served but to *serve*, and to give his life as a ransom for many" (Matt. 20:28). Jesus served us by his sacrificial death. But if we are disciples, we submit to him. He most pointedly does not submit to us (Matt. 16:23!), or it would destroy the meaning of his being our Master, and our being the disciples. Kings who are wise *serve* their subjects by their leadership, their laws, and their judicial judgments. But the people, not the king, submit. The word *submit* is not a synonym for *serve*.

Likewise, husbands are to *serve* their wives, as is evident from the comparison in Ephesians 5:22–33 between a husband's calling and the example of Christ, who "loved the church and gave himself up for her" (v. 25). It is a most challenging and humbling comparison for husbands. If husbands succeeded in imitating Christ in this way, women would have nothing to fear from their authority. Once again the principle holds: proper authority, properly exercised, blesses and benefits those under it.

The point then is that husbands are supposed to serve their wives but do not submit to them. The discussions of so-called mutual submission are in the end confused and incompatible both with the comparison made in Ephesians 5:22–33 and with the irreversible roles of men and women in the marriage relationship.

Second, the Greek word for "submit" does not occur in Ephesians 5:22. But it does occur in verse 21 and is to be understood as carrying over to verse 22. Greek syntax regularly permits elision, that is, the omission of a repeated item, and such a syntactical device does not undermine the meaning of verse 22. The word *submit* occurs in verse 24, with similar implications.

Third, the meaning of the instructions in Ephesians 5:22–33 was reasonably clear to its first-century readership, because readers lived in a culture where relations of authority, including authority in marriage, were culturally accepted. Our difficulties arise because our contemporary culture generates tensions with these instructions.

Fourth, objectors sometimes argue that Paul's instructions in Ephesians 5:22–33 were intended only narrowly for first-century culture, and not for our modern culture. This claim is implausible, given that Paul appeals both to the analogy with

---

[8] See, for example, John Piper and Wayne A. Grudem, eds., *Recovering Biblical Manhood and Womanhood: A Response to Evangelical Feminism* (Wheaton, IL: Crossway, 1991); Grudem, *Evangelical Feminism and Biblical Truth: An Analysis of More Than One Hundred Disputed Questions* (Sisters, OR: Multnomah, 2004); Andreas J. Köstenberger and Thomas R. Schreiner, eds., *Women in the Church: An Analysis and Application of 1 Timothy 2:9–15*, 2nd ed. (Grand Rapids: Baker, 2005).

Christ and the church, and to the verse in Genesis that forms the divine creational foundation for the institution of marriage (Eph. 5:31, quoting from Gen. 2:24). If objectors insist nevertheless on trying to remove contemporary application, they remove also the power of these verses to transform marriage in a Christlike direction. No one is going to be helped in a practical way by cutting off part of the redemptive stream that God has given us in this passage, which is designed to heal the destructive effects of sin on marriage and on wives in particular.

Subtlety and Depth in Sexuality

Human sexuality is both subtle and deep. Much could be said about this important dimension of human relationships. Sexuality is subtle because it is intimate. Man and woman in marriage should share intimacy, not only physically, but spiritually, intellectually, economically, emotionally, and in all kinds of ways, including ways that they do not explicitly articulate in words. The language of "one flesh" hints at this (Gen. 2:24; Eph. 5:28–33). Men and women are similar, both made in the image of God. But they are also subtly different, and the differences extend beyond obvious differences in the physiological organization of their bodies. Men find fulfillment in completing tasks; women in their personal relationships. But even that difference is subtle. The subtlety makes it difficult to put into words exactly what the differences are. Moreover, one man differs from other men, and one woman from other women. So simple generalizations run the danger of becoming overgeneralizations.

Human sexuality is deep as well as subtle. It goes down to the roots of who we are. That depth is again related to intimacy. Deep aspects of who we are come out the most in intimate relations. God shows the intimacy of marriage when by analogy he describes himself as acting like a husband to Israel his wife (Ezekiel 16; Hos. 2:2, 16). This Old Testament relationship finds fulfillment when Christ acts as the husband to the church as bride (Eph. 5:22–33). Husbands are commanded to love their wives as Christ loved the church (Eph. 5:25). That goes deep.

The subtlety of difference tempts egalitarians to overlook the differences. They can say that husband and wife are merely equal partners and pretend that differences do not affect authority. The subtlety can also mean that some complementarians, who believe in differences, could stereotype the differences and force them into an oversimple mold. The depth in sexuality calls for humility, in which we admit that we do not know everything, and that God knows best. We need to let God's way continue to mold us and to conform us more deeply to the pattern of Ephesians 5:22–33. God knows us better than we know ourselves, and better than our culture and its theories know. He also knows how to remedy what is amiss in us. In the end, taking Ephesians 5:22–33 seriously boils down to trusting him.

26

Classifications of People

The rich and the poor meet together;
the Lord is the maker of them all.
—Proverbs 22:2

N ow we consider another area of complexity and controversy, namely, the differences between people and the ways in which those differences come to expression in classifying people into distinct categories.

Both the insiders to a culture and its outsiders notice differences among people. Some of the differences receive common recognition among insiders and so are characteristic ("emic") in the culture's thinking. Each act of classifying people results in a distinct *category*. These categories are of many different kinds: by age, by hair color, by education, by musical preferences, and so on. In modern America, one major kind of category is a classification according to socioeconomic status: we speak of the "middle class." But other categories cut across this kind of classification.

Kinds of Categories of People

Categories of people, like behavioremes and institutions, show contrast, variation, and distribution.[1] Each individual is an instance of the category and shows *variation* in comparison with other individuals. The category has characteristic

---

[1]The terminology of contrast, variation, and distribution derives from Kenneth Pike, *Linguistic Concepts: An Introduction to Tagmemics* (Lincoln: University of Nebraska Press, 1982), 42–65; see chap. 18. Pike uses the term *class* for what we are here calling *category*. We use the word *category* in order to avoid confusion with socioeconomic class.

features that enable us to identify members of the category and to distinguish them from nonmembers. These features are *contrastive-identificational* features. And each category and each member of each category has functions in the larger society. These functions show the *distribution* of the category in its social context. As usual, these three interlock. Categories depend on trimodal interlocking, and this interlocking images the Trinity.

The contrastive-identificational features that distinguish a particular category can be of many kinds. Whatever distinguishes human beings from others can become a criterion for classification.

Classes and Power

Many modern studies of society concern themselves with a few features that interest us—in particular, class, race, and gender (male and female). *Class* here means socioeconomic class, as distinguished mostly by income and monetary wealth. Even a superficial examination of the Bible shows that similar classifications were known to cultural insiders in biblical times. There are rich and poor (Prov. 22:2, 7); there are men and women (Gen. 1:27; 2:22); there are foreigners ("sojourners") and natives (Gen. 23:4);

The distinction between the foreigner and the native is not really racial in the narrow sense, but political and cultural. Our modern idea of race in the narrow sense identifies racial categories mostly by skin color and a few facial features. But the tensions arising from racial prejudice lie next door to tensions arising from cultural prejudice. They are of a piece. Foreigners who speak or dress or act differently can receive hostility, even if their facial features give no indication of their foreignness.

The Bible also recognizes that differences in class standing open the possibility for exploitation and oppression. Amos mentions

> those who trample the head of the poor into the dust of the earth
>   and turn aside the way of the afflicted. (Amos 2:7)

God expresses particular concern for bringing justice to the weak: "He [God] executes justice for the fatherless and the widow, and loves the sojourner, giving him food and clothing" (Deut. 10:18). The verse mentions three categories of people: the fatherless, the widow, and the sojourner. The fatherless person is likely to be poor and powerless; the widow, as a woman, has less social power than a man in ancient society; the sojourner is seen as not belonging. All three types of people are more vulnerable to exploitation and to not obtaining what is right for them. Other passages confirm this vulnerability:

> You shall not pervert the justice due to your poor in his lawsuit. (Ex. 23:6)

You shall not wrong a sojourner or oppress him, for you were sojourners in the land of Egypt. You shall not mistreat any widow or fatherless child. (Ex. 22:21–22)

Interestingly, the Bible recognizes that the temptation can arise not only to favor "the great," but unjustly to favor the poor, maybe out of pity for his needs:

You shall do no injustice in court. You shall not be partial to the poor or defer to the great, but in righteousness you shall judge your neighbor. (Lev. 19:15)

Justice

What the poor deserve is not merely pity or favoritism, but justice. Justice is a large subject. We cannot enter into its many dimensions here.[2] Justice includes impartiality:

You shall appoint judges and officers in all your towns that the LORD your God is giving you, according to your tribes, and they shall judge the people with righteous judgment. You shall not pervert justice. You shall not show *partiality*, and you shall not accept a bribe, for a bribe blinds the eyes of the wise and subverts the cause of the righteous. Justice, and only justice, you shall follow, that you may live and inherit the land that the LORD your God is giving you. (Deut. 16:18–20)

Impartiality in judgment means that a judge renders judgment on the merits of the case; he refuses to favor one party because of who he is by social standing or friendship or age or any other factor irrelevant to the case.

This impartiality can also be called *equity*. All people are equal before the law in the sense that the law should treat them impartially. All people are also equal before God in terms of his divine law and divine judgment.[3] They are all made in the image of God, and they are all guilty for their sins against him.

But this fundamental equality is compatible with many differences in other respects: male and female, old and young, rich and poor, healthy and sick, beautiful and homely, skillful and unskillful, talented and untalented, married or single. God created each one of us (Ps. 139:13–16) and made us unique individuals with a unique cluster of characteristics (contrastive-identificational features; see Ex. 4:11; Prov. 22:2). He has also placed us in our particular situation in a larger group of family, relatives, friends, acquaintances, and ethnic groups.

---

[2] I offer further discussion in Vern S. Poythress, *The Shadow of Christ in the Law of Moses* (Phillipsburg, NJ: P&R, 1995), especially part 2.

[3] The Declaration of Independence of 1776 picks up the language: "all men are created equal."

So we may classify people in many ways. Economic class, race, and gender are only the beginning. Consider a list: speech dialect, educational level, knowledge in chemistry, skill in sewing, skill in farming, occupation, marital status, age, month of birth, money in the bank, overall wealth, location of home, style of home, pattern of TV watching, pattern of reading, experiences in travel, experiences in illnesses, religious views, religious practices (both public and private), criminal record, spelling of one's name, handwriting style, hair style, physical condition, strength and character of relationships with brothers, sisters, parents, or children—and on and on. All of these characteristics lead to categories that make sense to cultural insiders in American culture. All of them are valid classifications; all are significant in some way or other. All of them are ordained by God. None of them completely defines a person, nor do all of them together. Only the Lord knows us completely (Psalm 139).

Political Implications

We have seen that justice includes equity. So how does justice fit together with human differences? For example, younger children need adult care, and they are required to submit to their parents rather than having equal authority. Civil law ought to recognize the sphere of parental authority and the needs of children.

Working out the implications requires wisdom. Such wisdom grows out of fundamental biblical principles: (1) because we are made in the image of God, we all have a sense of justice; (2) justice brings practical blessings to the society that enjoys it; and (3) God himself is the standard for justice, and he expresses his justice in the Bible.[4] He is the standard; we are not.

Close reflection then shows that many modern ideas about justice have some truth in them but are distortions of the full truth found in God's word. Societies must accordingly undergo transformation, not merely in their *practice* of justice and in their institutions for justice,[5] but in their *ideas* about justice as well. This transformation includes transformation of our ideas about the limits of government, as discussed in the previous chapter.

The principle of transformation is all the more important because many people are overconfident about their own ideas. Often people hold confidently to ideas about justice that they have grown up with or have absorbed from education or peers or communications media. They have not thought about where they got their ideas. They have not thought either about whether their ideas agree with

---

[4]The three aspects of justice correspond to John Frame's existential, situational, and normative perspectives. See Frame, *The Doctrine of the Christian Life* (Phillipsburg, NJ: P&R, 2008).
[5]See the critique of prisons in Poythress, *Shadow of Christ*, especially chap. 15, and the broader critique of present-day penal laws in the same book, part 2.

God's. They *assume* their ideas are sound because they have an inward sense of justice. They are often not aware of the subtle ways that sin in both individual and societal forms can distort our ideas of justice. We have only to think about the widespread confidence in the pre–Civil War Southern United States that Southern slavery was not morally wrong. It happened there. If so, it can happen to me, and it can happen to you.

27

Social Equality and Inequality

Whoever trusts in his riches will fall,
but the righteous will flourish like a green leaf.

—Proverbs 11:28

We may now venture a little into the vexing questions of true justice by looking at the issue of equality.

Equity

Human beings are made in the image of God (Gen. 1:26–27), and that is the basis for a fundamental judicial equality (equity). The courts are supposed to be impartial. Every human being made in the image of God also has a sense of right and wrong, reflecting God's ultimate standard of right and wrong. We all therefore have an instinct for impartiality and equity, but it can be suppressed or twisted by sin. We have to be careful and submit ourselves to God's wisdom.

Judicial equity can be distorted by favoritism, as we have seen. We are tempted to favor those of the same ethnicity, or those who are friends or relatives, or those who are "respectable," or those who are powerful and who we hope will later show favor to us. A person's friends may encourage him to be partial in his dealings. Rhetoric may provide him with excuses: his friends are "more worthy," and foreigners are "inferior." These temptations appeal to deeply rooted sins in the human heart. They will not go away easily, though they may be mitigated by circumstances that discourage their expression. In America, a judge or prospective juror is supposed to avoid a case if he is a personal friend of one of the parties in the case.

But this concept of equity has limits. It is compatible with many inequalities that are not merely due to injustice (chaps. 25–26). Children are supposed to obey their parents (Eph. 6:1–3). People are supposed to submit to governmental authorities (Romans 13).

People in Need

One of the inequalities in the world consists in the fact that some people are in need and others are well off. God counsels us to be generous and to look after those in need:

> By this we know love, that he laid down his life for us, and we ought to lay down our lives for the brothers. But if anyone has the world's goods and sees his brother in need, yet closes his heart against him, how does God's love abide in him? Little children, let us not love in word or talk but in deed and in truth. (1 John 3:16–18)

> If a brother or sister is poorly clothed and lacking in daily food, and one of you says to them, "Go in peace, be warmed and filled," without giving them the things needed for the body, what good is that? (James 2:15–16)

> Religion that is pure and undefiled before God, the Father, is this: to visit orphans and widows in their affliction, and to keep oneself unstained from the world. (James 1:27)

> Whoever despises his neighbor is a sinner,
> but blessed is he who is generous to the poor. (Prov. 14:21)

These commandments are not merely optional. They are requirements, not advice. God's command is to "love your neighbor as yourself" (Matt. 22:39). These needs continue as long as we struggle within human societies affected by the fall into sin.

Many people today think that the government should take over the duty of caring for those in need. They are right that the needs exist, and frequently the needs are painful and pressing. Moreover, sometimes people are in need because they have been sinned against; someone else has mistreated or exploited them. Civil government does have an authority to deal with cases of mistreatment. But it may fail to track down some of the cases. And it cannot always repair damage already done.[1] We can make external improvements. But we must also be aware that the root of the mistreatments is in sin, which is difficult to uproot.

---

[1] See Vern S. Poythress, *The Shadow of Christ in the Law of Moses* (Phillipsburg, NJ: P&R, 1995), part 2, which talks about limitations, but does at least attempt to show that civil government can do better than its current practice by following biblical principles with respect to crimes.

People also need to consider what we have said in chapter 25 concerning the limits of civil government. Using government as the remedy can have unintended consequences. In particular, indiscriminate use of government can actually increase the temptations toward personal and family irresponsibility. A person may tell himself, "The government will take care of me," and it becomes an excuse for refusing to do what he can to take care of himself and his family. Even when our intentions are sincere, lack of wisdom can make things worse rather than better.

Christians need to continue to listen to God's commandments to exercise love and generosity, whether or not government undertakes to produce a bureaucratic substitute. They also need to be circumspect, recognizing that true compassion pays attention to whole people in whole situations, and does not settle for quick Band-Aid solutions to deep problems.[2]

Egalitarianism

People in genuine distress need help, but the need for help is not a need to become exactly equal to everyone else in every respect. People who are genuinely concerned about human poverty and suffering can become confused. The desire to overcome poverty and suffering can become in their minds a broad principle of misguided "equality."

By what standard do we evaluate when an inequality is morally bad? God ordains social order that ought to include equity in the law. But it may also include many kinds of inequality. God himself established David as king over Israel. David as king was not equal in status to a commoner. But David—unlike some of his later descendants—was a good king, and his rule was a blessing rather than a burden to the people under him.

Once the idea of equality is detached from God's character, it can be conceived of as a universal, impersonal abstract. The desire for equality becomes *egalitarianism*. Egalitarianism is an ideology that takes a moral stand in favor of maximizing equality of human beings in many, if not all, respects. It is important for us to reckon with, because it has an atmospheric influence in many modern societies. Many people are unconsciously influenced, even though they have never worked through the principles or set up a general argument for equality.

In principle, almost *any* kind of differences between human beings can be regarded as onerous. Extreme egalitarianism is possible, and I think there are people who long for it even though they realize that it is impractical. It has been called "equality of result": everyone should have equal income; everyone should have equal education (but will not some people want to specialize in different

---

[2]Marvin N. Olasky, *The Tragedy of American Compassion* (Wheaton, IL: Crossway, 1992), contains lessons both about damaging programs and programs that genuinely help. Compassion needs guidance from Christian wisdom.

directions?); everyone should wear the same clothing (it came close to that in Chairman Mao's China); everyone should be equally beautiful! Any kind of differentiation leads potentially to envy, and from there to conflict.

But we then need to ask, what is the real difficulty? Is it differentiation—differences in possessions, in education, in skills, in physical appearance? It would be boring if everyone looked and acted exactly alike. So what is the difficulty? Is it envy? And if it is envy, what is the remedy?

The biblical answer is different from the world's. It involves, as usual, both unity and diversity. We are all valued as creatures made in the image of God but are deserving of utter disgrace and humiliation because of our sins. And when we are redeemed by the work of Christ, we have the privilege of fellowship with God. That high privilege not only outweighs all earthly differentiations, but can enable us to respect people who are different from us. We can rejoice in the gifts given to others because we see reflected in them the goodness of God rather than being stirred by our selfishness.

God's redemption in the Bible also provides us with a healthy basis in our attitude toward people with few privileges. God commands us to be generous, as we have seen. In addition, we are not supposed to appreciate people or value them merely because of their vocation or their public achievements or their class or their measurable skills. Each person is valuable in the sight of God. We ought to love our neighbors as ourselves. We should extend respect and compassion to minorities, foreigners, the handicapped, the aged, the sick, and babies in the womb. These people need particular attention because they are more vulnerable. The Bible also gives instruction to honor those worthy of honor, whether because of their position, age, or wisdom (Prov. 31:28; Rom. 13:1, 7; 1 Tim. 5:1–2, 17; 1 Pet. 2:17–18).

Loving is difficult. It requires going out of ourselves. Christ came to redeem us not only so that we might be reconciled to God, but also so that the Holy Spirit might fill us and transform us, and we would receive power to become Christlike and to become loving people. True love results in *action*, not simply in good feelings (1 John 3:16–18).

We should also recognize that the people of God have frequently not lived up to God's instructions. Already in the first century, James had to take people to task who were showing favor to the rich (James 2:1–9; see also 1 Cor. 11:18–22). Prejudice and lack of concern are particularly ugly when they crop up among people who profess to be new creatures in Christ.

Equality of Opportunity?

Personally caring for needy people does not, however, produce complete equality. Should we push for equality? People who long for full equality of *result* may realize its impracticality and then retreat into equality of *opportunity*. Everyone must have equal opportunity, it would seem. Everyone must be able to become what he wants. We have all heard the message, "You can be whatever you want to be."

But it is not true. And it can never be true within this life. You cannot become an NFL football player if you are a five-foot-tall grandmother. You cannot become a fighter test pilot if you have a serious, incurable heart condition. You cannot become the world's greatest mathematician if you have an IQ of 80. A society can try to have open educational opportunities so that those with talent in football or in mathematics can rise to the level of the fullest exercise of their talents. But talents are unequal. If "equal opportunity" means an equal *ability* to do or become anything, it is not true.

So we have to scale down our expectations for equal opportunity. Equal opportunity does not mean equal *ability*, but merely opportunity to develop whatever unequal abilities people have.

Even opportunities qualified like this are not equal. Cities have cultural and educational opportunities that rural living does not afford. Farms have opportunities to be around and care for animals that cities do not afford. Living in China gives you the opportunity of learning Chinese from native speakers. Being a neighbor to a kind, loving family offers you an opportunity to learn kindness and love. We cannot equalize this kind of opportunity without putting each person into solitary confinement in a prison cell. Extreme efforts to equalize opportunity end up leveling the playing field by depriving people of opportunities.

Influence of Parents

One of the biggest of all inequalities of opportunity comes from parents. We come into the world as babies. We do not have the opportunity to choose our parents. God ordains who will be our parents. And that is shockingly unequal. Every parent is different from every other parent in a huge number of ways. Did you miss out on the opportunity to become a great football player partly because you did not have an expert football coach as your father? Did you miss out on the chance to become a famous actress partly because your mother was not an actress?

The reaction can be, "It's not fair." Does "fair" mean "just"? Are these inequalities unjust? Not by biblical standards (Ex. 4:11; Ps. 113:9; 139).

Who our parents are affects not only extraordinary opportunities that we miss, but ordinary influences. Parents have enormous influence on children through their example, their instruction, and their discipline. These influences push children in one direction or another. What about times when a parent thoughtlessly or selfishly says something that humiliates a child? Or when a parent by his example or his lack of discipline encourages a child in evil? Redemption through Christ offers a remedy for sins like these. But they will not be completely cured until God brings the consummation, the new heavens and the new earth. Political adjustments, such as egalitarians dream of, will not eliminate inequalities or troubles from this life. Our sickness is too deep.

Can you equalize this influence across all families? Only by abolishing the family, as the Soviet Union disastrously tried to do at one point by trying to put in place state-sponsored care as a substitute for parents (really, universal orphanages).

Does it matter whether your parents are wealthy or poor? It does. On the average, the son of wealthy parents has a greater chance of ending up wealthy than does the son of poor parents. Is this unjust? There are people who think so. But I am raising the question of whether justice according to biblical standards is being confused with equality of possessions. By biblical standards, possessions do not define who we are. We need to help deliver people from being captivated by preoccupation with riches, which can lead to money being an idol.

God's Way

Your parents make you *unequal* to others. But the biggest inequality of all concerns fellowship with God. We do not all have equal opportunity to hear the gospel message of how to be reconciled to God. And if we do have opportunity to hear it, we all reject it unless God draws us to himself (Mark 4:11–12; John 6:44, 65). We do not deserve the salvation that we receive from God (1 Cor. 4:7). We are not equally privileged with respect to God's gifts and his grace. Grace would not be grace if we could claim that God *owes* it to us by some principle of equality (Rom. 11:6).

Egalitarian ideology is seductive. It has an attractive side. It tells us to pay attention to those without power or wealth or prestige or social standing. And that exhortation is in tune with biblical teaching about the dignity of human beings made in the image of God, and with exhortations to care for those in distress. But the valid appeal for compassion is subtly invalidated when it is changed into an abstract principle for maximizing all kinds of sameness. The principle of sameness has evil effects when it makes people concentrate on envying and wanting what other people have.

28

Episodes

My counsel shall stand,
and I will accomplish all my purpose.

—Isaiah 46:10

God has purposes and accomplishes them. By analogy, human beings have purposes, and they endeavor to accomplish their purposes. If they do, the accomplishment usually has a unity as a single act—what we have called a behavioreme. We describe these purposes and their accomplishment in stories. Stories and storytelling vary from culture to culture, but stories everywhere tell about human action in its natural unities. These unities go back ultimately to the unities in God's purposes, which human beings imitate. So, even across the differences of culture, we can make some useful generalizations about human purposes and their accomplishment.

Let us begin with God's actions. God has a "story," namely, world history. God has purposes from the beginning, and these are executed in time. At the center of world history God has the climactic history of redemption brought about in the life of Christ.

Plot

God's world history has a beginning, a middle, and an end. In the beginning God created the world. Shortly after the beginning of the human race, the fall disrupted the original harmony. God then acted in the midst of history to redeem human beings. The end comes with the consummation, the new heaven and the new earth (Rev. 21:1).

God's actions exceed what human beings can do. And yet there are still similarities. We may relabel God's history as a plot consisting in commission, work, and reward (chap. 12). Using this more general labeling, we can see similarities with human action. Human beings imitate God's purposes on smaller scales. Purposeful human action has an action "plan" of sorts; it has purposes. It also involves a concrete action and its result (fig. 28.1).

Figure 28.1. Plot

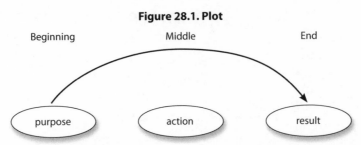

This pattern occurs both in real human actions in history and in fictional stories. Human actions endeavor to overcome obstacles and to arrive at a goal. Achieving the goal is a small-scale analogue of redemption. Unity of purpose, from plan to achievement, naturally results in a unified plot, recognized by insiders. The complete execution of the plot may be called an *episode*.

Complicated purposes, with sub-purposes within them, may result in episodes embedded in episodes. For example, my trip to the store to buy groceries is a single unified episode, with a single unified purpose—buying the groceries. The trip as a whole contains within it the sequence of actions at the store, which is an embedded episode. And the actions at the checkout constitute a sub-episode, namely, the actual purchase. My filling up of the shopping cart also constitutes a sub-episode. Within the filling-up process, my acquisition of an item such as a bag of apples constitutes a sub-episode (see fig. 28.2).

Figure 28.2. Embedded Episodes

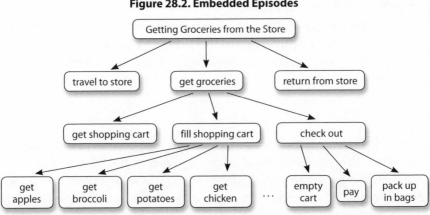

Success and Failure

Obstacles may arise in trying to accomplish the purpose of any one episode. For example, traffic may interfere with my getting to the store. Some of the items that I want to purchase may not be easy to find on the shelves or may be out of stock. The credit card that I intend to use may be expired or overdrawn.

Obstacles imply tension in the situation. Will I succeed, after all, in carrying out my purpose? The struggle against obstacles may be small or may be life-threatening. I may meet antagonists. The reality of conflict testifies to the effects of the fall. Human beings fight one another, and we meet obstacles from the lower creation as well.

Christ's redemption accomplished the fundamental deliverance from the fall. Our own struggles show analogies with that fundamental redemption. But in our case they may end in either victory or failure. Strikingly, Christ won the victory *through* the apparent defeat of the cross. Correspondingly, the life of a Christian, in imitation of Christ, involves not only instances of victory over sin, but instances of victory through suffering, victory through apparent defeat.

The themes of victory and defeat run strongly through the Bible. So its accounts have a relation to the classic idea of two kinds of plots: a comic plot ends in victory, while a tragic plot ends in defeat. Comedy and tragedy are two kinds of story, that is, two kinds of verbal account concerning human action. So how does personal action relate to verbal accounts of it? Each episode of action in the world has correlations with a verbal story or stories that we may tell to describe that episode. Our language correlates with the world by the design of God who made the world by speaking. Hence, much can be said about human interaction through looking at written accounts of happenings.

The central verbal account is the Bible's account of the history of redemption. Our stories about other events echo the Bible's accounts concerning great acts of redemption. The involvement of God in our actions can be inferred from the involvement of God in our language, including our accounts concerning our actions. Another book already deals at length with verbal accounts, and almost everything about verbal accounts has direct implications for understanding the structures of events and social interaction.[1]

For example, within stories the characters take on particular roles. We meet heroes, villains, helpers, and people who evaluate and reward the actions of others. Likewise, in our actions in life we take on roles. A man has the *role* of father to his son. The same man may also act as an employee to his employer, and has the *role* of employee. When I buy my apples using a credit card, I play the *role* of buyer and customer, and when I hand my credit card to the checkout clerk I

---

[1] Vern S. Poythress, *In the Beginning Was the Word: Language—A God-Centered Approach* (Wheaton, IL: Crossway, 2009), chaps. 24–29.

play the role of handing an item to another person. The innumerable kinds of action and social relationships and institutions include innumerable roles, some temporary, some lasting, some distinct, some overlapping.

But we need not repeat what can be learned by looking at stories. Let us proceed with some analysis that can complement what has been seen through stories. First, consider the issue of victory and defeat. God always accomplishes his purposes (Isa. 46:10). We, as finite human beings, cannot guarantee that we will accomplish ours. But we do have purposes. The purposes are worked out in time as we travel toward a goal. The actor determines the goal in his mind when he has a purpose. The goal corresponds to his purpose. If the goal is achieved, the result matches the initial purpose, and we have a case of victory. If the result does not match the purpose, we have partial or complete defeat.

We can see some of the complexities when we reckon with multiple actors. A group of actors can have a common goal toward which they work cooperatively. Or they may have independent goals. Or they may have antagonistic goals. The fall introduces fundamental disharmony into human life. Human beings are alienated from God and become antagonistic to his purposes. They also become alienated from one another and work at cross-purposes. Margaret Mead even classified whole societies by the predominance of competitive or cooperative or individual work.[2]

These structures in human life echo God's life. The interplay between individuals and groups within human life expresses the theme of the one and the many. Individual players on a football team function together as one team. The group is one, while the individuals are many. This human one and many derives from the archetype in God, one God in three persons.

Cooperation in human tasks also imitates God. The persons of the Trinity are in cooperation with one another in the execution of God's plans. Human cooperation expresses a unity of will, in imitation of the unity of the will of God.

Now, what about conflicts among human beings? God is eternally in harmony with himself, so at first glance we might conclude that conflict has no relationship to God. But the truth is more complex. Once evil enters the world, God is antagonistic to it and fights against it. God is animated by zeal for justice. Justice belongs to his own character, so that he is, in a sense, zealous for himself (Ps. 119:137). Or we can say that the Father is zealous for the glory of the Son, and the Son for the Father (John 13:31; 17:1).

Human fighting and struggle echoes the divine war against evil. But human beings are not always on the right side. They can call evil good and good evil (Isa. 5:20). Even when they do, they still imitate God in a sense. The evil fighter

---

[2]Margaret Mead, *Cooperation and Competition among Primitive Peoples* (New York: McGraw-Hill, 1937), 15–16.

makes himself into a god, in that his own preferences become the standard for which he is zealous and for which he fights. Not only wars but conflicts between individuals or institutions depend on God as their archetype.

Social Patterns of Harmony and Conflict

Does a particular culture value cooperation or conflict? It depends on the culture. Research on tribal cultures has found some that are warlike, others that are peaceful. And of course there are complex combinations. Americans typically value competition, but also share respect for political election processes that depend on cooperation. Social institutions like schools and businesses depend on a group of people sharing understanding of their purposes and functions. This sharing is fundamentally a form of cooperation. Students cooperate with the teacher and with one another; employees cooperate with the employer or supervisor and with one another. Without cooperation, the school or the business would cease to function. At the same time, individual employees may find themselves at odds with their employer or with fellow employees on some issues. They may fight for more power or more privileges. Neither cooperation nor conflict completely characterizes their situation.

In fact, without some kind of minimal cooperation, there is no culture or society at all. Culture implies common understandings and common participation in some patterns of behavior. But the existence of cooperation does not constitute a moral endorsement. God is the ultimate moral standard. A whole culture may go astray and cooperate in evil, just as the builders at the Tower of Babel did or as Jesus's religious opponents did.

Different forms of sociological analysis prioritize either cooperation and harmony, on the one hand, or tension and conflict, on the other. The "structural-functional" approach to sociology analyzes society with the purpose of understanding how various practices promote cultural stability. It therefore puts its emphasis on harmony. By contrast, the "social-conflict" approach focuses on disharmonies.[3]

In a fallen world, we may expect both cooperation and conflict to be present, both mixed together in complex ways. A lot depends on evaluating where conflict is morally right or wrong, and where harmony is morally right or wrong. And many situations call for a mixed response. We do well to try to change practices that are morally wrong; but in most cases change need not overthrow the entire social system in a revolutionary break. In fact, people being what they are, they cannot corporately make a complete break with the past. Even in situations of violent revolution they carry over from the past ways of thinking and behaving and understanding.

---

[3] John J. Macionis, *Sociology*, 11th ed. (Upper Saddle River, NJ: Prentice Hall, 2007), 16–20; see appendix E.

When it comes to practices that are *not* morally wrong, change can still be useful. In a business, for example, the current employee habits may cause inefficiencies in production. Do coffee breaks or casual conversation distract from concentration on work? Inefficiency and casual conversation are not morally wrong, in and of themselves. But if the employer expects consistent hard work, the distractions may become a way in which the employees in practice are defrauding their employer. Even if the employer has been allowing inefficiency before, it may be advantageous for him to try to change habits for the sake of efficiency. On the other hand, even in a business where production is the main goal, it need not be the exclusive goal. Employee morale matters. Care for the well-being of employees matters. And this care extends to coffee breaks and to a relaxed, friendly work atmosphere. The employer who contemplates changing the routine for the sake of efficiency ought to ask whether it is worth it.

Structure through Purpose

In sum, episodes of various kinds have cultural meaning because they have purposes, both cooperative and conflictive. These personal purposes, expressed by individuals and by groups, imitate the capacity of God, whose purposefulness is the archetype for any purposeful living.

29

Transactions

To make an apt answer is a joy to a man,
and a word in season, how good it is!

—Proverbs 15:23

Episodes in our social life are of various sizes. A single, short interaction between two people can be an episode. Cheryl asks a question and Julie gives an answer. Or maybe Julie is evasive, or maybe she is offended by the question and walks away. Cheryl may not succeed in getting from Julie the response that she desires. The question of success or failure is real, and therefore there is at least a minimal tension and a short plot. A question-answer sequence is a small-sized episode. So is a command followed by obedience to the command. So is the giving and receiving of a gift.

Failed episodes are still episodes. If Julie walks away in response to Cheryl's question, her walking away is still a response to the question, and it closes the episode with failure. Or Sam puts out his hand for a handshake. Tim puts out his hand in return, and the two shake hands, completing the transaction. Or Tim fails to notice Sam's gesture, and after a while Sam just withdraws his hand so as not to embarrass Tim. Or Tim conspicuously refuses to put out his hand because he is angry with Sam. This refusal also constitutes the completion of the transaction—but a completion by failure.

Once we notice such patterns, we can see that they are quite common. They are understood by insiders to a culture (they are "emic"). Let us call these regular patterns of initiative and response *transactions*.

Imitation of God

Transactions imitate God, as we might expect. The archetype for human transactions is divine transaction. The Father "gives the Spirit" to the Son (John 3:34). This eternal giving is a divine transaction, with the Father initiating and the Son responding by receiving the gift. This and other divine transactions are the original, which human beings imitate. The Father and the Son and the Holy Spirit are in harmony in their purposes, even though each has a distinct role: the Father is the giver, the Son is the recipient, and the Spirit is the gift. Each understands not only his own role, but also how his role fits the other persons and their roles. Likewise, human beings must be in harmony, both in understanding and performing their own roles and in understanding how the complementary roles of other human beings fit their actions.

The Challenge of Cooperation and Understanding

When I give my credit card to the grocery store clerk, I perform a transaction, namely, the transfer of the credit card to the clerk. I play a distinct role in a transaction; I give, while the clerk receives. The transaction would fail if I could not find my credit card, or I couldn't get it out of my pocket, or the clerk refused to touch it. The clerk must do his part, which is not the same as my part. We both have to understand what the other person ought to do. And we must be ready to be creative if something unusual happens, such as not being able to find the card. The cooperative and complementary roles for buyer and clerk may continue in their harmonious interlocking even when the credit card does not turn up. Or one or both of the people may become angry or frustrated, and human harmony may begin to break down.

Even though conflict can arise in transactions, the continuation of social relations depends on the presence of harmony in the society as a whole. If chaos were total, we would lose the experience vital to identifying transactions as transactions, and we would not know what to expect from other people to whom we wish to relate. The newcomer who is trying to adjust to a foreign culture meets a challenge of this kind, where he does not know what is expected. He puts out his hand for a handshake. But Japanese culture expects a bow instead. The insiders to the culture may recognize that he is a foreigner and be patient with him. Or they may consider his foreignness a threat and may expel him.

Transactions with the Subhuman World

We experience complex transactions when we interact with fellow human beings. But some analogues to these transactions crop up when we interact with the subhuman world (animals, plants, and nonliving things). The subhuman world can respond, metaphorically speaking. Subhuman creatures do not respond with the complexity that we have come to appreciate in other human beings. But higher animals nevertheless have some degree of complexity in their responses. We can train a pet dog to shake hands or to sit down on command. We then have a pattern of command and response.

In the grocery store I interact personally with the clerk. I give him my credit card in a transaction. I also interact with the items for sale when I am in the process of filling my shopping cart. I hunt for the apples; I pick out a bag; and I put it in my cart. The search for apples is an episode, with purpose, tension, and success or failure at the end. I may not find the apple counter. Or the bag of apples may be stuck to the counter. Or the bag may have a hole in it, so that when I pick it up, apples begin to fall out. In all these ways the apples "respond" to my initiative, in a metaphorically extended analogue to human responses. So is the process of getting the bag and putting it into my cart a transaction? It just depends on how broadly we want to use the word. It may be valuable to reserve the word for situations that involve the response of a fellow human being or at least an animal—not merely a bag of apples. On the other hand, it could also be valuable to extend it to subhuman interactions in order to show how far-reaching is the pattern that God has established of initiative and response.

Even simple transactions show both dependence on God and imitation of the original divine pattern of initiative and response.

30

Action in Steps

A man's steps are from the LORD;
how then can man understand his way?

—Proverbs 20:24

What we have called an episode in human action has unified purpose, and the purpose "holds together" the various pieces of action, whether by one human being or by several. Episodes, as we have seen, come in various sizes. Episodes can be embedded in episodes. Transactions are one kind of small-sized episode. So how far can we go in breaking down human action into smaller bits?

From the point of view of a physical scientist, events can be broken down into very small segments, a millisecond ($1/1000$th of a second, 10^{-3} second) or a nanosecond ($1/1,000,000,000$ second, 10^{-9} second) or less. But human purposes no longer consciously control such minute events. They are in focus for scientists, within their viewpoint as insiders to their subcommunity. They are not in focus for ordinary participants in a culture.[1]

God's focus is comprehensive. He understands both the scientist's point of view and the participant's point of view. And he understands down to the nanosecond level and beyond the range of current human investigation and curiosity. At the same time, having created human beings and pronounced the creation "very good" (Gen. 1:31), God validates human perspectives as truthful and meaningful even though they are not comprehensive. He himself, when he communicates to us

---

[1] In the terminology from chap. 18, minute, millisecond events are "emic" for a scientist with an analytical goal; they are "etic" for the ordinary participant.

in the Bible, communicates with focus that human recipients can understand. Typically he describes human action at the level of ordinary participants, not at the level of movement of each atom.

The Smaller Pieces

Some human actions, like an involuntary twitch, do not express an actor's purpose. But much of human action has personal purposes. The degree of attention to smaller actions varies. I think that in many cases there is a kind of "threshold" of attention that does not descend consciously into minutiae, even though we are capable in principle, through conscious attention, of focusing on minutiae. For example, the father and son working on the jigsaw puzzle may focus on the placing of an individual piece. They typically do not focus on the smaller actions into which such placing can be decomposed:

1. Choose a piece that you think likely to fit.
2. Grasp it with your thumb and fingers (typically index finger).
3. Lift it up and convey it to the place where you think it will fit.
4. If necessary, orient it by an appropriate amount of rotation.
5. If it fits, put it in place; if it does not, return it to where it was or to another suitable place.
6. Let go of it.

These actions can be analyzed even more minutely. For example, the action of rotation in step 4 involves judgments with the eye as to the shape and color to be expected in the empty space into which the piece is going to fit. In the process of rotation, a person also continues to judge with the eye as to whether more rotation is needed or whether he has already achieved the purposeful goal of appropriate orientation. Purpose is clearly involved at this level. The purpose of solving the jigsaw governs the minipurposes in placing an individual piece, and these minipurposes govern the micropurpose in orienting the pieces. However, habit takes over most of the time at this kind of level, unless we are engaging in some kind of special analysis with a special focus, as we are doing at this moment.

Similarly, consider my episode at the grocery store. I am aware of having to find the bag of apples and put them in my cart—particularly if I have to search for where the apples are in the store. Finding the apples and putting them in the cart constitutes an episode. It is of course part of the larger embedding episode of filling the cart with all the items that I want to purchase. I am usually not focused on the distinct smaller steps of putting out my hand, grabbing the bag, moving the bag into the cart, and letting it go once it is in the cart. These actions I may call steps rather than episodes. God knows about them. I am capable of focusing on them, particularly if arthritis or trembling in my arm is giving me difficulty. But for the most part I do not focus on them. They are still purposeful, but the purpose in each distinct small step is, as it were, nonfocal.[2]

Coinherence in Smaller Actions

Steps in action show coinherence just as larger episodes do. Grabbing the bag of apples involves my intention (plan), my execution (the grabbing motion), and actual effect (the bag firmly in the control of my hand). All three must hang together. To have human significance, each must be embedded in a larger structure of human purposes—in this case, to purchase the apples, bring them home, and eventually eat them. The small steps have purpose coherently fitting into larger purposes.

Human purposes exist because they reflect God's divine purposes. Human actions cohere in the carrying out of the purposes because they reflect the coinherence in divine action. Even at this small level, we depend on God, who sustains and holds in harmony human action.

---

[2]Note the discussion of various kinds of focus in Kenneth L. Pike, *Language in Relation to a Unified Theory of the Structure of Human Behavior*, 2nd ed. (Paris: Mouton, 1967), 78–82, 98–119. "There are lower limits beyond which the ordinary participant in a church service does not normally go in changing focus. If he does so, he has become an analyst, rather than a worshiper—or 'critical' rather than 'enjoying it'" (ibid., 80). "Whenever a certain change in focus is necessarily accompanied by a sharp change in observer attitude or participant type, we may say that a THRESHOLD must be crossed to pass from one to the other. Such a threshold is crossed when one passed from a participant kind of observation to an analytical kind of observation of the same events" (ibid., 111).

31

Subsystems for Human Action

Jesus said to them again, "Peace be with you. As the Father
has sent me, even so I am sending you." And when he had said this,
he breathed on them and said to them, "Receive the Holy Spirit."

—John 20:21–22

The complexity of human beings reflects itself in complexities in human action. One of these complexities reveals itself especially in language. Language shows multiple subsystems that we use in communication. Specifically, a language has a referential subsystem, enabling us to refer to things and to communicate content; it has a grammatical subsystem, maintaining internal structure; and it has a phonological subsystem, enabling transmission by sound.[1] We want to look more carefully at these subsystems in human action, because here also the presence of God reveals itself.

Subsystems of Signs

Meaningful action includes not only communication through language, but also meaning in personal action of other kinds, and meaning in institutions. Some of these kinds of meaning rely on subsystems. The study of language-like sign systems is called *semiotics*.[2]

---

[1] See Vern S. Poythress, *In the Beginning Was the Word: Language—A God-Centered Approach* (Wheaton, IL: Crossway, 2009), chap. 32. A written language also has a graphological subsystem, which plays a role analogous to the phonological subsystem when communication has a written medium.

[2] Daniel Chandler, *Semiotics: The Basics* (London: Routledge, 2001); Marcel Danesi, *Of Cigarettes,*

Signs can exist in a culture outside of the core of the language. For example, red and green lights in the context of a traffic signal mean stop and go. Even outside the context of a traffic light, a flashing red or orange light signifies that there is danger. Under the category "miscellaneous symbols" the Unicode standard for alphabets recognizes quite a few standard signs (see table 31.1).

Table 31.1

Symbol	Meaning
☢	radioactive hazard
☣	biological hazard
☮	peace
♀	female
♂	male
♔	king piece in chess
♙	pawn in chess
♠	spade (suit in cards)
♣	club (suit in cards)
♩	musical note
♭	flat (in music)
etc.	etc.

In order to understand more about how signs work, let us first consider natural language. A word like *dog* has both a meaning ("a canine creature") and a sound (*dôg, däg*).[3] The meaning belongs to the referential subsystem, while the sound belongs to the phonological subsystem (the sound subsystem). The meaning and the sound of *dog* are linked by social and linguistic "convention," which means that other languages can accomplish linkage in different ways: German *Hund* and French *chien* mean "dog," but they have sounds and spelling unrelated to the English word *dog*. The word *dog* also participates in the grammatical subsystem. It has two grammatical forms, the singular form, *dog,* and the plural, *dogs*.

Examples of Sign Systems

The signs in a traffic light make up a much simpler system than a whole language, but we can see analogues to the subsystems in language. The colors of the lights

---

High Heels and Other Interesting Things: An Introduction to Semiotics (London: Macmillan, 1999); Thomas A. Sebeok, *An Introduction to Semiotics* (London: Pinter, 1994).

[3]This double characteristic has been termed *double articulation*.

are like the sound of the word *dog*. They enable the light system to communicate through physical means to drivers, just as the sound of *dog* can transmit the word in the physical medium of the air. The meaning of the colors is at least partly a matter of convention. Why could not green stand for the idea of rest, while red could stand for the idea of hot or the idea of blood? An association with blood would not be purely conventional, since blood is red. But there is still an element of convention if, within a particular culture, red becomes a consistent symbol for blood, instead of being a general sign of warning (as it mostly is in American culture).

So we can say that with a traffic light we use a color subsystem that consists of three colors—green, red, and yellow—contrasting with one another. And we use a meaning or referential subsystem, namely, the meanings "go," "stop," and "'stop' is coming."[4] These two subsystems function jointly in practice; but they are distinguishable in theory because the contrasts are of different kinds.

We might also say that there is a kind of rudimentary "grammar" to the lights. Green, yellow, and red occur in sequence; and usually they interlock with green, yellow, and red signals that are being offered to cross traffic. Green, yellow, and red also occur in spatial order, with green at the bottom and red at the top. The sequencing helps people to process the meaning—even color-blind people can identify the colors by positional information.

In sum, the three lights in a traffic signal function by invoking three subsystems: referential, grammatical, and visual. These three subsystems interlock in a manner parallel to the subsystems in language. The subsystems in language reflect the origin of language in God. The referential subsystem reflects the origin of meaning in God the Father. The grammatical subsystem reflects the origin of grammar in God the Son as the Word. And the phonological subsystem reflects the origin of phonological articulation in God the Spirit, who is analogous to the "breath" of God.[5]

A traffic light represents a much simpler system. But in its triple articulation, it is analogous to language and therefore reflects God, who is the ultimate origin of human meaning and therefore of the traffic light's ability to convey meaning. When the traffic light functions, the three subsystems coinhere, in analogy with the persons of the Trinity. We see the meaning of the light because the meaning (referential subsystem) "coinheres" with its color (visual subsystem).

Instead of sound, the traffic light uses color and light as its physical medium. In the Bible this physical medium also becomes a medium for God's presence

---

[4] These meanings belong to the American system. There are some variations in the European. Also, flashing yellow (without a neighboring green or red) means "slow down and exercise caution; but you should not stop unless the need arises."

[5] Poythress, *In the Beginning*, chap. 32.

in *theophany*, the special appearance of God such as at Mount Sinai (Exodus 19). Theophany involves the work of the Spirit, who is closely associated with the glory and brightness of God's appearing.[6] Thus the use of subsystems is not confined to the medium of sound.

The four suits in a pack of playing cards also show a rudimentary form of three subsystems. The four suits are identifiable by physical shapes: ♠, ♡, ◇, ♣. The shapes contrast with one another and together form a geometrical subsystem. This system is the analogue to the phonological subsystem in language. The meanings of the suits are their meanings as spades, hearts, diamonds, and clubs within card games. These meanings are analogous to the referential subsystem. The meanings contrast, in most games, because two cards of the same suit will play against one another in a different manner than cards of distinct suits. The "grammar" of how the suits fit together may vary from game to game.

We can do a similar analysis of signs that have been more or less standardized for labeling the buttons on audio and video players. A square (■) on one of the buttons means "stop." A right-pointing triangle (▶) means "play." A double triangle (▶▶) or double chevron (») pointing to the right means "fast forward." Two vertical lines (‖) mean "pause."

Music

Music represents a much more complex representation of meaning. Written music has symbols representing the pitch and length of each note and the manner in which the notes occur in sequence. In music we have a system of symbolic representation that has at least two subsystems, the written subsystem with the notes on the page, and the music as played, sending out sound.

How might we further analyze the nature of music? Does it have reference and grammar in a manner analogous to language? People talk about the "language" of music, but that designation of music is metaphorical and does not by itself tell us how close a parallel we have.

One kind of music is vocal music, music with the human voice as the chief instrument. Usually, vocal music has words—the lyrics. Vocal music using words clearly has a close relationship to language, because it *is* language. It substitutes unusual and stylized sound patterns for the normal ones in prose speech. But the meanings are still identifiable, because the words have meaning and they fit together into sentences that have meaning. Like other examples of language, vocal music has the three subsystems: reference (content of what is talked about), grammar (structure of the sentences), and phonology (sound). We can say that

---

[6]Meredith G. Kline, *Images of the Spirit* (Grand Rapids: Baker, 1980); Kline, "The Holy Spirit as Covenant Witness," ThM thesis, Westminster Theological Seminary, 1972.

this kind of music is language, but with a variation on the sound patterns for ordinary speech.

Music belongs not only to human beings but also to God and the angels. Zephaniah 3:17 describes God as rejoicing over his people "with loud singing." Jesus sang a hymn with his disciples in the upper room before going to Gethsemane (Matt. 26:30). Hebrews 2:12 indicates that Christ sings praise to God the Father for his victory. The angelic beings sing praises in the presence of God and the Lamb according to Revelation 5:9–10.

What about written music? The written score for vocal music uses the conventional system of musical notation, which is a graphological subsystem. This graphological subsystem corresponds to the sound subsystem used when the vocal music is performed. Thus the written music and the performed music correspond to one another in a manner parallel to the correspondence between written and spoken language.

If vocal music represents a variation on language, does the variation make a significant difference? It does. Music somehow enhances meaning. Emotion can come through strongly. We may suspect that, by analogy, similar principles might be true in mysterious ways for singing by God and his angels. For us at least, musical accompaniment enhances expression, in ways that are difficult fully to penetrate. We may find ourselves strongly moved by a song without being able to say exactly what it is about the song that makes it more moving than the same words without music.

Emotive Meaning

Emotional expression and "being moved" by communication are part of "meaning," in the broad sense. Meaning belongs not merely to the words and the sentences, but also to the enhancement that they receive through music. Music itself has meaning—though the meaning typically is not isolated from how the music reinforces the words.

We may suspect that emotional and communicative meanings in music are not purely "conventional." A dog is a dog, whether it is called a *dog* in English or *chien* in French. The link between meaning and sound is "conventional." Is it the same with the emotional impact of music? Probably not. Is there a link between dissonance and emotional distress, or harmony and emotional rest? Is there a link between the rhythm of marching music and the vigor of bold action? It is hard—maybe even impossible—exactly to separate what is "in our blood," acquired more biologically, and what we have learned unconsciously from cultural associations built up over a long period of time.

It is clear as well that associations can build up between certain styles of music and cultural stances. Rock-and-roll music, at least in its origins, comes associated with a broader social movement. Is that association a product of its sounds, its lyrics, the lives of its musicians, the teenage fans who were drawn into it because their parents disapproved, or some combination of influences?

We do need to leave space for variations in culture, even in music. The same exact sound sequence may not have the same significance within two disparate cultures. But music does get into our bones and our blood, and the way it does suggests that its power has a culturally universal side. In the end, we need not make a precise decision about what is cultural and what is natural. God created us as flesh-and-blood creatures, and the beat of our hearts can operate in time to the beat of music. He also designed us as cultural creatures. So the overlay of culture is not in the end an accident, or a merely human choice. It is God's choice as well. So God gives us music to be appreciated for what it is within its full cultural context. All the meaning is *real*, as ordained by God. The integration of nature and culture in musical effects is part of what music is, and we need not tear apart what God has joined.

Vocal music is clearly a form of language. Music without words is vaguely analogous to language. The analogy does seem to extend to the subsystems, since music has sound together with meaning. The link between sound and meaning may be in part natural rather than conventional, but the link is there. Sound and meaning coinhere, and in this way music as a human product reflects God, who is the origin of human creativity and human expression.

Visual Art

Our observations about music can now be extended to visual art and other forms of human expression. God is the original artist, who made the world and made it beautiful. God instructed the Israelites to include music in their temple worship, and visual artistry played a role in both the tabernacle and the Solomonic temple (Ex. 31:1–11; 25:18–19; 28:2; 1 Chron. 16:4–36; 25:1; 28:19; 2 Chron. 2:14; 3:10–14; etc.). The artistry ultimately reflects the beauty of God himself (Ex. 24:10; Ezekiel 1). Likewise our modern artistic expression reflects the meaningfulness of God in that man was created with the capacity for creative artistry.

Visual art has distinct subsystems similar to what we have already seen. A painting or a sculpture has meaning, appreciated by the viewer. That meaning composes the referential dimension. And the art object has shape and form and color and texture, which form the physical basis for the communication of meaning. That physical substratum belongs to the visual subsystem. Both are necessary. They coinhere, since only through the one expressing the other can meaning be communicated through physical means.

Analog versus Digital Communication

Visual art is language-like in some respects. But it is not literally a language. It is not a sign language or a written text. What makes the difference? Many things, perhaps. Each creature and each artifact within it belong to a larger world of meaning, but each is also unique, not simply the same as anything else.

But we can go partway in noticing some of the differences between visual art and language. One of the differences lies in the question of conventional versus "natural" meaning. The word *dog* has the meaning of "dog" "by convention," we say, because it is different in French. Music and visual art may have some elements influenced subtly or dramatically by convention. But they rely on natural bonds as well. The landscape painting looks like a landscape, and the portrait looks like a person. The connection between form and meaning is not purely conventional. The artist is directly imitating God, who created the landscape as part of his world of creation.

A second difference comes to light when we consider the difference between analog and digital communication. Digital communication uses as its basis black-and-white, yes-or-no contrasts. For example, the letter *b* is distinct from all the other alphabetic letters. The *b* sound in English is distinct from all the other sounds in English. Ordinary language is mostly digital in substance. Each alphabetic letter and each word is distinct from every other letter or word. It can therefore be transmitted in written form over thousands of years, with no degradation except in the case of accidental copying errors that are in principle avoidable.

On the other hand, the difference between a loud and a soft sound is an analog difference, because there is a smooth gradation between the two. There is no exact boundary between a loud sound and a soft sound. We can specify the loudness of a sound with some precision using a numerical scale like decibels. But the specification never exactly captures the analog original. Characteristically, digital information can be exactly reproduced; analog information cannot. Copying analog information multiple times results in gradual, irreversible degradation in the quality.

We can see illustrations in music. Written music is mostly digital. (I say mostly, because a few elements, like the labels for loudness or speed or mood of performance, allow for a good deal of interpretation and are not purely digital.) Sound can vary in pitch by minute amounts. But Western music breaks up this analog-like continuum into discrete, "digital" pieces, namely, the notes on one of several standard musical scales.[7] In principle, such music can be copied exactly. On the other hand, an actual musical performance can never be copied exactly,

---

[7] In a chromatic scale beginning with middle C, these can be labeled C–C#–D–D#–E–F–F#–G–G#–A–A#–B. Then the sequence repeats at the next higher octave or the next lower octave. Each note is digitally distinct in pitch from every other.

because the exact length, timbre, and loudness of each note cannot be completely captured. They are analog in nature.

Ordinary languages have words with stable meanings. The words and their meanings contrast with one another, so at the level of meaning as well as the level of sound the subsystems are digital in nature. How does music compare? Music has meanings, in emotional expression. But are they expressed digitally, by something analogous to words? At least most of the time it does not appear that music without words has an exact analogy to word meanings. Musical meaning is much closer to being analog in character. Only its basic sound subsystem is digital.

Large stretches of languages, whole discourses, using context as well as choices about arrangements of words, can express delicate nuances and precision beyond the functions of a single word. Taken in large amounts, language is more like the analog expressiveness of music.

Visual art like painting and sculpture appears to have an analog structure in its visual subsystem as well as its referential subsystem. In neither painting nor sculpture are there clearly identifiable digital units with convention-based contrast to other units. Yet they still express meaning, and the meaning is distinguishable from the mere physical appearance. Schools of painting and of sculpture can endeavor to express meaning in particular ways, and certain stylizations can have regular meaning. Even here, then, meaning and form coinhere. Their coinherence depends ultimately on God, who made man with capabilities for communication in many media. God ordains both digital and analog media.

The Use of Systems for Meaning

Musical expression or expression in painting uses the systematic resources offered by music or painting as a medium of communication. Let us think briefly about these systematic resources.

We can again use language as our starting point. The language system of English includes patterns like the patterns for use of English tenses, or the patterns for sounds in English words. Since man is made in the image of God, his speaking ability images God's speaking ability. When God speaks, there are three aspects: (1) God has his purposes, (2) he has a knowledge of truth against the background of which he speaks, and (3) he speaks a specific utterance. Consider the example where God says, "Let there be light" (Gen. 1:3). "Let there be light" is the specific utterance. God's purpose is the creation of light. What language did he use? Later he had the utterance recorded in Hebrew (Gen. 1:3). But at the initial point at which he created light, God was not speaking to any human being, so the utterance would not necessarily be in any (later) known human language. If God spoke in a particular human language, he would use the resources of that particular language system (a system that he himself fully controls). The system offers possibilities for many distinct utterances. But what God said still contrasts with many other things that he might have said. The deeper "system" behind all human languages is the system of God's truth and his wisdom, which he uses in creating the world (Prov. 8:22–31). He knows all the possibilities for what he might have created, and all the possibilities for what he might have said. Thus we have three aspects to God's speech: his purposes, the system of his wisdom, and his specific utterance (see fig. 31.1).

Figure 31.1. God Speaking

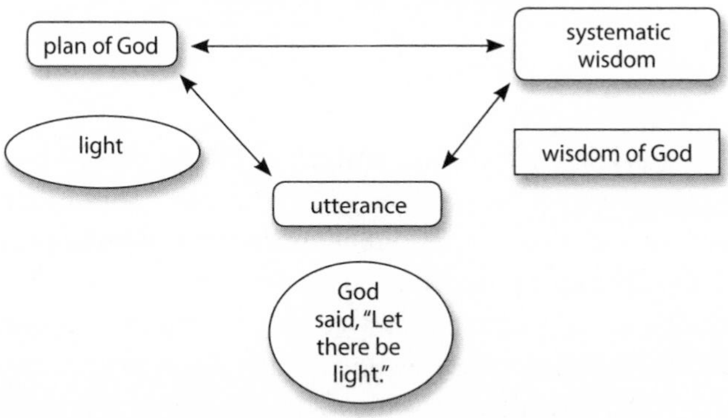

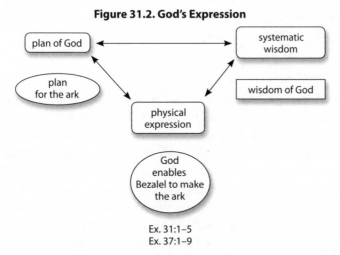

By analogy, God's artistic expression involves three aspects: his purposes, his expression, and the system of wisdom against the background of which he chooses his particular expression (see fig. 31.2).

Figure 31.2. God's Expression

God's activity in artistic expression has its ultimate foundation in his Trinitarian character. The plan of God is the plan preeminently of the Father. The systematic wisdom of God is found in the Son, "in whom [Christ] are hidden all the treasures of wisdom and knowledge" (Col. 2:3; see 1 Cor. 1:30). And the Holy Spirit is like the breath of God that empowers his specific works (see fig. 31.3). Thus the artistic activity of human beings displays an image of the Trinitarian character of God.

Figure 31.3. God in Trinity

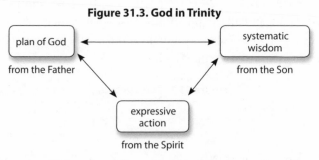

Now let us consider a particular example: Amy composes a piece of music for trumpet. Western music as a system, with notational conventions, must have resources for enabling Amy to carry out her purposes in writing a specific piece. In order to fulfill Amy's purposes, music as a system has resources for expressing meanings: emotions, moods, struggles, victories, relating to innumerable human purposes. These resources for expression are the referential subsystem. Music also has resources for articulating the use of the medium of sound—specifically, the sounds made on a trumpet. The stable resources for this purpose are the system of sounds, that is, the phonological subsystem. A Western musical scale is the starting point for this system. Finally, music as a system offers resources for regular ways for building structures that combine both sounds and referential resources together in an internally consistent way. This internal structuring takes the form of the grammatical subsystem.

Human Dependence

The three subsystems in music, and their analogies in other artistic media, have their ultimate foundation in God's Trinitarian nature. Human purposes using the referential subsystem imitate God's purposes, and more specifically the purposes of God the Father. Human expression with sound or shape or color imitates God's expressiveness, which he executes through the power and "breath" of the Holy Spirit. Human articulation of meaning uses the systemic resources of music or of painting, in imitation of God who uses the systematic wisdom of God the Son. The interlocking between meaning, media, and system reflects the coinherence among the persons of the Trinity. Human beings must rely on the interlocking of these functions whenever they communicate artistically. They are using a gift from the Trinitarian God.

32

Signs and Their Meanings

He [Abraham] received the sign of circumcision as a seal
of the righteousness that he had by faith
while he was still uncircumcised.

—Romans 4:11

What is a *sign*? Roughly speaking, it is an item with significance.[1] Words and sentences have significance, and in this sense they are signs. We know their significance because we use them all the time. *Dog* means "a canine." For native speakers of a language, a large amount of this knowledge is tacit. We know how to use words, but we seldom concentrate on them explicitly. When linguists do undertake to analyze words in detail, they find startling complexity.[2]

Language is the richest resource for signification. But cultures have other means of signification, as we have seen. And God himself gives us signs in the form of the miracles recorded in the Bible. Let us consider one of the miracles and then an ordinary sign from today's world.

God's Signs to Us

In Luke 5:12–16 we have an account of Jesus healing a leper. The physical, visual side of the healing is one side of the total significance of the account. But the healing also has a spiritual significance. In the Old Testament, leprosy made

---

[1] Technical discussion can be found in *semiotics*, the study of signs. See, for example, Daniel Chandler, *Semiotics: The Basics* (London: Routledge, 2001).
[2] See Vern S. Poythress, *In the Beginning Was the Word: Language—A God-Centered Approach* (Wheaton, IL: Crossway, 2009), especially chap. 33.

a person ceremonially unclean, which disqualified him from approaching the presence of God that was symbolized in the tabernacle (Leviticus 13). Leprosy was a ceremonial symbol for sin. So the account about Jesus healing the leper symbolizes that Jesus comes to heal our spiritual disease, that is, sin. This spiritual meaning of the healing is a second side of it.

The two sides, the physical healing and its spiritual significance, cohere with each other. The physical side has relationships with a kind of physical subsystem, consisting of all kinds of physical actions and physical health and disease. The spiritual side has relationships to all the meanings involving our relationship with God, and the breaking of that relationship through sin. That side belongs to a kind of referential subsystem, where the deeper meaning of the healing has relations to all the meanings associated with relationship to God.

In addition, we can speak of a kind of "grammar" of the healing. The episode of healing has a sequence that fits together naturally. It starts with the leper's recognition of Jesus. Then it goes to the leper's request, and from there to Jesus's touch and healing. Likewise God's action in healing us from sin has phases: (1) our recognition of Jesus, (2) our prayer requesting forgiveness, and (3) Jesus's spiritual touch and healing. God shows who he is and what he is doing in redemption through physical signs. The grammar, the spiritual significance, and the physical actions cohere with one another.

Miracles as signs have a special, central role in God's work of redemption. But they also show what is true in a less intense way in God's providential action. Every time that God supplies food, he gives people a physical sign, namely the food, which signifies his goodness: "He [God] did good by giving you rains from heaven and fruitful seasons, satisfying your hearts with food and gladness" (Acts 14:17).

An Example with the Symbol for Playing a CD or DVD

The pattern that we see in God's signs to us is analogous to the pattern in signs that human beings use. Let us see how this works using a particular example. Consider the symbol ▶ for "play." This play symbol appears on a button on a cassette player, CD player, DVD player, or other playback device. It labels the place that we are supposed to push or click to start the playback device, which then begins playing whatever medium has been placed within it. The play symbol is a *sign*. It has meaning, namely "play," or more precisely, "start play," usually from the current position.

Multidimensional Relationships for Signs: Referential Relations

Signs interact with all three of the subsystems of signification that we examined in the previous chapter. First, signs have referential relations, relations to meaning content. The play symbol means "start playing." It is not fully equivalent to the clause "start playing," but signifies that the place where it appears is to be pushed or clicked in order to start the playback device of which it is a part. It has a specific relation to the actions of people who want to start a device. The people execute their purposes by a finger push at the spot designated by the sign.

It gets more complicated, because we have remote-control devices. These devices usually have a button with the play symbol on it. Pressing the play symbol starts internal electronic activity within the remote-control stick. But the whole point of this internal activity is to send a signal to the playback device that actually holds a CD or a DVD placed within it. Typically the remote-control stick generates an electromagnetic signal that goes through space to the playback device (say, a DVD player). The signal sent through space has its own electronic means of signification, though this is invisible to the casual user. The play symbol enjoys meaning relations to the signification sent through space, and this new means of signification must convey the same message as did the original finger push in order that the physical playback device may respond correctly.

The playback symbol also enjoys meaning relations to other symbols found on playback devices and on remote-control sticks. We earlier mentioned the stop symbol (■) and the fast-forward symbol (▶▶). Others could be added. The meaning of the play symbol contrasts with the meaning of these other symbols. The other symbols belong to a common field of meaning (technically called a *semantic domain* or *semantic field*). They all have to do with various operations performed on the medium (say a DVD disc) that has been inserted in the playback device (say a DVD player). Similar symbols can also be found on computers, where images may represent the computer analogue to a DVD player (for example, the VLC computer program emulates a physical audio or video player). The play symbol means what it means in the context of the choice offered for other options. Do you want to play at normal speed or fast forward?

You can also use the play symbol in combination with other features to have a more specialized experience. You can turn up the sound, turn it down, or turn it off altogether. Depending on your situation, you may be able to adjust between a "full-screen" view of a video or a box view or a cropped view. The play symbol can encompass this variety—the variations in the exact manner of playing cohere with the general meaning of the play symbol.

We mentioned that the play symbol is part of a semantic domain consisting of the symbols for the various kinds of playback options (and sometimes options for recording and not merely playing). This semantic domain may be called the domain of media-playing options. But this domain interlocks with other domains of meaning. It has meaning as part of still larger groupings of action, including all kinds of recreational and leisure activities, educational activities (an educational video), and business activities (a training video). Human interaction with a video interlocks with human interaction, if several people are watching the video and interact while they are watching.

The play symbol also has meaning relations to signs that are near to it in meaning. The conductor raises his hands and his baton, and a stylized motion signifies to the orchestra that it is supposed to begin playing. A light in the backstage of a theater could signify to the actors that they are to come on stage and begin acting.

Relations in the Visual Subsystem

Next, the play symbol has relations in its appearance to a visual subsystem, analogous to the system of sounds in a language. The play symbol has a distinctive shape. It is a triangle, oriented with one point toward the right. It is similar to triangles with other orientations (and indeed, such triangles may appear on remote-control sticks). It contrasts with these triangles in orientation, and it contrasts with the square symbol used to signify "stop playing." It can have variations in size and shape, and still be recognized as the play symbol.

Its being recognized as the play symbol also depends on context, what we have called *distribution* (chap. 18). In a context in a geometry class, a triangle is just a triangle, not the play symbol. One of my computer monitors has a button with a right-pointing triangle, but these buttons adjust the features of the monitor. Nothing is played.

Relations in the Grammatical Subsystem

Finally, the play symbol has relations in grammar within the grammatical subsystem. As we observed, it can be used in combination with other adjustments, in sound and in visual size and quality. More fundamentally, its meaning depends in a sense on a simple grammar. The play symbol in its effect is like an activity and corresponds within language to an active verb: *play*. The medium inserted in the DVD player is like an object. It is a "patient" or recipient of the action, and corresponds within language to an object: "this DVD disc." The button plus the position of the DVD disc together determine the action as a whole: "play this DVD disc."

There is also a kind of "grammar" for working your way through the menus and possibly submenus on a typical DVD disc in order to get from the disc the one particular piece that you select. Suppose, for example, that you wish to show to a friend a particular scene from a DVD movie. You have to go through a menu or two to start the movie, then fast forward until you get close to the scene, then shift to regular play in order to play through the scene at regular speed. The play symbol is used in the process along with other buttons in order to maneuver toward the scene and then enjoy it. The grammar also provides ways to "back out" of the results of a button if you make a mistake.

Tacit Knowledge of Relations

Anyone who has learned to use DVD players and other such devices knows the meaning of the play symbol. He does not just know the meaning in total isolation. He tacitly understands a multitude of relations.[3] The relations are an essential part of knowing how to recognize and use the symbol. The user has to know relations in meaning to other symbols and to the world in order aptly to choose when to press the play symbol and when to make other adjustments first. In addition the user has to know the properties of the symbol in visual appearance in order to identify it correctly.

For the adept user (the insider) the play symbol enjoys all these relations in a unity. Take away the visual appearance, and the entire symbol disappears. Take away the meaning, and the symbol disappears. (We may still imagine the appearance of the triangle, but without the meaning it would be just a triangular shape, not a symbol.) Take away the grammar, which includes the fact that pressing the symbol initiates an action on a particular object, and nothing of substance remains. The three aspects of symbol interlock. As we saw in the previous chapter, this interlocking reflects the coinherence of persons of the Trinity. It also reflects the coinherence in signs that God gives to us, both extraordinary signs in the miracles and ordinary signs like food.

An immense amount of complex learning goes into mastering the meaning of a sign. Some people do not understand the latest technology and may fumble if they try to use it. But many others do it effortlessly because they are not conscious of the knowledge that they have. We owe all of this heritage to God. It is God who made us in his image.[4] And one implication is that we have the capacity to learn and use signs—at least insofar as the capacity has not been damaged by physical effects such as brain damage. But it is not only a capacity, an innate ability. God in his providence also has put us in families and in environments where signs are used, and day by day gives opportunities to learn new signs. Both children and new adult users of technology utilize these opportunities. The opportunities eventually issue in mastery of new signs.[5] The immensity of richness of any

---

[3] On tacit knowledge, see Michael Polanyi, *The Tacit Dimension* (Garden City, NY: Anchor, 1967); Polanyi, *Personal Knowledge: Towards a Post-critical Philosophy* (Chicago: University of Chicago Press, 1964).

[4] It is God also who multiplied the languages at Babel (Gen. 11:1–9). This multiplication, as a result of the fall into sin, reminds us that there can be competing and confusing systems of signs, and that signs can be used deceitfully or for destructive purposes.

[5] In this and in other ways we can find sad exceptions within a fallen world. On occasion children are abandoned or grow up in dysfunctional families, or in conditions of famine or war, where their

particular sign system reflects the immensity of richness in the gifts that God has given to us. The immensity understandably becomes the fascination of those who study languages and sign systems professionally. Even those students who profess not to know God see his wisdom, beauty, order, and richness in the object of their study.

Aspects of Signs: Features, Variation, and Context (Distribution)

Let us now consider the play symbol in terms of another triad of interlocking aspects of signs: features, variation, and context (distribution). We introduced this triad in analyzing the behavioreme (chap. 18). In fact, behavioremes are of many different sizes. An entire basketball game is a behavioreme. So is a single utterance, a single sentence within the utterance, or a single sign such as a hand gesture. So also is the inscribing of the play symbol on a button by the manufacturer. A sign, then, can be characterized by its contrastive-identificational features, its variation, and its context (distribution). In discussing the play symbol above, we have for the most part focused on contrastive-identificational features. But we have already said a few things about context (distribution). The play symbol occurs in the distributional context of human activity. A human being interacts with electronic playback devices in order to receive the meaningful content on a DVD disc or other medium.

Another kind of context (distribution) for the play symbol is its distribution in relation to other button actions that can substitute for it in a particular larger sequence. Any of the buttons that are pushed result in action in relation to the DVD disc inside the DVD player. Each represents one possible action in relation to this disc. In this sense they are substitutes for one another within a certain larger structure.

Now consider variation. The play symbol can vary slightly in appearance. It can be black or gray or some other color, depending on the device and its color context. It can be relatively large or small. We can see it in dim light or bright light. Such variations are in visual appearance. But there is also grammatical variation in the fact that the play symbol can occur in any number of possible sequences with other buttons in the process of searching for a particular scene. The play symbol can be used by many different people in many different situations. Each use is a particular instance of its variation. Contrast, variation, and context (distribution) of the play symbol interlock. Here is another reflection of coinherence.

---

opportunities with respect to sign systems are severely curtailed. Access to special, technical sign systems like mathematical signs or signs on playback buttons also depends greatly on cultural privileges not open to all.

33

Foundations for Unified Signs

O Lord, how manifold are your works!
In wisdom have you made them all;
the earth is full of your creatures.

—Psalm 104:24

Signs are complex in their structure of relations. To a native user (the insider) it seems simple to use them. We do it without thinking about it. But there are challenges when it comes to seeking wisdom through the use of signs or categories of thought. Thought largely takes place in connection with signs, so the signs we use can have an influence on our thought.

The Search for Pure Concepts

From as early as the ancient Greeks, philosophers have reached out for wisdom about the fundamental character of the world. Metaphysics or ontology is the study of the fundamental kinds of things that there are. In thinking about the world, we use signs from language. It has been tempting to philosophers to treat these signs as if they are pure ideas, without any embodiment. For the play symbol, this approach treats the *idea* of playing as all-important. The physical manifestation in the triangular shape is purely accidental and dispensable.[1]

---

[1]For further discussion of the philosophical quest for pure ideas, see Vern S. Poythress, *In the Beginning Was the Word: Language—A God-Centered Approach* (Wheaton, IL: Crossway, 2009), chap. 33, and appendix D.

There is a grain of truth in the search for pure ideas. God did make us so that we could recognize unified ideas, such as the idea of the play symbol: "start playing (whatever is in the playback device)." God's word and God's power ordered the world, so that it has unified patterns. But the order of the world is a multidimensional order, an expression of the richness of God's word and the richness of his plan. It expresses the richness of his language and his signification. God does not start with preformed "ideas" that are superior to him and to which his acts of creation must conform. The ideas are his ideas. And using the word *idea* is not apt in this context, because we are dealing with the infinite richness of God's mind, not with merely a list of terms—*dog, chair, horse, man, playback.*

Avoiding Reductions

In fact, signs are not pure abstractions. They are form-meaning composites, having both meaning and form.[2] The meaning of the play symbol has to do with its function in the referential subsystem and its relation to the activity of starting playback. The form of the play symbol is the visual appearance of the symbol. The play symbol is not "pure" meaning with no form. A pure meaning could not be used, because we could not designate it or point to it. We need form (sound or visual appearance) for communication. And even when symbols are in our minds, they have relational ties to their use in practical activities, including not only the ties to visual appearances but also ties to the things for which we have seen the symbols used.

The One and the Many

Our body plays a role in learning about the play symbol. We learn about individual instances of the symbol and also about the class of all such instances (the play symbol as a generality). There are many instances of the play symbol, but there is one class. In our bodily experience, the two are involved in one another. When we see an instance of the symbol, we classify it as the play symbol and

---

[2]See the previous chapter. The search for a pure meaning, detached from all form and from all bodily manifestation, represents an unreachable ideal. And at least in some cases it may be a distorted ideal. It may express a desire to escape our finite condition. And in some cases it may be a reduction of the richness of what God has given us. The ideal of "pure" meaning can sometimes take the route of trying to reduce the three aspects—the referential, the grammatical, and the physical/phonological—into one alone, namely, the referential, in order to master it perfectly and completely. In that case, it may be a desire for Unitarianism. Unitarianism is the theological position that says that there is one God but not in the Trinity, the three persons in the Godhead. Unitarianism has a final unity but no coinherent diversity. The analogue to Unitarianism within signs is to claim that there is a final unity, the unity of the meaning of a sign, with no diversity—in particular, no diversity in physical manifestations and grammar.

thus use the general idea "play symbol." Conversely, we learn the general idea of the symbol by experience of individual instances, either from teachers or from life in general. The relation of these two has been called the problem of the one and the many. The universal category of the play symbol is "the one." The particulars—many particular instances appearing on playback devices—are "the many." How do they relate?

In medieval discussions, there were two parties. The *realists* said that the universal category, the play symbol, was the starting point, and that individual instances were embodiments of the prior, real idea. By contrast, the *nominalists* said that the particular instances were the starting point, and that the general category was a convenient kind of grouping together of the particulars under one name or one idea, the play symbol.

Our examination of signs suggests that neither of these accounts is completely right. The contrastive-identificational features of signs, particularly those related to the referential subsystem, are the focus of the realists. The meanings of signs are stable, and that stability suggests to the realists that the generality, the totality of general features of meaning, is more ultimate than the particulars. The nominalists are closer to focusing on variation. And some forms of modern *structuralism* constitute a kind of third alternative that focuses on distributional context: everything boils down to relations. All three of these approaches are partly right. But they become wrong if they insist that they have the whole account. All three aspects are necessary, and all three interlock. All three are ordained by God in their relations to one another.

Real instances of the play symbol show a unity among different instances. The unity goes back to the unity of the plan of one God. The diversity among different instances of the symbol goes back to the diversity in the plan of God for a diversity of human activities. And that diversity in the plan of God has its foundation in a diversity in God himself, in that he is three persons. So creation itself is a reflection of God.

But suppose a person does not want to acknowledge the role of God as the source of unity and diversity. He may claim that the unity of the play symbol, the unity in the general idea, is simply a unity that is just "there" without any further explanation. Then how can it come about that the idea of the play symbol ever has a particular embodiment in a particular instance? How do the particulars come about, and how do they come to have a relation to the general idea? There is no explanation, if the "one" is the only ultimate, of how the many come about. A converse difficulty arises if we start with the particulars. If the particulars are just irreducibly "there" without further explanation, how does it come about that we can unite them under the heading of one general idea? Extreme nominalism might say that the unity is simply a unity imposed by the human mind. But if so, it is ultimately illusory in comparison with how the things themselves are related to one another. And how can it come about that different human minds could agree on the unities?[3] We need God as Creator to form the unity among human beings created in his image.

God's Self-Disclosure

We can see the challenge in another way if we consider what the Bible indicates about God's name. God's name is a *sign* that signifies God. What are the implications for our thinking about signs?

In modern American culture, personal names often have little meaning. But in ancient Hebrew culture names often had meaning. For example, "The man called his wife's name Eve, because she was the mother of all living" (Gen. 3:20). In Hebrew, *Eve* resembles the word for living. So, too, God says to Abram, "No longer shall your name be called Abram, but your name shall be Abraham, for I have made you the father of a multitude of nations" (Gen. 17:5). *Abraham* means "father of a multitude."

In the same way, the name of God has meaning. For example, after Hagar's experience of encountering the Lord, "she called the name of the LORD who spoke to her, 'You are a God of seeing,' for she said, 'Truly here I have seen him who looks after me'" (Gen. 16:13). Hagar spoke a name that expressed something about her previous experience with God. God in speaking to Moses reveals his name as "I AM WHO I AM" (Ex. 3:14), in contrast to the earlier name "God Almighty" (Hebrew, *El Shaddai*). A name for God reveals something of his character. It is not just an arbitrary sound. So when God says concerning the "angel" (that is, the messenger) of the exodus that "my name is in him" (Ex. 23:21), it implies that God's character is in him, that is, that the messenger is himself divine.

In the end, a name for God designates the entirety of God, no matter which particular name or description we start with. The "name" of God is a condensed or summary version of his character and so implicitly points to the whole of his character.

Visual appearances of God also manifest his character. The thunder and lightning on Mount Sinai underline the power of God. The bright cloud accompanying God's appearing shows his splendor. The figure on the throne in Ezekiel 1:26–27 manifests God's character as King and Judge of the world.

When the Son becomes incarnate, we are told, "And the Word became flesh and dwelt among us, and we have seen his glory, glory as of the only Son from

---

[3]Once again we can see a relation to some themes in postmodernism. Postmodernists, in order to protect the diversity, are tempted just to give up on unity—except that they want everyone to agree about giving up, and in doing so they still cling to a final unity, even if it is a second-order negative unity of jointly giving up on unity concerning first-order human judgments.

the Father, full of grace and truth" (John 1:14). The "Word" communicates who God is. He is "full of . . . truth." He shows the character of God, and this idea is very close to the function in the Old Testament of the name of God. In the Old Testament, God put his name on the temple of Solomon (1 Kings 8:29). When the Word "dwelt among us," he was the replacement or antitype for the temple of Solomon. It follows that God's name was on him. He revealed God's character in climactic form.

In his incarnation the Son is also the climactic visual manifestation of God. Jesus says, "Whoever has seen me has seen the Father" (John 14:9). The language of "glory" in John 1:14 echoes the mention of glory that accompanies God's appearing in the Old Testament.

The name of God in the Old Testament is a sign: it has a physical side, namely, its sound and pronunciation. It has a meaning side, namely, its designating God. The appearances of God in the Old Testament likewise have a physical side, in the visual display, and a meaning side, namely, in the display of God's character. Both of these aspects are fulfilled in Christ.

Christ reveals God, both in his words and in his actions. But that revelation needs to be received if we are going to profit from it. The Holy Spirit enables us to see this revelation for what it is. Christ signifies God to us through the Holy Spirit.

God himself is therefore the archetype or original for signification. He is the foundation for all signification, whether in language through names or through visual phenomena. Signification has an origin in the character of God the Father, who is the meaning or significance of verbal and nonverbal revelation. Signification takes place through the manifestation of the Son, who displays the character of God to human view. The Son as one person unifies the physical manifestation with the divine character. And the Holy Spirit opens our eyes spiritually to the physical manifestation.

This archetypal revelation is unique. But since it reveals God's character, we can expect that it is reflected dimly in signification in general. Signification in general owes its significance to man being created in the image of God.

Signification in God's revelation of himself involves God's character as signified, God's Son as the unified channel, and the Holy Spirit as the signifier who conveys the signified to the recipients. By analogy, signification in general involves signified meaning, unified manifestation, and a conveying signifier. The play symbol, for example, has the meaning "start playing," expressed in a unified manifestation: button, together with label (the triangle), together with a connection of the button to activation of a device. The physical appearance of the symbol, together with transmission of light, together with human visual capacity, convey the meaning to the human actor.

The Origin of Signs

So we see in God himself the logical origin for signs. Signs do not come out of nowhere. Out of his bounty, his goodness, God has supplied human beings with all the signs in all the particular systems of signs. He has not given signs in isolation but signs that are tied to and related to one another in their meanings, their appearance, and their ability to form larger patterns that act in the world. And it is not a gift that is unrelated to the giver. The gift reflects the giver in mysterious ways. Signs, with their ability to signify, reflect God who signifies himself, as is hinted at in his self-description, "I AM WHO I AM." God describes himself to himself in the communication and communion of the persons of the Trinity, in unity and diversity. And then that unity in diversity is reflected in the unity (contrastive-identificational features), diversity (variation), and interconnectedness (distribution) that exist in any one sign. When you use a sign, you rely on God. Each sign shows God's eternal power and divine nature (Rom. 1:20). Each sign comes to you in a situation that depends on God's creation of you and your environment. In its coinherence of aspects, each sign images the coinherence in God's Trinitarian character.

Human Action as Signifying

The play symbol is a specific sign within a specific sign system. But the observations that we have made can apply by analogy to the larger question of significance. Human actions have significance, related to human purposes. So we can see some analogies to sign systems.

Consider again the example where I give my credit card to the grocery store clerk. That action has significance. In analogy to the visible appearance of the play symbol, my action has a visual and tactile side. To understand what I am doing, the clerk has to receive physical input. This visual and tactile side is analogous to the phonological subsystem for language or the visual subsystem for the play symbol.

The action also has a meaning side. Given the context of American life, the cultural understanding of credit cards, and the agreement of the credit card company, my signature on the credit card receipt signifies that I am willing to have the grocery store transfer money from my credit card account to the store's account. This meaning coheres with a larger system, the credit card system, and the familiarity that system has in the mind of the American public. This system is the analogue of the referential subsystem of language and the referential aspect of the play symbol ("start playing").

Finally, the credit card transaction has a kind of "grammar." The credit card with its numerical identification has a role in a kind of grammatical operation in which the local human action with the clerk results in bringing together (1) my personal monetary balance with the credit card company, (2) a transfer of money from the credit card company, and (3) a delivery of money to the store. In this transfer we can see a kind of analogue to a sentence in language. The order to transfer money is like the verbal part of the sentence, that is, the verb *transfer*. The agent in the transfer, namely, the credit card company, is like the subject of the sentence. The two pieces fit together grammatically in a manner analogous to the subject and verb in a sentence: "The credit card company transfers . . ." Then there is the amount to be transferred, let us say $2.50. It functions like the object in a sentence. "The credit card company transfers $2.50 . . ." Finally, there are two monetary accounts, which are analogous to source and destination within a sentence. The two accounts are "my balance with the credit card company" and "the store's account." The full sentence then runs, "The credit card company transfers $2.50 from my credit card account to the grocery store account." The actual transaction may take place without anyone using a sentence to describe it. The transaction is nevertheless sentence-like in its structure. It has a "grammar" linking the credit card company, the activity of transferring, the amount transferred, and so on.

Thus, a credit card transaction involves the use of and interaction of three "subsystems" of the action, a visual subsystem, a referential subsystem, and a grammatical subsystem. These, as usual, interlock in a harmony, in imitation of the Trinitarian character of God.

34

From Signs to Perspectives

The kingdom of heaven is like a grain of mustard seed that a man took
and sowed in his field. It is the smallest of all seeds,
but when it has grown it is larger than all the garden plants
and becomes a tree, so that the birds of the air come
and make nests in its branches.

—Matthew 13:31–32

Signs are relatively stable in meaning, but they also have flexibility. Over time the meaning of signs can shift around. Today the play symbol means "start playing." But it did not always mean that. It is similar in shape to the stylized head of an arrow, which has a more generic meaning: "this direction (toward the tip of the arrow) is marked (for some purpose, to be discerned from context)."

The point here is that meaning develops. Meaning can come to be firmly associated with a sign by a series of steps. The steps may build on earlier, related meanings. Or meaning can be created suddenly, by a striking new association. In scientific and technical fields, new symbols can be created as need arises.

Associations

How is it that we can "stretch" the meaning of a sign in a new direction or create a completely new sign? This creativity goes back to God.

When we use the field perspective on meaning, we focus on the relation that a particular sign like the play symbol has with various aspects of its normal meaning, as well as further associations that it may have with neighboring meanings and contrasting meanings and "stretched" meanings. We can apply a similar field perspective to words used in describing God. A name for God, or an attribute of God such as "gracious," designates his character. It is a kind of condensation or summary of one aspect of his character. But his character is a whole. God is righteous and gracious and loving and holy and all-powerful. When any name is used to designate God, it designates the God who has all these characteristics. Thus any one name for God does two things simultaneously. It singles out or focuses on some one characteristic of God or a small number of related characteristics. And, second, it designates God and all that he is, and so invites us to associate with it all the other things that we know about God. A name is like one perspective on God.[1]

A Sign as a Perspective

If a name for God can be used as a perspective on God, can we do the same with other signs? Take the play symbol as a sign. Can that sign be expanded into a perspective on life? Yes, it can. We start with more or less the literal meaning, "start playing." Why is the action of starting to play significant in human experience? The button is part of a larger process in which we receive an audio or video recording. We become recipients of meaning, musical meaning or speech meaning or video action. This reception of meaning coheres with reception of meaning in all of life. The recording medium provides the possibility of transmitting and reproducing meaning over gaps in time and space.

The play symbol represents part of a process of communicating meaning. So it can be viewed as one instance within a larger domain of many types of personal communication. It therefore can serve as a perspective on personal communication in general. Human reception of meaning depends on divine meaning, and human communication of meaning depends on the original divine capacity for communication of meaning, including communication not only from God to man but also from God to God among the persons of the Trinity. In fact, all of God's action, within the Trinity as well as from God to the world, can be viewed as communication of meaning. So now the original example of starting to play a DVD disc has become a perspective on all communication, including divine communication.

God has always been communicating among the persons of the Trinity. He never *started* but always exists. Yet even the idea of *starting* to play a DVD depends

---

[1]For further discussion of perspectives, see Vern S. Poythress, *Symphonic Theology: The Validity of Multiple Perspectives in Theology* (Grand Rapids: Zondervan, 1987; repr., Phillipsburg, NJ: P&R, 2001); John M. Frame, *Perspectives on the Word of God: An Introduction to Christian Ethics* (Phillipsburg, NJ: Presbyterian and Reformed, 1990); Frame, *The Doctrine of the Knowledge of God* (Phillipsburg, NJ: Presbyterian and Reformed, 1987); and other books by Frame. More on the name of God can be found in Vern S. Poythress, *In the Beginning Was the Word: Language— A God-Centered Approach* (Wheaton, IL: Crossway, 2009), chaps. 33–34. The name of God in Ex. 3:14 is special because it defines God by referring us to God.

on constancy before the start. The relative constancy within the created world depends on the eternal constancy of God, who had no beginning.

We can reach a similar conclusion if we start not with the reception of meaning but with the meaning received. What are the contents of the audio or video recording to which the play symbol intends to give access? Those contents involve human and divine action and so become a perspective on the larger vistas of action. These larger vistas eventually encompass all of world history. And world history depends on God who governs it.

Signs in General as Perspectives

Making a sign into a perspective on everything may be easier with some signs than with others. But the potential is there with any sign as a starting point, because signs exist in relationships, as the field perspective emphasizes. Following the relationships out from one point to another connects us with a never-ending web of relationships, and the relationships end up by including everything. We can rephrase this phenomenon by thinking in terms of the mind of God. The relationships that we see are relationships that we were not the first to create. God is the source for and controller of all relationships. He knows all the relationships in his own mind, as part of his plan for the entirety of history.

Our own knowledge is a partial image of God's knowledge. So in using a sign as a starting point for exploring relationships, we are tracing in our minds some of the patterns that exist first of all in God's mind. God's plan is harmonious and coherent, and so all the relationships hold together; everything is genuinely related to everything else.

Perhaps another account can be given of the capabilities of perspectives. We saw in the previous chapter that God's name was a special case for understanding signs. The name of God is climactically revealed in Christ, who is the Word of God according to John 1:1–3. The character of God is summed up in Christ. Christ is in this sense a "perspective" on the whole of God; but the word *perspective* is too weak, since he is himself God. The second person of the Trinity, as the Word of God, is also the archetype for all signs. So do all signs enjoy a structure that is analogically related to the one archetypal Word? If so, the use of any sign as a perspective is an analogical image of the name of God, who is the Word. The flexibility of signs in this way reflects the original dynamics of the Word who reveals the Father. "No one has ever seen God; the only God, who is at the Father's side, he has made him known" (John 1:18). When you use a sign perspectivally, you are relying on God, who holds together literal meanings and their perspectival uses.

All signs depend on God. But creaturely signs do not *become* God. God remains God, and we remain his creatures. What is creaturely reveals God in his wisdom.

PART 5

Applications

35

A Jigsaw Piece as a Perspective

That which we have seen and heard we proclaim also to you,
so that you too may have fellowship with us;
and indeed our fellowship is with the Father
and with his Son Jesus Christ.

—1 John 1:3

We may illustrate the function of perspectives by using a piece of a jigsaw puzzle as a perspective on relationships.

Reaching a Solution to a Puzzle

We have considered the situation where a father and a son are putting together a jigsaw puzzle. The father's movement of a single piece into place is part of the process. The movement of the piece contributes to the endpoint, the solution of the entire puzzle. The solution, when it is achieved, represents a tiny achievement of a goal, and this achievement of human purpose imitates the grand purpose of God, the achievement of the goal of the consummation, the final "solution" to the "puzzle" of life in a fallen world.

Cooperative Solution

We may also consider the solving of the puzzle from the standpoint of relationships. The father undertakes to solve the puzzle with his son not merely for the purpose of the puzzle but also for the purpose of his relationship with his son. The father and the son work together, and this working together is itself part of the point. The father and the son share in the struggle and may help one another by collecting pieces of one color or pattern. They also share the triumph when the puzzle is finished.

The work on the puzzle thus integrally involves the family relationship. If the puzzle solving goes well, the father through his fellowship with the son expresses and confirms his commitment. Every single piece laid in place expresses the relationship, though the implications of the relationship only become visible through the accumulation of a large number of individual steps. In the process the father is committed to helping and guiding his son both with the puzzle and with life. The expression of love and concern for his son in the puzzle solving underlines the larger concern that he has with the son living his whole life. We might say that the father's commitment is covenantal, both because it is a personal relationship with intimacy and because the relationship is mandated by God. Fathers are required by God to look after and raise their children (Eph. 6:4).[1] The covenantal commitment between a human father and son imitates or reflects the commitment that God the Father has to his people, whom he treats as sons: "It is for discipline that you have to endure. God is treating you as sons. For what son is there whom his father does not discipline?" (Heb. 12:7). God has established us in a relationship of sonship because of his unique Son: "But when the fullness of time had come, God sent forth his Son, born of woman, born under the law, to redeem those who were under the law, so that we might receive adoption as sons. And because you are sons, God has sent the Spirit of his Son into our hearts, crying, 'Abba! Father!'" (Gal. 4:4–6). The passage in Galatians is speaking of *redemptive* adoption, which is based on Christ the Son being sent to accomplish redemption. God the Father relates to God the Son redemptively. Behind that redemptive relation stands the eternal relation of love between the Father and the Son, a relation that holds true even apart from creation and redemption.

Hence, the jigsaw puzzle piece points to the human father-son relation; the human relation points to the divine relation in redemption; and the divine relation in redemption points to the eternal Father-Son relation in the Trinity. This pointing remains in operation even when human action becomes perverted by sin. Sin corrupts and distorts and inverts the relationships. Even in the midst of distortion, however, they depend on God.

---

[1]God's fatherhood is helpful also to those children who grew up with no father in the home or who had an abusive father. God offers fellowship with himself as the true father, in contrast to the lack of a true father that a child experienced in growing up.

Figure 35.1. Reflection of Relationship

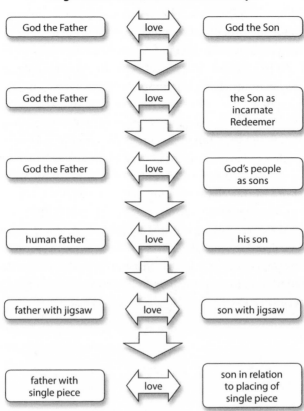

Subsystems to Meaning

We can also analyze the placing of jigsaw pieces using what we have learned about subsystems of meaning (chap. 31). A jigsaw piece is a physical object. It has color, shape, and tactile presence. Its color and shape make it identifiable as a distinct physical object. It contrasts with pieces of different color or shape, and these relationships with other pieces, from the same or from different puzzles, form part of a visual subsystem for jigsaw solving. The color and shape are also clues to where it will fit. So they function with a certain "grammar" in relation to the other pieces in the same puzzles.

Finally, the piece contributes to a scene that has meaning. Often a solved jigsaw puzzle reveals an artistically pleasing photograph or artistic rendering of a landscape or some other interesting scene. The meaning then lies in the appreciation of the completed scene, to which each placing of a piece contributes.

In addition, the solving of the puzzle has added layers of social meaning for the father and son and their participation together in the process. The placement of one piece is a physical action, involving sight and touch. That dimension enjoys relations with the whole subsystem of the human body detecting color and shape and tactile sensations. The physical sensations belong to the physical subsystem for the process of moving a piece into place. But the moving of a piece also has a personal, social significance, because it expresses the sharing of father and son in a process and a goal. That human significance is part of a referential subsystem involving relations to other expressions of social bonding. The moving of a single piece also fits together in a kind of "grammar," in that the physical process of moving one piece fits with the physical processes for other pieces, while the human meanings for one piece fit with the human meanings for other pieces. These acts of gradually fitting together, in the two dimensions, cohere with one another, so that the physical solving of the puzzle goes together with the human expression of victory, which is achieved when the whole puzzle comes together. Grammar may not here occupy a distinct "layer" from the other systems. Instead, it is merely the coherent link between the two sides, the physical and the social.

God has designed coherence for the three subsystems for puzzle solving. He has also designed human relationships in imitation of and in reflection of his own eternal relationships.

36

Living in Relationships

And walk in love, as Christ loved us and gave himself up for us,
a fragrant offering and sacrifice to God.

—Ephesians 5:2

How extensively do we meet with relationships? We meet them in all of our social life—family, business, education, economy, law, art, sports. Our relationships with animals, plants, and nonliving things are subpersonal. But even in these relationships, we also have a relationship to God, who gives and ordains the animals, plants, and nonliving things to which we relate. Our relationship with God is inescapable.

Attributes of Lordship

Let us remember the three attributes or perspectives on lordship: authority, control, and presence. God is the Lord. As an attribute of his lordship, he has authority over all his relationships to human beings and over all our relationships to one another. His authority extends even to those things that human beings may never notice: a single cell in a muscle fiber in a finger moving to grasp a jigsaw piece. God's authority specifies what is right and wrong in relationships. He requires the father to serve as wise guide for the son, and the son to respect the father.

Second, God controls the relationships. He controls everything in every human relationship and institution and artifact and culture throughout the world. His control is what imparts power to our human control and gives significance and meaning to our human significances.

Third, God is present in his wisdom and truth in the midst of human meanings, purposes, and attempts at control. He confronts us not only with his goodness and his name, but also with his holiness and his requirement of truthfulness and moral responsibility on our part. Personal relationships are not something that we are to be involved in as we please, independent of all moral standards. If people tried consistently to abandon moral standards with respect to relationships, no one could be trusted, and social life would be full of failures as well as treacheries. God makes the social world generally livable. But in a fallen world, there may indeed sometimes be anarchic situations and evil groups where human destruction rises to horrible heights. Short of completely reforming and purifying people as God will do in the consummation, he rules over a world that still contains treacheries in human relationships.

Acting in Relationships

Within this world we have the privilege of acting and reflecting on our relationships. In our actions, in our creativity, we draw out and make manifest meanings that God has already ordained. We depend on meanings all the time—the meanings in the episodes and the meanings in our motives and the meanings in the effects on others.

At every point in relationships we depend on God, even when we are not aware of it. Our duty to God is not to become perfectly aware of everything, which would be impossible anyway. Our duty is to love the Lord our God with all our heart, soul, strength, and mind, and our neighbor as ourselves (Matt. 22:37–40). Love, not knowledge, is our prime duty. But how shall people be changed when they have rebelled against God and turned in hatred against him? We must not pretend that we are not sick with sin and rebellion.

We must come to Christ, the source of our redemption, and live from his authority, control, and presence. We must live in his truth (John 14:6), being sanctified by his word (John 17:17). We must walk in his truth, and speak the truth (2 John 4; 3 John 3–4; Eph. 4:25). We may express our gratitude to God for our relationships, not only by praising him when we think of their marvels, but also by serving him even when we are not thinking of those marvels.

Situations with Non-Christians

We may also grow in our appreciation of the struggle that non-Christians have. They live in God's world, and according to Romans 1:18–25 they know God in his eternal power and divine nature (1:20). God is present to them in their every breath and every interaction in human relationships. And that is not pleasant, because they do not want him there.

Non-Christians cannot get God's presence out of their relationships. That is something different from the question of whether they can cease consciously to think about God. Clearly they can. But to abolish God's presence would be to abolish relationships themselves, including every significance of every smile, every sign, every episode, every step, every jigsaw piece.

Some people have tried to do so. Eastern forms of meditation often involve the practice of emptying the mind and trying to bring thought to an end. The goal is to be one with the universe or to experience union with "the All," that is, with a god who is conceived pantheistically. Allegedly, such a union dissolves the restlessness of the human mind in order to advance toward the goal of final peace. The Buddhists want nirvana, which is the dissolution of the mind and the person and all human relationships into the cosmic "All."

Yes, the mind is restless. The mind involved in human relationships is restless. "Our hearts are restless till they find their rest in You."[1] What we need is a renewed relationship with God—fellowship with God and reconciliation with God, not nirvana. The paradox of Eastern mysticism is that it seeks by heroic mental, spiritual, and bodily efforts to arrive at a god, when all along God, the true God, is already there. He is there right in the structures of persons and their relationships. "In him we live and move and have our being" (Acts 17:28).

You do not have to cease to think, and you do not have to empty out meaning to get there. God is already there with persons in their fullness, in their relationships. Fill your mind with him, rather than emptying it. In fact, emptying it is retreat from God into one more idolatry, where a person pretends that the self is identical with the One, identical with a god. Non-Christians do not see how to receive God, this God who is closer than thought itself. In fact, no one on his own initiative does. We are rebels. "No one can come to me unless the Father who sent me draws him" (John 6:44). God must give light, through his Son (John 8:12; 9:5). And then, when God casts off the darkness and fog in our minds, we may begin to understand how much God was present to us all along, in our relationships as well as other ways. He was present even while we rebelled, hated, and fled.

---

[1] Updated language, from St. Augustine, *The Confessions of St. Augustin*, vol. 1 of *A Select Library of the Nicene and Post-Nicene Fathers of the Christian Church*, ed. Philip Schaff (Grand Rapids: Eerdmans, 1979), 45 (1.1.1).

Interaction with Other Approaches to Society and Relationships

APPENDIX A

René Descartes's Method

The fear of the LORD is the beginning of wisdom;
all those who practice it have a good understanding.

—Psalm 111:10

René Descartes in his *Discourse on Method*[1] struggled with the issues of the influence of society and the influence of teachers. On the one hand, he recognized that he could learn from others. On the other hand, he discovered the unreliability of received opinion. Here are his own words concerning philosophy:

> As to philosophy, I shall say only this: that when I noted that it has been cultivated for many centuries by men of the most outstanding ability, and that none the less there is not a single thing of which it treats which is not still in dispute, and nothing, therefore, which is free from doubt, I was not so presuming as to expect that I should succeed where they had failed.[2]

> Already in my college days I had been brought to recognise that there is no opinion, however strange, and however difficult of belief, which has not been upheld by one or other of the philosophers.[3]

---

[1]René Descartes, *Discourse on the Method of Rightly Conducting the Reason and of Seeking for Truth in the Sciences*. I have used the translation by Norman Kemp Smith in *Descartes' Philosophical Writings* (London: Macmillan, 1952).
[2]Ibid., 121.
[3]Ibid., 127.

And then concerning the opinions of ordinary people:

> Yet, here again, so long as I gave thought only to the manners and customs of men, I met with nothing to reassure me, finding almost as much diversity in them as I had previously found in the opinions of the philosophers. The chief profit I derived from study of them was therefore this: observing that many things, however extravagant and ridiculous they may in our view appear to be, were yet very generally received and approved *by other great nations*, I learned not to be too confident in any belief to which I had been persuaded merely by example or custom.[4]

Descartes discerned the influence of upbringing:

> Bearing also in mind how the selfsame man, with the mental equipment proper to him, if *nurtured* from infancy among the French or the Germans, would come to be different from what he would have been had he lived always among the Chinese or the cannibals; and how, in respect of fashions in dress, what pleased us ten years ago, and which will again please ten years hence, appears to us at the present moment extravagant and ridiculous. Thus I came to see that *custom and example* have a much more persuasive power than any certitude obtained by way of inquiry.[5]

Wrestlings with Confusions in Knowledge

Descartes struggled with some of the same issues that we have addressed in this book. The fall introduces confusion into human knowledge, and this confusion has a social dimension. Human teachers are not completely trustworthy, not merely because they can be consciously deceitful, but also because they belong to a larger tradition that over a long period of time may have gone astray from the truth.

Descartes might have added that many differences in custom fall on a different plane than differences about truth. We have made the point that diversity among human beings and diversity among cultures is not always bad or unacceptable; it may sometimes be a created diversity compatible with God's universal truth, or it may sometimes be a contradictory diversity in which one or several views go astray from truth (chap. 17).

A Christian Remedy?

Descartes could have said, in responding to the difficulty, that we need God to straighten us out. We need God to act in redemption, and we need him to

---

[4]Ibid., 122 (italics original).
[5]Ibid., 127–28 (italics original).

speak in order to instruct us. That would have been an answer in line with the Bible's teaching about the fall and its remedy. But Descartes does not take this route. Religion falls under the same uncertainty as does everything else because Descartes observes the plurality of religious notions. As part of his "method," Descartes indeed proposes as a practical measure to follow the precepts of the religion with which he has grown up.[6] But this practice is temporary. Descartes has in effect treated religion as a social phenomenon, as opinions and practices of multiple societies across the world. So treated, it cannot yield certainty. He has not asked himself directly about God and whether God has revealed himself in special revelation through the deeds of Christ and the words of the Bible.

Autonomous Reason

Instead, as a fundamental principle of his method, Descartes proposes accepting as true only what is clearly evident: "The first [rule] was to accept nothing as true which I did not evidently know to be such. . . ."[7] Together with this rule go three others that have to do with dividing difficulties and arranging thoughts. Descartes says concerning the rules, "I came to believe that the four following rules would be found sufficient."[8] And then, "But what pleased me most in this method I had discovered was that it afforded me assurance that in all matters I should be employing my reason, if not perfectly, at least as well as it was in my power to do."[9]

Later reflection has rightly called this method *autonomous reason*.[10] Descartes pictures reason as functioning independently of God's revelation. This picture is itself a ghastly mistake, because the social uncertainties in knowledge arise from human rebellion and its long-term effects. Descartes does not reckon with the fall or its remedy. Or rather, he has a false remedy, a remedy that continues the rebellion of Adam and Eve, who wanted to think independently of God's instruction.

Descartes has some complimentary things to say about the religion in which he was raised. But he thinks that he cannot rely on it. And he indicates why:

> I revered our theology, and would be as desirous as anyone to reach heaven, but being reliably given to understand that the way to it [heaven] is not less open to the

---

[6]"The first [maxim, part of "a provisional code of morals"] was to obey the laws and customs of my country, adhering unwaveringly to the religion in which, by God's grace, I had been educated from my childhood . . ." (ibid., 133).

[7]Ibid., 129.

[8]Ibid.

[9]Ibid., 132.

[10]Cornelius Van Til, *A Survey of Christian Epistemology* (n.p.: den Dulk Foundation, 1969), 103–4.

most ignorant than to the most learned, and that the revealed truths which afford us guidance are above our power of understanding, I did not dare to test them by the feebleness of my reasonings. I recognised that to enter on an examination of them, and to succeed in so doing, I should require to have some special help from above, and to be more than man.[11]

Descartes is in danger of making a polarity between human "reasonings" and divine truths, which are "above our power of understanding." By making a polarity, he suggests that the divine truths are then left totally mysterious. A person would have to "be more than man" to understand them. Maybe this expression about being "more than man" is qualified by the neighboring clause, which speaks of "special help from above." Does Descartes mean that we need the Holy Spirit? We certainly do. But then the logical response is to ask God and to humble ourselves before him, acknowledging our need. By God's grace we can then come to know him, to know Christ, and to know the way to heaven. But Descartes does not follow this route.

On the other hand, the expression "be more than man" could effectively bar the door to almost everyone. Taken at face value, it seems to make genuine human knowledge of God impossible. If we give up on such knowledge, human reason is left free in its own sphere to conduct its operations independently of God's presence and his instruction. The freedom on the human sphere then boils down to the exercise of autonomy, self-reliance *independent* of divine instruction and communion.

The biblical view of God's truth, on the other hand, brings the two sides, reason and revelation, together.[12] Our modes of reasoning need to be transformed through communion with Christ in the power of the Holy Spirit, so that we may examine both "religious truth" from the Bible and ordinary affairs and philosophical issues with minds trained in knowing God and his ways. That is what I am trying to do, albeit imperfectly, in this book. We can know God without becoming "more than man" because in Christ God has acted to redeem us, to have fellowship with us, and to instruct us. When we know him, we have his guidance as we sort through the mixture of truth and error in human tradition and the training we receive from human societies.

Descartes as Sociologist

Descartes's discussions come long before the rise of sociology as a distinct scientific discipline. But in some ways they lay the foundation. Descartes lays out the

---

[11]Ibid., 120–21.

[12]See, in particular, the discussion of divine transcendence and divine immanence in John M. Frame, *The Doctrine of the Knowledge of God* (Phillipsburg, NJ: Presbyterian and Reformed, 1987), 13–15; Vern S. Poythress, *In the Beginning Was the Word: Language—A God-Centered Approach* (Wheaton, IL: Crossway, 2009), appendix C.

difficulty: the unreliability of human opinion. And he discerns that this unreliability stems from the social dimension of human knowledge and learning. But he provides a "solution" that sends people off in fundamentally the wrong direction. He in effect counsels them to rely on themselves rather than on God. Whether or not he actually intended it that way, the practical effect is to encourage ignoring God's instruction in Christ and in the Bible and try to build up knowledge by an independent exercise of rational discernment.

This counsel offers an alternative way of salvation. The difficulty is to know the truth in important matters. Descartes's method proposes a way to save ourselves, with reason as the instrument for our salvation. All modern methods of knowledge that are at bottom self-reliant rest on the same principle. Rely on yourself, on your reasoning powers, and thereby save yourself. By contrast, the Bible offers another way: "The fear of the LORD is the beginning of wisdom" (Ps. 111:10). God himself, speaking in the Bible, counsels us to rely not on ourselves but on him.

Assumptions

Descartes wanted not to rely on any assumptions that were not clearly evident. But from a different point of view we can see that he had plenty of assumptions. He seems to have assumed that his reasoning powers, and those of other human beings as well, were fundamentally intact, rather than being corrupted by the fall. He assumed that religion could be treated fairly when treated sociologically, apart from reckoning with the presence of God and God's revelation of his character. He assumed that the difficulties with unreliable human opinion were in the end merely intellectual, rather than moral and spiritual and therefore due ultimately to rebellion against God. He assumed that it was morally all right to search for a method self-reliantly. He suppressed the knowledge of the fact that such self-reliance recapitulates the desire for self-reliance in the fall of Adam and Eve.

Descartes's own rules for his method were not clearly evident. I would guess that he was not troubled by the fact, because he did not claim that the method itself was knowledge. But how can we know that the method will be conducive to knowledge? And even if, in practical experience, we find that it is a practical aid to knowledge in some ways, how do we assure ourselves that it does not contain some fatal flaw that leads us astray in subtle ways? In particular, does it contain the fatal flaw of ignoring the fear of God by seeking instruction without reference to divine revelation?

Broader Difficulties

I mention Descartes because his difficulties are not unique to him. In some ways he speaks for the Western world. How do we conceive of human reasoning? Is it built to function most effectively when on its own or when in communion with God? Western science is certainly infected with this difficulty.[13] So also is the process for reflectively analyzing the nature of human relationships, the nature of society, and the nature of what we can expect to know when we are social creatures who learn from our parents and teachers and peers.

Descartes hoped to train himself to become critically aware of the influence of society. Modern sociology may do the same thing. This critical awareness represents a form of reflection, of standing back from our immersion in practical living. We stand back to take a view of ourselves, our relationships, and their meaning. We stand back in a form of transcendence (chap. 11). But if we claim an absolute viewpoint, we take the place of God. That is the bad kind of self-reliance. That kind of transcendence will fail us because it is rebellious. Descartes fell into it in his desire to transcend the limitations of human opinions in the various cultures that he encountered. Modern sociological analysis can fall into it if it wants transcendent insight without relying on God's guidance.

---

[13]Vern S. Poythress, *Redeeming Science: A God-Centered Approach* (Wheaton, IL: Crossway, 2006).

APPENDIX B

Modern Sociology

Be not wise in your own eyes;
fear the Lord, and turn away from evil.

—Proverbs 3:7

Observations about social life go back into the distant past. The book of Proverbs is an outstanding example of such observations. Confucius, Plato, and Aristotle all thought about society and its organization.[1] The Reformation and, later, Descartes wrestled with the issue of tradition, including the possibility that social influence can pass on untruths and encourage us to adopt them (see appendix A). But the academic study that we call sociology arose somewhat later. In 1838 Auguste Comte invented the term *sociology* to describe a new way of looking at social life.[2]

Distinctives for Sociology

Sociologist John Macionis, in his textbook introduction to sociology, defines sociology as *"the systematic study of human society."*[3] He then delineates four features distinctive to a "sociological perspective."[4]

---

[1]John J. Macionis, *Sociology*, 11th ed. (Upper Saddle River, NJ: Prentice Hall, 2007), 13.
[2]Ibid. Considerable variation occurs among different approaches to sociology (ibid., 14–21, 33–39). In this and the following appendices I focus for convenience on Macionis's textbook *Sociology* as an important representative. It claims in the preface that it and its paperback companion *Society: The Basics*, 10th ed. (Upper Saddle River, NJ: Prentice Hall, 2008), are "chosen by far more faculty than any other text" (Macionis, *Sociology*, xxiii). Later (appendix G) we consider postmodern directions that do not surface much within Macionis's account.
[3]Macionis, *Sociology*, 2.
[4]Ibid., 2–5.

First, the sociological perspective sees "the general in the particular." Macionis illustrates with a generalization about women's hopes for marriage:

Lillian Rubin (1976) found that higher-income women typically expected the men they married to be sensitive to others, to talk readily, and to share feelings and experiences. Lower-income women, she found, had very different expectations and were looking for men who did not drink too much, were not violent, and held steady jobs.[5]

But such generalizations are not unique to modern sociology. The book of Proverbs is full of generalizations, such as

The vexation of a fool is known at once,
    but the prudent ignores an insult. (Prov. 12:16)

So how does modern sociology differ from the book of Proverbs or other ancient observations about society and human relationships? Is the key difference in the *systematic* character of sociology? Perhaps. But Plato's and Aristotle's discussions of society have some elements of systematization. What about the book of Proverbs? Can we say that the proverbs, unlike modern sociology, are not a "systematic" study? It depends on what we are looking for. The biblical proverbs could easily be arranged in larger categories, such as wisdom and folly, riches and poverty, wise and foolish speech, diligence and laziness, and of course human relations to God. That would be a "systematic" arrangement and would differ little in basic content from the book of Proverbs as we have it. And how do we tell whether some of the proverbs derived from "systematic" rather than merely casual observation of human life?

Second, according to Macionis, the sociological perspective sees "the strange in the familiar." Macionis explains, "We are used to thinking that people fall in love and decide to marry based on personal feelings. But the sociological perspective reveals the initially strange idea that society shapes what we think and do."[6] He calls the idea of social shaping "strange"; but he also indicates that this "strangeness" has a connection with the fact that "we live in an individualistic society." Other societies therefore might not find the idea strange, but might be quite accustomed to socially oriented thinking. The Old Testament includes situations of "arranged marriage," where the parents take the initiative in bringing together the future marriage partners (see Genesis 24). Proverbs provides examples of social influence, both in its many observations about wisdom being acquired from parents, and in its particular examples:

---

[5]Ibid., 2.
[6]Ibid., 3.

My son, if sinners entice you,
  do not consent. (Prov. 1:10)

An evildoer listens to wicked lips,
  and a liar gives ear to a mischievous tongue. (Prov. 17:4)

Third, the sociological perspective sees "personal choice in social context." Macionis gives as an example the difference between high-income countries, where women have two children or fewer, and low-income countries, where the average number of children may be anywhere from three to seven.[7] The Bible also provides examples. A just or unjust king has an effect on the whole country; so does idolatry. Individual choices are influenced by such contexts, and even if an individual resists the prevailing social atmosphere, he cannot escape its effects in the form of injustice and suffering that issue from the society as a whole.

By justice a king builds up the land,
  but he who exacts gifts [bribes] tears it down. (Prov. 29:4)

When the righteous triumph, there is great glory,
  but when the wicked rise, people hide themselves. (Prov. 28:12)

Fourth, the experience of living in the margins of society and the experience of social crisis help people to think sociologically. "No African American grows up in the United States without understanding the importance of race in shaping people's lives."[8] The Bible provides examples of this experience also in observations about the poor and despised: "The poor man's wisdom is despised and his words are not heard" (Eccles. 9:16); "Those who are well have no need of a physician, but those who are sick. I [Jesus] have not come to call the righteous but sinners to repentance" (Luke 5:31–32). Moreover, in a good deal of the history recorded in the Bible, the Jews lived comparatively "at the margin" of great imperial powers, such as Egypt, Assyria, Babylon, and Rome.

Scientific Sociology

So what is sociology?[9] The "sociological perspective" claims to offer a distinctive way of thinking about and analyzing society and social relations. But is this analysis

---

[7] Ibid., 5.
[8] Ibid., 6.
[9] For more interaction with sociology from a Christian point of view, see David Lyon, *Christians and Sociology: To the Challenge of Sociology—a Christian Response* (Downers Grove, IL: InterVarsity, 1976); Russell Heddendorf and Matthew Vos, *Hidden Threads: A Christian Critique of Sociological Theory* (Lanham, MD: University Press of America, 2010).

really distinctive to modern sociology, or has it characterized many reflections about society and culture throughout history? Is sociology just another label for reflecting self-consciously about social relations? We could say that sociology is whatever is taught in sociology classes and what is practiced under the label of "sociological research." But that does not succeed in telling us what is truly distinctive about it.

I think there *is* something distinctive about modern sociology. But what is it? That is not so easy to say, and a textbook introduction to sociology can easily gloss over the question.

Transcendence through a Sociological Perspective

In many situations new perspectives help us to see things that previously escaped notice.[10] We understandably become excited with what we are discovering. We wonder how it could have escaped us so long, and we give credit to the perspective. The same is true for a sociological perspective. It offers us genuine benefits and insights. Many people raised in monocultural situations have never asked themselves questions about society. And even those exposed to multiple cultures may not ask deeper questions about the functions of social interaction and culture.

Asking questions about society means standing back from the immediacy of our circumstances, and the immediacy of our immersion in mundane action. The book of Proverbs provides an example. So the practice of standing back is not unique to modern sociology. It is nevertheless one feature.

In standing back, we exercise *transcendence*. We survey the field of human life. This human ability for transcendence imitates divine transcendence (chap. 11). But then it is influenced by whether we are wanting to be a god, self-sufficient in our knowledge, or we acknowledge our dependence on the ultimate transcendence of God. Religious influence, based on our communion with God or our rebellion against him, affects the operation of our transcendence. It also affects the operation of transcendence by way of our conception of the rules or regularities observed in society. Do these regularities depend on God and manifest God's character, or are they merely there as impersonal somethings (chap. 9)?

So the development of a sociological perspective has potential both to give insight from a kind of transcendence and to become an instrument in furthering our communion with God or our rebellion against God, as the case may be.

Critical Analysis

Sociological analysis can attract us for both good and bad reasons. It attracts us because it offers fresh insights, and that is good. It attracts us also, perhaps,

---

[10]On perspectives, see chaps. 4, 7, and Vern S. Poythress, *Symphonic Theology: The Validity of Multiple Perspectives in Theology* (Grand Rapids: Zondervan, 1987; repr., Phillipsburg, NJ: P&R, 2001).

because it offers transcendence that promises *superiority* of a certain kind. At the end of the analysis we have ideas about society that make us feel superior to the blundering, unselfconscious participant. We have become critically aware of social influences, whereas the ordinary participant just drifts along in subjection to the influences.

Alternatives to Modern Sociology

Critical awareness is a popular and sometimes a heady acquisition. It has its value as a perspective, just as we have affirmed the value of many other perspectives. But sociology does not always discuss as critically as it might the very decisions that lead to modern sociology. If one of the characteristics of sociology is to have some critical awareness, critical awareness can apply to sociology itself.

For example, we can ask ourselves whether social analysis might proceed in other ways besides what is offered to us in a typical form of modern sociology. Why this way rather than another way?

To its credit, Macionis's textbook raises this same question indirectly by expounding not one but three different approaches to sociological theory, and three ways in which people do sociology.[11] We want to look at these approaches a little later. But the same question about foundational choices arises even earlier, in Macionis's account of the origin of sociology with Auguste Comte.

As noted earlier, Auguste Comte first introduced the term *sociology* in 1838. Comte claimed that thinking about society passed through three historical stages. In the first stage, the *theological*, "people took a religious view that society expressed God's will."[12] According to Comte, this view prevailed until the end of the Middle Ages in about AD 1350. In the second stage, the *metaphysical* stage, "people saw society as a natural rather than a supernatural system."[13] The final, third stage was the *scientific* stage, in which the scientific approach to physics and the natural world was applied to society. Comte "believed that society operates according to its own laws, much as the physical world operates according to gravity and other laws of nature."[14] According to this account, sociology is distinct from everything that came before in that it is *scientific*.

Macionis's textbook is intent on summarizing Comte's thought briefly and in merely descriptive fashion. So he does not raise all the questions that might be raised. But we will go ahead and raise the critical question: Why is a scientific approach superior to the theological and the metaphysical? If sociology is to be

---

[11]Macionis, *Sociology*, 14–21, 33–39.
[12]Ibid., 14.
[13]Ibid.
[14]Ibid.

established on a sound basis, this question asks to be debated. The historical fact that one approach has taken over from another does not imply by itself the superiority of the later approach.

We have the modern idea of progress to assist us. We live in a society where science has prestige, where the later development of an idea is typically assumed to be superior to the earlier, and where respect for the prestige of a long-standing academic subject tells us that the founders of the subject must have had good reasons for preferring their choices. The result, unfortunately, may be to lead the unthinking reader merely to accept the status quo for modern sociology. Instead of engaging in critical analysis of the sociological forces at work in the founding of sociology, the reader just accepts the prestige of the academic tradition. Accepting this prestige unthinkingly is all the more delightful because, as we observed, it offers the student superiority to the ordinary individual.

We may focus particularly on what is called the theological stage. In this stage, according to the textbook summary, "people took a religious view that society expressed God's will."[15] Actually, Comte's thought on this point is complex. But a simple summary like this one makes it easy for a student to dismiss a theological approach as antiquated and simplistic. Such a dismissal, however, depends on caricaturing theology.

Let us see how. The textbook summary talks about "God's will." Does it have in mind God's decretive will or his preceptive will (chap. 5)? The decretive will of God expresses his plan for whatever will happen. If this will is what the textbook summary has in mind, it may make it sound as if an appeal to God's will eliminates all study of society. It suggests that the religious person says, "God has ordained it," and thus there can be no more discussion or reflection.

Such an understanding is a caricature. Actually, God's decretive will is compatible with secondary causes operating within the created world. Human actions have consequences, including social consequences. The book of Proverbs in fact contains *both* observations about God's sovereignty over social life *and* observations about secondary causes. Some verses indicate that God is primary cause:

> Commit your work to the LORD,
>   and your plans will be established. (Prov. 16:3)

Elsewhere in Proverbs human beings function as secondary causes:

> Iron sharpens iron,
>   and one man sharpens another. (Prov. 27:17)

---

[15] Ibid.

Whoever tends a fig tree will eat its fruit,
 and he who guards his master will be honored. (Prov. 27:18)

Like an archer who wounds everyone
 is one who hires a passing fool or drunkard. (Prov. 26:10)

Proverbs is full of such observations of life. Saying that God ordains the order of society does not end reflection but in the book of Proverbs is a beginning for reflection on the details and many dimensions of that order.

The summary about "God's will" given in the sociology textbook could also have in mind God's preceptive will, his moral will (instead of his decretive will). It would then mean that people thought they were merely supposed to submit to the existing social order because it was the moral will of God, and nothing was supposed to change. Indeed, religion has sometimes been perversely used to stifle dissent and to excuse oppression. But that is quite contrary to what the Bible offers. The Old Testament prophets, Jesus, and the apostle Paul had critical things to say about some existing social practices and some aspects of the status quo. They exhorted people to follow God's precepts, which were not at all identical to the status quo.

The summary of the "theological stage" can lead quickly to dismissing the stage. But the dismissal takes place by means of an impoverished conception of what it would mean to look at society theologically. My own reflections within this book offer one example of such an approach. Such an approach is not confined to looking at the book of Proverbs or at the Bible's direct teaching about society. The Bible's instruction should give us a foundation. But then we can go out and make observations about our own society and those around us, as Proverbs indirectly encourages us to do. We could include quantitative, statistical analysis of data as well. Nothing prohibits this kind of integration of a theological framework with careful attention to detail.

APPENDIX C

"Scientific" Sociology

Can papyrus grow where there is no marsh?
Can reeds flourish where there is no water?

—Bildad the Shuhite, in Job 8:11

Wₑ can approach the issues of modern sociology in another way by asking what it means for a discipline to be "scientific."

What Is "Scientific"?

Macionis's textbook account indicates that Auguste Comte's approach, called positivism, involved an oversimple parallelism with natural sciences: "We [sociologists] now realize that human behavior is far more complex than the movement of planets or even the actions of other living things. We are creatures of imagination and spontaneity, so human behavior can never fully be explained by rigid 'laws of society.'"[1] So Comte's attempt to distinguish modern sociology on the basis of a clear delineation of its "scientific" character sounds like a failure. Yet, Macionis says, "Most sociologists still consider science a crucial part of sociology."[2] In what way?

Ways of Doing Sociology

Macionis's textbook explains "three ways to do sociology." These are (1) "scientific sociology," which relies heavily on quantifiable and reproducible measure-

---

[1]John J. Macionis, *Sociology*, 11th ed. (Upper Saddle River, NJ: Prentice Hall, 2007), 14.
[2]Ibid.

ment, often based on statistics and statistical analysis; (2) "interpretive sociology," which endeavors to focus on the human meaning of social activities—here the researcher exercises empathy with people and how they understand their activities; and (3) "critical sociology," which endeavors to highlight the injustices and inequities in a society and to suggest or implement changes.[3] A fourth way that Macionis does not mention, namely, postmodernist critical analysis, will receive our attention later (appendix G). There are also combinations of approaches, and variations within the approaches.[4] A detailed consideration of variations would lead us into a great deal of complexity. It is best for us to make some general points using Macionis's simplified classification into three approaches.

So let us consider these three approaches one at a time. Of these three approaches, only the first has the clear aspiration to be "scientific" and "objective." But when we analyze its ideas, numerous difficulties come into view.

First, the decision to focus on what is quantifiable is selective about the objects of research. The object is no longer really society, or social relationships, or social institutions, or social behavior, but *only* those aspects of society that are quantifiable. Who knows beforehand what crucial insights we are leaving out, insights that might come from nonquantifiable aspects? Given what we naively know about human beings, quantifiable aspects cannot be expected to plumb the depths of what we typically find most fascinating, most mysterious, or most revealing about what it means to be a person.

Suppose, for example, that we undertake a quantitative analysis of a father and a son working to solve a jigsaw puzzle. We may measure the speed at which a father and a son complete the puzzle. That is quantifiable. But we ignore their social interaction because it is not quantifiable. Or perhaps we draw up a questionnaire about jigsaw puzzles and give it to a large number of people. We can get quantitative results if we ask yes-or-no questions or multiple-choice questions, but a lot will depend on just what questions we ask. The results will be insightful only if the questions are insightful. And we may doubt whether any stereotyped series of questions will reveal much about the special feelings shared by one father-and-son team. The discipline of "scientific sociology" appears to condemn itself at the outset to being one-sided and limiting. Or else it will be question begging if it postulates that it can tightly correlate some interesting feature like talent to some quantifiable variable like a test score.

---

[3]Ibid., 33–39.
[4]For an introduction to some of the complexities, see Russell Heddendorf and Matthew Vos, *Hidden Threads: A Christian Critique of Sociological Theory* (Lanham, MD: University Press of America, 2010).

The Challenge of Spurious Correlations

Second, even if we restrict ourselves to quantifiable observations, there are still too many possible ways to interpret the quantities. We need to explain this difficulty.

The usual procedure in "scientific sociology" uses statistical data and statistical correlations. Macionis's textbook provides an example. Statistical comparison shows a numerical correlation between the housing density of young people's living situations and delinquency rates. The denser the housing, the higher the delinquency.[5] The analyst can then be tempted to conclude that dense living conditions *cause* delinquency (or are at least a significant causal factor in it).

But the conclusion does not follow. Macionis explains that further research shows that income level has an influence. *Both* housing density and delinquency vary with income level. If we return to the statistics and look only at the statistics for a single level of income, the correlation between housing density and delinquency rate disappears. Hence, there is no direct causal relation between crowded housing and delinquency. Rather, both are dependent on level of income. The correlation between the two was, in Macionis's terms, a "spurious correlation."[6]

So far so good. But we can ask a further question, which goes beyond what Macionis's textbook presents. Since income level correlates with both housing density and delinquency, can we conclude that differences in income *cause* differences in housing density and delinquency? One of the diagrams in Macionis's textbook suggests that it does.[7] But the same pattern of reasoning shows that we cannot draw this conclusion. The relation between *all three* may be spurious.

To find out whether the correlations are spurious, we have to look for the possibility of still *other* causative factors. What factors might be involved that affect both income level and delinquency? What about whether a household has a father as well as a mother who is present for the family and who is responsible? Such a father will probably be earning income, supplementing a mother's income, and the joint income of the household will be higher. Might the presence of a responsible father also discourage delinquency of his son or daughter? Can delinquency arise in a rich household with a workaholic father who pays no attention to his children? The presence of a responsible father may conceivably have an influence that overrides the factor of income. Thus, the observed correlation

---

[5]Ibid., 36.
[6]Ibid.
[7]Ibid., figure 2-1 (d): "This finding leads us to conclude that income level is a *cause* of both density of living conditions and delinquency rate" (italics mine).

between income and delinquency might be "spurious," because another causal factor, the presence or absence of a father, is affecting both statistics.

And how do we know whether the presence of a responsible father is also a spurious correlation? What other factors might be behind that?

People who set up statistical research have to choose which features to look at. Each feature, when converted into a quantity, becomes a mathematical "variable." There are innumerable variables, because there are innumerable ways of classifying human beings (chap. 26). Researchers do not have the time to investigate in detail every possible classificational feature. So how do they decide? They have to have some prior sense of what features might most plausibly be causal factors. Nonquantitative human understanding is at the back of their judgment. We know from long experience that loving fathers help children to grow into responsible citizens. And the Bible confirms it.

Consider now the statistical correlation between income and housing density. Is this causal? Or is it too a "spurious correlation"? And how do we know? At this point a sociologist might think that he can safely terminate his research questions. He knows that people with higher incomes seek more comfortable housing based on those incomes. But how does he know that this is a causal relationship? He knows because he has broader, nonquantitative knowledge of how he himself and others tend to treat income. They understand its value for spending and do not merely hoard it. But in a hypothetical society filled with hoarders, there might theoretically be no correlation between income and housing. So the correlation with income turns out not to be a real cause. The real cause lies in people's desires and in their understandings of the possible human significances of income.

Some people are committed in principle to a "simple lifestyle." No matter how much income they have, on top of a bare minimum, they might choose to live in the same housing. Their desires and attitudes, not income in and of itself, turn out to be the real cause of their housing choices.

Racial or cultural discrimination in housing may also be a factor. If landlords consistently reject tenants from one ethnic group, or sellers reject buyers from that group, members of the group may end up in poorer housing not related to their incomes.

Of course when we claim that income is a cause of housing density, we need not be claiming that it is the *only* cause. Other factors may enter. The difficulty is that these other factors might actually show that the correlation with income is a spurious correlation.

Statistical correlations *may* suggest an underlying causal relation. But it seems that they can never establish it. We cannot succeed in eliminating the possibility that other, deeper factors might be the actual causes.

Falsifying Causal Hypotheses

On the other hand, might statistics at least *falsify* some causal hypotheses? If statistics cannot *establish* a cause, at least they might be able to refute a false idea of cause. For example, the inclusion of statistics about income level refutes the hypothesis that crowded housing contributes to delinquency.

But here again we need to think critically and ask ourselves whether this kind of reasoning has flaws. When income level is brought into the equation, the correlation between crowding and delinquency does indeed disappear. But how do we know whether the *disappearance* of correlation is itself spurious? Perhaps something about income level is interfering and masking what in many circumstances still *is* a causal relation between housing and delinquency. Perhaps crowded housing *does* tempt teenagers to delinquency (for example, they are more irritated by the close quarters and more likely to rebel against their elders). And perhaps some other factor is working in the reverse direction, making the causal relation statistically invisible.

The statistical test demands that we reanalyze the statistics after we "control for income." That is, we look only at one level of income at a time. For each level of income, we then examine which families *within that level* are in more crowded housing. This procedure might seem to eliminate other factors, but it does not, at least not completely.

Using nonquantitative reasoning, let us ask ourselves why families with the same income might select different levels of housing. Why does not each family with the same income choose about the same level of housing? Various other factors might be at work. One factor might be ethnic discrimination in housing offers. Another factor might be desire to be with a certain kind of people—artists in Greenwich Village, or Ukrainians in a Ukrainian area in the city. One family may have a principled commitment to a "simple lifestyle." Another family might perceive spiritual values as more important than material and want to give more to charity. Another family may want to save more for the future (college education of the children, for example). Or they may be using money for children's tuition to a Christian school. Another family might choose crowded housing in an area with a better school system, in preference to less crowded housing in an area with poor schools. Any of these other factors might possibly be causative, pushing the rate of delinquency down.

But even if there are other causative factors, would these factors exactly balance the causative factor of crowded housing (if it is a causative factor)? Statistics might still be able to detect a small correlation. But a small correlation may well be a statistical artifact of imperfect sampling. Statisticians know that they cannot show that a small correlation is "statistically significant." And suppose the correlation goes the other way? Suppose there turns out to be a negative correlation between crowded housing and delinquency? That negative correlation could indicate, not that crowded housing causatively inhibits delinquency, but that other factors, like the family principles for use of income, have suppressed the amount of delinquency more than crowded housing increases it.

Intuitions

If the statistics do turn out with correlations in a counterintuitive direction, some researchers will be tempted to ignore them or consider them a statistical fluke. By contrast, correlations that confirm our intuitions are likely to be attended to. In both cases, we are influenced by nonquantitative personal impressions as to what induces people to do what they do.

There are still other possibilities. Maybe crowded housing contributes to delinquency only in some situations. Maybe it creates more opportunity for anger and irritation that can lead to rebellion. But maybe some kinds of families (with certain religious or ethical or financial principles) have resources that enable them to defuse anger. Irritating circumstances become an occasion for exercising love, which binds the family together and heads off the otherwise destructive paths for anger.

As in other cases, so here, there are a large number of variables. Many of these might be difficult to quantify adequately. The presence or absence of quantitative statistical correlations establishes nothing by itself. It must be interpreted, and it is always going to be interpreted against the background of broader ideas about what makes people function.[8]

Difficulties in Achieving "Scientific Rigor" with Multiple Variables

Scientific sociology would have liked to imitate the rigorous experimental procedures of physical science. In physical science, the researcher may set up an experimental environment in the laboratory in which he tries to control all variables except a single one. He can then see the effects of that one variable and be confident that he is not seeing interference from other factors. Sociological research, on the other hand, researches people, and they cannot be controlled in the same way.[9] Hence, there is a much larger possibility that other variables, not under the inspection of the researcher, are influencing outcomes.

---

[8]See Macionis, *Sociology*, 36–37.

[9]Ibid., 36. In some cases sociologists can set up special experimental situations. Macionis provides interesting examples with the "Stanford County Prison" (ibid., 43) and Solomon Asch's and Stanley Milgram's researches on group conformity (ibid., 171–72). But such opportunities are limited, because not all aspects of society can be shoehorned into a laboratory environment.

Moreover, close inspection of these experimental cases shows that they have some artificial dimensions. In the Stanford County Prison experiment, Philip Zimbardo set up a prison-like

We might compare the difficulties to the situation with medical research on allergies and autoimmune diseases. Modern medicine has achieved impressive success in understanding invasive, infectious diseases and in devising cures. This kind of disease is usually due to a single agent, a bacterium or virus or parasite. Single-agent causation makes the cause of disease easier to track down. And once the agent is identified, medical research can look for weak points to attack in order to destroy or disable the agent.

Allergies may also arise from a single agent, an allergen. But the immune system of a human being is a holistic system, with interacting parts, and reaction to one threat tends to put the entire system on the alert for all kinds of threats in other directions. The immune system can "overreact," and we can see one of the effects when a person's whole body breaks out in a rash because of a reaction to an allergen contacted at only one point.

Likewise, may we suggest that understanding people in their social relationships involves the interaction of multiple aspects? For one thing, the body affects the whole person. A person who is tired or sleepy may react inconsiderately. A person who is depressed or angry about some one aspect of his life may prove less capable of giving gracious responses in other areas. Abject poverty can "grind people down," in nutrition as well as in hopelessness, so that they are listless even when an opportunity arises to pull themselves out of their situation. Religious views also have their effects. Nurses can tell of patients whose religious faith gives them confidence and good spirits even when facing death. On the other side, a fatalistic religious view may paralyze a person by making him feel that nothing

----

environment in the basement of the psychology building of Standard University. He recruited volunteers and divided them into two groups, "guards" and "prisoners." The situation went from there. In this case, all the volunteers knew that their situation was a mock situation. We cannot easily tell what influence this knowledge had on their behavior.

Asch's and Milgram's research set up experimental situations where volunteers were told that the focus of research was on visual perception (Asch) or on the relation of punishment to learning (Milgram). The actual research focused on the volunteers' actions, and the influence of peers or authorities on them. The volunteers did not realize that others around them were accomplices for the true experimental setup. The essential artificiality in these setups lay in the fact that the research directors lied and the accomplices practiced duplicity. Of course all of us have to deal with the possibility of lying and duplicity in real life. But a professional experimental situation puts volunteers off guard, so to speak. They see no reason in the context to suspect a lie. Precisely because of the prestige of science, including its ethical dimensions that demand truth in experimental reporting, the volunteers are more easily lulled to sleep than they would be even by a normal authority figure. The volunteers also assume that the same high ethics governs the other participants, whom they therefore assume are volunteers rather than accomplices.

In all these cases the research depended substantively on artificial factors that do not match normal life experience. These artificialities cannot be "controlled" for *within* the experiment, by turning them on and off while leaving everything else the same. Hence, they affect the results in uncontrollable ways.

he does can make a difference. Finally, sin in the heart affects a person's social relationships. It is a whole person who acts and responds. Many aspects interact. We cannot produce a second person who is a carbon copy of the first person except for a change in one variable.

Motives for Giving Preference to Science

We may reflect on the motives that have encouraged people to seek a "scientific" sociology in spite of difficulties. Some positive motives are obvious. Hard sciences like physics, chemistry, and astronomy have displayed impressive rigor, and over time their progress becomes plain to all. It is natural to see whether, by imitating methods characteristic of hard sciences, we might achieve similar positive results in studying society. Only after we try does it become clearer that human beings, especially in their social relationships, display intractable complexities, and that an attempt to force social relationships into the one-dimensional pattern of studies in hard science can artificially restrict what we consider relevant.

More problematic motivations can also arise. For many people, modern science seems to offer a way to knowledge independent of religion and independent of God. Auguste Comte's idea that the theological stage is now over comes as a relief. The sense of relief may arise partly from the way in which religion—including Christian religion—has too often been used by the powerful to suppress dissent, to protect their power, and to keep "in their place" people under them who are feeling boxed in by rules that are falsely alleged to have God's moral approval. But it is good to remember that atheist ideology is also capable of boxing people in, or even slaughtering them wholesale,[10] through rules that are falsely alleged to be for the benefit of humanity.

One concealed motive that we do not want to admit is the motive of flight from God. Since the fall we have been rebels against God (chap. 13), and we do not want him to interfere. This desire expresses itself in the natural sciences when scientists form an idea of scientific law that is independent of a personal God instead of an expression of his character.[11] Since natural sciences have led the way in this move, social sciences can follow in the trail already blazed.

In a way these trails have come to seem natural because they are common in modern life. And they seem to many people to offer a way of moving beyond controversies in religion. But, as I see it, they avoid the older controversies only by making false assumptions about the irrelevance of God to their subject.

---

[10] I am thinking of the massive loss of life in the Stalinist Soviet Union and Maoist China (chap. 25).

[11] See Vern S. Poythress, *Redeeming Science: A God-Centered Approach* (Wheaton, IL: Crossway, 2006).

Leaving God out in thinking about people has a further consequence. We can also leave out sin. We then use social research about people to reassure ourselves that the problem with human beings is of some other kind.

Scientific sociology would say that it wants to be "objective" and not be influenced by the personal views of the scientist.[12] But no investigation of the world can operate without some idea of what kind of regularities it might expect—in this case, regularities in social life. Social order is regularity, and that regularity is ordained by God and manifests God (chap. 9). So escape from God is an illusion. Moreover, if we do not see sins and their effects for what they are, we will see them as something else. And that falsifies our account.

Scientific sociology tries to escape by the same route that natural science has tried to escape, namely, by replacing divinely ordained regularity with impersonal, mechanical regularity—regularity that is just "there" without further explanation. That replacement, as we observed (chap. 9), is a form of idolatry, substituting a false god for the true one. In this case, the false god or God-substitute is social regularity conceived of as impersonal. This act of replacement is neither neutral nor objective. It is not neutral because it takes a religious stand against the true God. It is not objective because it determines at the beginning to distort what it studies, namely, the regularities. It also distorts social relationships by excising God as a person in relationship with us, and by excising from our human relationships the presence of God. Finally, it distorts sin by seeing it merely as a disorder of some kind and not a violation of God's moral standards.

This kind of sociology is nevertheless attractive. It seems to promise not only intellectual independence from God in our thinking, but also practical independence from God in our social life and its transformation. This book is written partly to disillusion those who think they will escape God in such a way. They are not escaping but simply perpetuating an age-old rebellion described in Romans 1:18–25.

A Biblically Based Alternative

From a biblically based point of view, there is nothing wrong with quantitative statistical research on human beings. God has ordained the quantitative aspect of our world. Moreover, quantitative research can sometimes suggest directions in which to ask more questions about why people do what they do. But any quantitative data are interpreted in a larger context. The context includes what we think people are and what we think are reasonable motivations to expect. The context includes God himself, who enters into social relations with us, who ordains the regularities of human social life, and who sustains social life by his presence with us. And it includes the fact that human beings mistreat others. They sin.

---

[12]Macionis, *Sociology*, 37.

APPENDIX D

Empathetic Sociologies

When he saw the crowds, he had compassion for them, because they
were harassed and helpless, like sheep without a shepherd.

—Matthew 9:36

I n addition to "scientific" sociology, Macionis's textbook describes two other
major sociological approaches: *interpretive sociology* and *critical sociology*.[1]

Interpretive Sociology

Macionis's introductory description of interpretive sociology helps to capture
its distinctiveness:

> Scientific sociology focuses on actions, what people do; interpretive sociology, by
> contrast, focuses on the meaning people attach to their actions. Second, scientific
> sociology sees an objective reality "out there," but interpretive sociology sees real-
> ity constructed by people themselves in the course of their everyday lives. Third,
> scientific sociology tends to favor *quantitative* data—numerical measurements
> of people's behavior—and interpretive sociology favors *qualitative* data, or how
> people understand their surroundings.[2]

The human meanings in interpretive sociology are not quantifiable. A good
deal depends on the empathy of the sociologist rather than on some mechanically

---

[1]John J. Macionis, *Sociology*, 11th ed. (Upper Saddle River, NJ: Prentice Hall, 2007), 38–39.
[2]Ibid., 38.

reproducible technique. It then becomes hard to distinguish such an approach from the observations in Proverbs, particularly observations that display acuteness (think of the description of the young man falling victim to the lure of an adulteress, Prov. 7:6–27).

So can interpretive sociology be scientific? It depends on how expansive a term *scientific* becomes. Certainly an interpretive approach can still exercise care. A researcher can observe and interact with a large number of participants in culture, rather than only one or two. He or she can keep detailed records of observations and interviews. He can try to be aware of his own biases. He can try to ask questions that probe many dimensions of human life. He can interact with previous research done on the same or analogous social groups. But might not the same be said of serious research in many areas of humanities, including theology? Interpretive sociology can be considered an academic discipline, but the word *scientific* is not an apt word if it suggests, as it will to many people, a special affinity to natural science as opposed to the humanities.

"Scientific sociology" aspires to objectivity, an objectivity that becomes most rigorous when it focuses on quantitative data. It aspires to be free from and independent of the personal commitments of the researcher, that is, moral commitments, political commitments, personal preferences, and personal meanings imported by the researcher. All of these more personal dimensions are more freely embraced by interpretive sociologists, because they know that only by bringing in personal meaning and moral evaluation do they make themselves able to discuss directly some of the issues that most interest us about people.

But if a researcher includes his personal meanings in his research, he himself is an inextricable part of his research. That is the price that is paid. And the personal meaning, more obviously than the quantitative data, includes the influence of his relation to God, because God ordains the personal meanings. Who the researcher thinks God is may have a subtle influence on who he thinks other people are. Or, better put, every sociological analyst relies on God or gods or impersonal substitutes for gods. The "laws" or regularities of social action are transcendent over the particulars of the action. Depending on whether the laws are from God or gods or are impersonal, the sociologist will tend to analyze other people as like God or like his gods or impersonal. But he may still be inconsistent and is even *likely* to be inconsistent, given what the Bible tells us about fallen human nature.

Critical Sociology

A third approach to sociology, *critical sociology*, commits itself to critique and to change. This approach clearly displays a tension with the approach of "scientific sociology," which aspires to exercise moral neutrality. Scientific sociology will worry that critical sociology has compromised objectivity by mixing evaluation with description.

Moral evaluation does raise questions about our moral foundations. Where does the sociologist derive the standard by which he judges what is unjust, what is inequitable, and what changes would be healthy (chap. 27)? Moral standards go back to God. God has implanted a sense of right and wrong in each of us, so that even if we cease to be in communion with God, we continue to evaluate situations as just or unjust. But our evaluation can be distorted by sin. Plato and Aristotle evaluated society but did not see slavery as wrong. Neither did the Greek society around them (at least if we query the citizens, not the slaves!). We see slavery as wrong, but why? Is that just our individual or social preference? Are we merely a product of our social upbringing, just as Plato and Aristotle were?

Most sociological study happens to take place in academic settings within Western cultures or within settings heavily influenced by Western cultures. Within these settings, the desire for human equality is strong. The discussion will tend to be influenced by egalitarian thinking.[3] But that influence could be dismissed as merely a local Western phenomenon. Is the West morally superior? If social standards are merely derived by looking at the opinion of the majority in a society, then all we will find is that standards vary with the society. What kind of absolute moral claims remain? If sociology evades the issue of absolute morality, no basis is left for evaluating a society from outside as good or evil at a particular point, except by using the standards of some *other* society.[4] And who is to say that the moral standards of one society are purer than those of another? The basis for critique and change is radically undercut.

Confronting Evil

Sociology confronts fundamental moral issues in a painful way when it brings us face-to-face with the breadth and magnitude of people's sufferings. We can read heartrending accounts of poverty, cruelty, and prejudice even within the United States. Moving to a global perspective introduces statistics about millions of people who starve or are on the verge of starvation, people with no health

---

[3]On egalitarianism, see chap. 27. We may use Macionis's textbook *Sociology* as an example of the tendency. Most of the time the textbook is descriptive, but the selection of topics and subtle remarks gently push readers in the direction of affirming the egalitarian ideology characteristic of much of the academic world. For example, the textbook asserts that patriarchy is one of the "negative aspects of family life" (475).

[4]Of course we could also undertake to evaluate a society according to its own standards and accuse it of being inconsistent. But in such a case, we still remain stuck with the question of which is better, the official standards or the actual social behavior. Nothing in the society gives us a transcendent basis for deciding in favor of one rather than the other.

care, people under oppressive governments.[5] A sensitive heart veritably screams protests. We instinctively ask big questions. What remedy can there be? What are we supposed to *do*? At a point like this, we do have to be reminded not *just* to overflow with emotion or with protest. It is fitting that we study and do not merely react emotionally. Precisely because the situation is so desperate, we want to understand it rather than act precipitously.

But how do we understand moral horror? First, do we really know what it is? Most of sociology has cut itself off from God, and without God it cannot adequately tell us the depth of this horror. If all of the universe is merely the product of chance, and life and human nature are the product of blind chance, and God is nowhere to be found, are we seeing merely molecules in motion? Is our own moral indignation merely a figment, an aberrant evolutionary product of a one-time useful warning to help selfish genes survive?

Sociology poses the problem in another form if it claims that our moral indignation is merely the product of socialization into our particular society. Our particular society has taught us to be indignant about starvation, but if we had been raised in a xenophobic society, we would see nothing wrong about the starvation of hated foreigners.

Beyond a certain point the practice of mere description, which is the principal voice of scientific sociology and interpretive sociology, no longer satisfies. That voice has insights, yes. But descriptive language does not address the issue of morality as an absolute, rather than as personal or social preference. If we do choose to address morality as absolute, we run into difficulties because, partly for social reasons, people in different societies, and sometimes people within the same larger society, do not agree about what are the absolutes.

In part, sociologists may just be acknowledging the reality. People in the various societies of the world do not agree, and sociology by design avoids taking a stand in any area on which evaluations disagree.

In a way this self-limitation on the part of sociology is understandable. But it leads to more questions. Absolute morality, if it really exists, is surely an essential component of what it means to be human. And it affects us socially as well as individually. The disagreements over moral absolutes are also of great importance, partly because they can lead to painful clashes between parties who disagree. Sociology is indeed concerned about descriptive analyses of such things. But if it decides to remain on the level of description, it misses something essential about humanity, namely, the existence of the absolute and the explanation for why societies and individuals nevertheless deviate from the absolute. In biblical

---

[5] I might add still one more form of suffering to the list: millions live without saving knowledge of God in Christ. The fact that this kind of suffering gets left out of most lists today is part of the story of selective attention.

terms, we would say that sociology leaves out God, who is the source of moral absolutes, and sin, which is the source of disagreements. If sociology will not discuss these matters, its account of humanity is necessarily truncated.

It would not be so bad if everyone admitted the truncation. But the prestige of "science" can hover around sociology and give people the idea that sociology—possibly along with other social sciences—can give us the ultimate or "deep" account of what human beings are.

Let us put it another way. Lack of discussion of some questions, namely, moral absolutes and the ultimate source of disagreements about them, can easily be understood as implying the lack of relevance of these questions to understanding humanity and its sufferings. Sociology is then alleged to imply that whatever difficulties we have are social, not due to sin; and their remedy must be social, not divine.

Critical sociology at this point differs from the other sociological approaches. It does have an answer, namely, that our moral indignation is proper. But it has no explanation for why it is proper (remember, this indignation may still be a product of socialization) or for how we know when our own indignation has gone astray, as it did in the products of communist revolutions. In fairness, I should observe that good intentions can go astray anywhere, including within organized religion. Those who ran the Inquisition possessed what they thought were good intentions. They wanted to protect people from the soul-destroying effects of heresy. But they perpetrated terrible injustices.

> The heart is deceitful above all things,
>   and desperately sick;
>   who can understand it? (Jer. 17:9)

Let us face it: moral horror is horror because it is horror first of all to the holiness of God and second to the human heart. But we are sick at heart. The horror of human suffering should turn our screams in desperation to God. The more we see of sins and their effects, the more desperate we should be for God's healing, because we cannot heal ourselves. But even in distress our hearts can be hard. Some of us will turn elsewhere, anywhere else besides God. We will turn to one more proposed human remedy. That remedy, of course, will be one more alternative to the Bible's teaching about the way of salvation. But it should be clear that neutrality in religion is an illusion. People who propose a moral remedy are tacitly proposing a "way of salvation" even when they think there is no God and no sin.

The difficulty here for a secularized sociology is that it cannot remain genuinely neutral. If it disclaims to have a moral voice, it shows itself to be artificial—it is "scientific" at the cost of being less than human. Or if it claims to have a moral voice, it will offer a humanist-based way of salvation. In this latter case, sin is redefined, perhaps as the capitalist structure for the means of production, and humanity is redefined to conform to the new conception of sin.

Or a sociologist might leave it up to the reader to undertake moral evaluation. The reader may still have tacitly learned from the whole orientation of sociology that egalitarian ideology is the correct moral stance and that sin is nonexistent. The reader tacitly infers from reading sociology texts that if sin did exist, sociology would mention it because it would be a part of the human condition. Since it is not mentioned, one infers that sin does not exist. Therefore, the problems with humanity are of another kind, and sociological and political and economic reforms are the only possible remedy. But down that route lies the wreckage of countless unintended consequences, because the plans of the reformers are no longer reckoning with the reality of sin and the depth of the difficulty it poses. At the end stands a warning sign with the maxim, "Extreme moral passion minus reality equals mass death."[6] If, as some sociobiologists suspect, violence is endemic to human nature, there is no remedy.

Biblically Informed Empathetic Sociology

I believe there is a remedy, but God, not man, is the author. That does not mean that we as human beings can do nothing. Within the context where we come to know God and are reconciled to him, the Bible says, "Love your neighbor as yourself" and makes it plain that love leads to action.

Action includes intellectual action, that is, reflection. Reflection on society and on social relations can develop in a way that is informed by a biblical worldview. I have tried to make a beginning in this book. We do have an absolute moral standard in God. The Bible also shows how subjective moral evaluations arise from human hearts made in the image of God but corrupted by sin. The Bible also shows the social transmission of sin. By teaching us God's standards, the Bible gives us a transcendent basis for social criticism and social transformation, rather than leaving us with the merely immanent moral preferences that are typical of much secularist, humanist critical sociology.

We can be indignant and cry out to God in our indignation without being swept away by grandiose conceptions of our own righteousness and our own autonomous ability to set things right. We can begin to love God, and out of the love he shows us we can begin to love our neighbors as ourselves. God's instruction in the Bible, combined with his work to transform us, can be the foundation for a biblically based "critical" approach to society.

---

[6] Jay W. Richards, *Money, Greed, and God: Why Capitalism Is the Solution and Not the Problem* (New York: HarperCollins, 2009), 21.

We can also respond to interpretive sociology. The Bible shows that unity and diversity in human nature have their ultimate basis in unity and diversity in the divine nature, that is, the Trinitarian character of God. That unity and diversity lead to the unity and diversity in contrastive-identificational features, variation, and distribution in the understanding of human action (chap. 18). Human action is purposeful, meaningful action, in imitation of God's meanings and purposes in his actions.

This meaning lays the foundation for empathetic interpretive sociology. God's comprehensive knowledge is the foundation for our derivative knowledge as human beings. Because God created man in his image, we have the prospect of genuinely understanding someone else's meanings, and even the meanings of a culture other than our own. At the same time, the diversity of societies and the diversity among analysts of society make us expect that different analyses will show the diversity of the differences of perspective of the different analysts, even if all the analyses are true and insightful. This kind of interpretation is not monocultural, monochromatic, or monolithic, and the attempt to crush diversity in favor of unity misunderstands the natural diversity in the human beings who do the analysis.

Sociological Models

The one who states his case first seems right,
until the other comes and examines him.

—Proverbs 18:17

In an early chapter Macionis's classic textbook sets forth three approaches to sociological theory that are loosely connected to the three methods we have discussed in earlier appendices. These are the *structural-functional* approach, which stands closer to scientific sociology; the *social-conflict* approach, with affinities to critical sociology; and the *symbolic-interaction* approach, with affinities to interpretive sociology.[1] A more fine-grained analysis would recognize combinations and variations in these approaches.[2] We will concentrate only on the three main approaches, leaving aside many of the complexities.

The Structural-Functional Approach

Macionis summarizes the nature of the structural-functional approach: "The structural-functional approach is *a framework for building theory that sees society as a complex system whose parts work together to promote solidarity and stability.*"[3]

---

[1]John J. Macionis, *Sociology*, 11th ed. (Upper Saddle River, NJ: Prentice Hall, 2007), 14–23, 39.
[2]See Russell Heddendorf and Matthew Vos, *Hidden Threads: A Christian Critique of Sociological Theory* (Lanham, MD: University Press of America, 2010), which mentions the *conflict functionalist theory* of Georg Simmel and Lewis Coser (80–81), the theme of Christian revolution in Jacques Ellul (88–90), exchange theory (111–27), and phenomenology and ethnomethodology (147–63), among others.
[3]Macionis, *Sociology*, 15.

Terms like *system, solidarity, stability,* and *structure* indicate that the structural-functional approach has the conviction that there *are* stabilities; there are regularities. It sends us back to our discussion of social regularities that reveal the God who authors them (chap. 9). Assumptions about God or a God-substitute are vital to the way this approach builds the particulars of its theories. If society "holds together" and shows stability, why is it so? Individual human beings show regular behavior, and some aspects of this behavior can be partially accounted for on the basis of biological and physiological regularities. But why do human beings acting together form cohesive organizations?

The structural-functional approach can postulate a distinct order of *social* regularity in addition to the regularities of individual behavior. This order includes the regular social behavior at a basketball game. But this distinct order remains merely a postulate, a projection, if society is not "real" but merely a chance collection of individuals who happen to be interacting. To postulate merely a mechanical order, an impersonal order, is to postulate something that seems like a convenient fiction. There is no social mechanism, as far as anyone can see, that would be a real entity analogous to the dome over a football field. Is the sociological analogue of a dome, in the form of a hypothesized social *order*, merely a projection of the need for order to "keep the rain out," the "rain" of chaos?

According to the Bible we do not merely "postulate" order, but receive from God instruction telling us that human beings are made in the image of God, and made with social relations to God and to fellow human beings already "built in" to who they are. That is a far different answer. God's order also includes a moral dimension. Sins exist, and they are morally reprehensible.

The impatient person may still ask, "Oh, but what difference does it make? Let's just go and study society." But it is not so simple, because our conceptions about what kind of order we are studying and what is "society" (including or excluding God as a person with whom we interact socially and personally) affect our study of society. Our moral evaluation is affected by whether we think morality is a real part of us as human beings in society. The structural-functional approach runs the danger of postulating a mechanical structure independent of God and thus supporting the illusion that God is absent or irrelevant in social life, and that life is amoral.

The Social-Conflict Approach

Macionis defines the social-conflict approach as *"a framework for building theory that sees society as an arena of inequality that generates conflict and change."*[4]

---

[4]Ibid., 17.

How do we evaluate the strengths and weaknesses of this approach? While the structural-functional approach stresses *stability*, the social-conflict approach stresses *conflict and change*. As we observed (chap. 28), both stability and conflict characterize a fallen human world. Sin causes conflict. God is in conflict with sin and evil. Stability characterizes the original creation of man, which has not been totally undone by the fall. Change also would have characterized the original created situation, because God designed that human beings would multiply and fill the earth and subdue it (Gen. 1:28).

Conflicts presuppose regularities for the way in which the conflicts take place. And the social-conflict approach need not deny it. In fact, at a practical level it cannot deny it, because any generalizations about conflict are generalizations that express regularities. Conflicts themselves form regular patterns, or we would not be able to analyze them and talk about them.

The social-conflict approach "sees society as an arena of inequality." Yes, it *is* an arena of inequality (chap. 27). But there are many kinds of inequality. And the social-conflict approach may too easily jump to the conclusion that all kinds of inequality are morally bad and that all kinds of inequality "generate conflict." God created the world good, and originally human beings were at peace with God and with one another. They were not in conflict. Conflict began with Satan and with the fall (chap. 13).

Conflicts have sin at their root, but they are of many kinds. For example, human beings are not equal to God in authority or power. This inequality "generates conflict" in the fall. But it need not be so. And that particular conflict is one in which the inequality is just. God is the Creator, and he has an authority that we do not. At the same time, other kinds of inequality arise from human misuse of power. How does the social-conflict approach distinguish between good and bad inequalities?

Within the world after the fall, all conflicts, whether just or unjust, take place within a world that God governs. God's conflict against evil is the foundation for human conflicts. God energizes those who fight against evil and injustice. But conflict still exists. Some people selfishly pervert justice. Some may be too lazy to fight against injustice. Others are confused about injustice, and though they may be ready to fight, their fighting is ineffective or even counterproductive. People on both sides of a conflict typically are convinced that they are in the right.

Does the social-conflict approach bring our attention to the foundation for the meaning of conflict in God's conflict against evil? Or does it treat conflict as something that is merely "there"? Without a moral foundation in a personal God, conflict easily becomes a contest between two limited personal opinions about justice. Worse, it may become sound and fury, signifying nothing. Is human conflict no different from animal conflict or "conflict" between two gravitational forces? Is it just "there" as part of the "system" of the universe, which has no innate morality? No. Once again, God gives us instruction that we need in order to see the world correctly.

The Symbolic-Interaction Approach

A third approach to sociological theory is the symbolic-interaction approach: "The symbolic-interaction approach, then, is *a framework for building theory that sees society as the product of the everyday interactions of individuals*."[5] Macionis explains further that, in contrast to the structural-functional approach and the social-conflict approach, the symbolic-interaction approach begins with individual people and small-scale interactions. Society as a large-scale institution is built up from the microlevel. "Society [in this view] is nothing more than the shared reality that people construct as they interact with one another. That is, human beings live in a world of symbols, attaching meaning to virtually everything."[6]

This description could merely mean that the symbolic-interaction approach prefers to start with individuals and uses individuals as a perspective on society as a larger whole. Nothing forbids such a perspectival approach. But we can see some possible pitfalls in the description. The expression "nothing more than" can easily lead to the exclusion of God. People "construct" society independently of God.[7] This kind of language can be interpreted as a flat denial of the fact that God ordains all social orders everywhere, and that he is constantly involved as people do innovative things such as creating new games, new businesses, and new families.

We can also ask where the symbolic meanings come from and what they attach to. Are they *merely* human invention, or do they also owe their origin to God's plan and *his* meanings? Just as the structural-functional approach depends on assumptions about regularities in social order that are in place, and as the social-conflict approach depends on notions concerning inequality, so the symbolic-interaction approach depends on assumptions about meanings and creative "construction." Are these meanings and constructions the product of divine meaning and action, which is then distorted in human interpretation? Or are the meanings conceived of as merely the combinations of individuals' human actions?

Combining Approaches

Macionis's textbook shows sympathy for all three approaches and shows how they can be combined in analyzing a particular domain such as sports.[8] The combina-

---

[5] Ibid., 20.
[6] Ibid.
[7] On the idea of constructing reality, see also chap. 18.
[8] Macionis, *Sociology*, 21–23.

tion is insightful. It shows that the three approaches can in principle be construed as offering complementary insights. This complementary character has affinities to what we have already observed about complementary perspectives.

John Frame has defined the normative, situational, and personal (existential) perspectives in Christian ethics.[9] The situational perspective has an affinity to the structural-functional approach, because this approach focuses on society as a systemic whole, a kind of "situation" in which people live. The normative perspective has an affinity to the social-conflict approach, because this approach tackles most explicitly the normative evaluation of society and social relations. The existential perspective has affinities with the symbolic-interaction approach, because it focuses on meanings *for persons*, for individuals, and includes their attitudes, motives, and evaluations.

In Frame's thinking, the three perspectives interlock and show both harmony and mutual dependence. None is ultimate in relation to the others. They can be guaranteed to have an ultimate harmony because all originate from God. God controls the situation by his power; God gives the standards by his authority; and God created and is present to the persons as a function of his covenantal *presence.*

Without God, the unity of ethics tends to disintegrate. Philosophical systems produce a normative or "deontological" ethics with too little connection with the situations and the persons, or situational ethics with too little connection with standards and persons, or existential, individual-centered ethics with too little connection with external standards and with situations.

We may ask whether analogous difficulties confront sociological theory. God ordained the total "situation," the society as a whole, which implies the pertinence of structural-functional study of the whole. This is the situational perspective in sociology. God's holiness provides the standard for evaluating social arrangements, which suggests the pertinence of social-conflict study of the conflicts and tensions. This is the normative perspective in sociology. God created the persons and their meanings, which gives warrant to symbolic-interaction study of individual personal meaning. This is the existential perspective in sociology.

All three perspectives interact; all three are complementary; all three are perspectives on the whole. All three are in meaningful harmony because all three have their anchor in God—his plans, his standards, and his meanings.

But if we try to leave God out of our picture, what picture do we have left? The three approaches are each "a framework for building theory."[10] If there are three different frameworks, must we not also ask how and why they can be expected to fit together? *Do* they fit together? Or are they competing ideas? Does the

---

[9]John M. Frame, *The Doctrine of the Christian Life* (Phillipsburg, NJ: P&R, 2008).
[10]Macionis, *Sociology*, 15, 17, 20.

structural-functional approach see the individual as a product of society, while the symbolic-interaction approach sees the society as the product of the individuals? And do the conflicts seen by the social-conflict approach destroy the stability seen by the structural-functional approach?

We can see some partial agreements. The conflicts emphasized in the social-conflict approach take place within an order, an order that forms a kind of system. Conversely, the structural-functional approach allows that conflicts and tensions exist within the social order as a system, and these conflicts produce change. Yet the two frameworks are different. Which is right? If both are right, how can they both be right as whole frameworks and not merely as piecemeal accumulations of observations?

We might expect that sociology would give attention to building a single theory that would incorporate the three smaller theories into a larger whole. But how? Macionis's example with the sociology of sports seems to let the three theories mostly stand alongside each other. Each offers its distinctive insights. There is no final picture incorporating all three. But how do we know whether these insights are really insights instead of distortions if no one theory offers us a true overview?

The fascination of sociology derives partly from the process of "standing back" and endeavoring to *transcend* our immersion in our immediate social circumstances. We try to build a picture of the whole. But is there a whole without God, without his greater transcendence?

APPENDIX F

Sociology of Knowledge

Bad company ruins good morals.
—1 Corinthians 15:33

Whoever walks with the wise becomes wise,
but the companion of fools will suffer harm.
—Proverbs 13:20

S ociology of knowledge is a subdivision of sociology that studies the social dimensions of the acquisition and transmission of knowledge.[1] It is a fascinating study.

People around us play a big role in what we learn, especially during our childhood years (chaps. 22–23). We learn from parents, from teachers, from TV, and from the Internet. We learn from children our age as well, but where do they get what they give us? A good deal comes from their parents and their teachers.

Modern societies have huge stores of knowledge. Such vast stores cannot be learned from scratch by each succeeding generation. The treasure must be passed on. The passing on takes place through social relationships.

---

[1]See Peter L. Berger and Thomas Luckmann, *The Social Construction of Reality: A Treatise in the Sociology of Knowledge* (Garden City, NY: Doubleday, 1966); Nico Stehr and Volker Meja, eds. *Society and Knowledge: Contemporary Perspectives in the Sociology of Knowledge and Science*, 2nd ed. (Edison, NJ: Transaction, 2005); Russell Heddendorf and Matthew Vos, *Hidden Threads: A Christian Critique of Sociological Theory* (Lanham, MD: University Press of America, 2010), chap. 11, pp. 165–81.

Acknowledgments of the Role of Society

People in every society experience the social transmission of knowledge, but sociology of knowledge draws explicit attention to it. The Bible draws attention to it as well and explicitly instructs parents to teach their children:

> And these words that I command you today shall be on your heart. You shall *teach* them diligently to your children, and shall *talk* of them when you sit in your house, and when you walk by the way, and when you lie down, and when you rise. (Deut. 6:6–7)

> I will open my mouth in a parable;
>   I will utter dark sayings from of old,
> things that we have heard and known,
>   that *our fathers have told us.*
> We will not hide them from their children,
>   but *tell to the coming generation*
> the glorious deeds of the LORD, and his might,
>   and the wonders that he has done. (Ps. 78:2–4)

> Fathers, do not provoke your children to anger, but *bring them up* in the discipline and *instruction* of the Lord. (Eph. 6:4)

The Bible also indicates that whole groups of people have distinct access to the truth:

> He [God] declares his word to Jacob,
>   his statutes and rules to Israel.
> He has not dealt thus with any other nation;
>   they do not know his rules. (Ps. 147:19–20)

> ... delivering you [Paul] from your people and from the Gentiles—to whom I am sending you to open their eyes, so that they may turn from *darkness* to light and from the power of Satan to God, that they may receive forgiveness of sins and a place among those who are sanctified by faith in me. (Acts 26:17–18)

> Now this I say and testify in the Lord, that you must no longer walk as the Gentiles do, in the futility of their minds. They are *darkened* in their understanding, alienated from the life of God because of the ignorance that is in them, due to their hardness of heart. (Eph. 4:17–18)

The Value of Focusing on Social Transmission of Knowledge

What can be the value of drawing attention to social influences on knowing?

First, we become aware of our finiteness. We do not know everything, and much of what we do know we owe to others who have taught us.

Second, we become more aware of the social dimensions of life and the influence of society on each of us. America has a strong tradition of individualism, including the image of the lone-ranger hero who triumphs single-handedly and needs no help from anyone. Awareness of social relations can help to balance this one-sided picture.

Third, we can become aware of the social power of sin. Each individual is responsible for his sin, but the consequences of sin include social effects. A greedy employer or a selfish parent causes damage to others. The same is true in the area of knowledge. Sin can distort our judgments about knowledge, because we come to want to believe untruths when they make us comfortable. Within a whole society, sinful distortions of the truth can be passed from one generation to another.

Transmission of Idolatry

The effects are particularly evident with idolatry. People worship idols rather than the true God partly out of fear about the spirit world, and partly because idols seem to offer people the hope that they can gain control in their lives.

Parents transmit idolatrous thinking and practice to their children. Or, conversely, they transmit knowledge of the true God. If a whole society falls into idolatry, the idolatry gets passed even more effectively from one generation to another because the society seems to confirm what a child hears from his parents.

Many modern societies have largely abandoned the practicing of worshiping physical idols in the form of statues. But money, pleasure, sex, and power can become objects of people's ultimate commitments; they can enslave people just as effectively as the worship of statues.[2] Our social environment encourages these modern forms of idolatry.

When passages in the Bible talk about Gentiles (non-Jews) being in darkness, they partly have in mind this effect. God made a special covenant with Israel and gave them explicit instructions, such as the Ten Commandments and records of God's care for them in previous generations (e.g., Genesis, and later the records in Samuel and Kings concerning the monarchy period). Most people in other nations did not have this instruction. And even if they heard about it, they would be tempted to ignore it because people in the society around them would assure them that Israel's God was not worth attending to, and that the gods they were

---

[2]Timothy Keller, *Counterfeit Gods: The Empty Promises of Money, Sex, and Power, and the Only Hope That Matters* (New York: Dutton, 2009); Herbert Schlossberg, *Idols for Destruction: Christian Faith and Its Confrontation with American Society* (Nashville: Nelson, 1983).

already worshiping were the "right" gods, or the gods belonging to their nation or territory, or the gods that could most effectively help them.

Before the coming of Christ, darkness—that is ignorance and confusion about God—covered the nations outside Israel. Israel had God's special instruction (Ps. 147:17–20). And even Israel, partly because of her own perverseness, but partly because she was tempted by neighboring societies (Egypt, and then the Canaanites), fell into idolatry herself. This darkness has a lesson. Human confusion about knowledge is difficult to eliminate, not only because of finiteness and social pressures, but also because in some key areas, confusion is spiritually more comfortable to sinners than is the light:

> And this is the judgment: the light has come into the world, and people loved the darkness rather than the light because their deeds were evil. For everyone who does wicked things hates the light and does not come to the light, lest his deeds should be exposed. But whoever does what is true comes to the light, so that it may be clearly seen that his deeds have been carried out in God. (John 3:19–21)

Confronting the darkness of the social effects of sin therefore offers a wonderful opportunity for us to appreciate more deeply the importance of God rescuing us, changing our hearts, and giving us pure instruction.

Insights from Sociology of Knowledge

Sociology of knowledge highlights these issues of finiteness and sin. Not all societies believe the same thing. What they believe is *heavily* influenced by what the previous generation believed, and what the present generation around them believes. A society has characteristic thought patterns, which make up a worldview (or multiple views if the society is divided). Sociology of knowledge claims that "reality [as seen within a particular society] is socially constructed."[3] The patterns of thought result in what have been called *plausibility structures*. New ideas are plausible when they fit in harmoniously with the prevailing worldview and its practices.

For example, believing in Marduk, the patron god of Babylon, is *plausible* if you live in ancient Babylon and everyone else around you believes the same thing. Believing in the God of Israel within a Babylonian society is *implausible*, not because it is untrue, but because the truth itself seems implausible when you are being urged by the surrounding patterns of thought in other directions. The Babylonians will tell you that the God of Israel has failed, which they think is evident from the fact that he let Israel go into exile (Jer. 25:8–12). Such is the

---

[3]Berger and Luckmann, *Social Construction*, 1. For a critique of the concept of social "construction," see chap. 18.

way that the Babylonians thought about any of their gods. If the gods failed to meet their needs when they called on them, the gods were failures.

Consider another example. The Greeks mocked the idea of the bodily resurrection when Paul proclaimed it at Athens, because they thought of the blessedness of the afterlife as consisting in being *freed* from the body (Acts 17:32). Their conception of the afterlife was part of their worldview. That conception made it implausible to accept a claim about bodily resurrection. A person can feel confidence even when he rejects the truth because he is relying on cultural assumptions that are not valid. But the person is unaware of his invalid assumptions. He may even have many in his society who assure him that his assumptions are both valid and natural. Sociology of knowledge makes explicit some of these dependencies in what we count as knowledge.

A Difficulty for the Foundations of Sociology of Knowledge

We confront a difficulty when we try to apply sociology of knowledge to itself. Sociology aspires to be knowledge. And it aspires to be a growing and developing discipline, which will continue from one generation to another. The continuation requires transmission, and the transmission falls under the domain of the sociology of knowledge. So what does sociology of knowledge imply about its own character as a social phenomenon?

Sociology of knowledge rests on plausibility structures, which seems to imply that we do not know if it is true. To its credit, Berger and Luckman's book on the sociology of knowledge recognizes this difficulty.[4] It specifically indicates that sociology of knowledge tends to make people skeptical, but that if they apply this skepticism to sociology of knowledge itself, the whole project dissolves in smoke.

This difficulty could suggest that human beings, when unaided, are radically insufficient to find out the real fundamental truths about the world. That would be right, and it should cause people to turn to God. But modern thinking has already immunized them against this route by giving them a plausibility structure that tells them that such a route is impossible. Sociology—or at least most sociology—considers religion merely as one more social phenomenon among others. Moreover, there are many competing religions, and they do not believe the same thing. Given that the plausibility structures of sociology and of modern secularism are already in place, differences among religions seem to indicate that no one can hope to know God as he is, but we can know only a plurality of human ideas about God.

All this reasoning seems eminently plausible. But it seems so because people are living and thinking within a framework of so-called knowledge that has imparted

---

[4]Ibid.

plausibility to it. Sociology of knowledge, along with much of modern society, has unconsciously adopted the assumption that serious reflection requires religious "neutrality" and that God is absent from our social life. These assumptions carry with them the difficulties that we have already seen for sociology as a whole (appendix B).

This framework for sociology of knowledge has its own weaknesses. One of the weaknesses is paradoxical. The framework implies that no one can know God, but only one's own ideas about God, ideas that are socially generated. What it conceals from itself is that it has to know a lot about God to make such an assertion.[5] How does anyone know that God cannot reveal himself and speak to people, as the Bible claims that he did to Israel at Mount Sinai (Exodus 19–20)? How do we know that the diversity of religions means that they are all *merely* human? Might one be the true religion while others are merely human? Or, worse, might one be true while the others are interacting with God's general revelation (revelation given in the very nature of the world, Rom. 1:18–25), but distorting it in various ways because of their sinful desire to control gods rather than submit to the true God?

Most of all, modern secular thinking conceals from itself its own dependence on God, the Trinitarian God who is really there and who sustains all our social relationships. That is part of the point that I have tried to make in this book.

Suppose a person agrees to go along with our society in its predominant thinking that God is fundamentally absent from human society and human relationships. It is understandable that he will find that God seems to be absent. A claim that he is present for us, or that he was uniquely present to Israel, then seems incredible (implausible). A modern person finds it incredible because modern plausibility structures are at work, and those structures are inherited from the processes of social transmission of what counts as knowledge. If, on the other hand, we commit ourselves to following Jesus Christ and his word, and we trust that his word in the Bible offers guidance into the truth (John 16:13; 17:8), we may find that the plausibility structures and assumptions of the society around us make untrue assumptions about God and human relationships. Starting from untruth, they persist in untruth, and the truth never dawns on them. Or if they do hear of it, it seems implausible.

---

[5]If religious ideas are merely humanly generated, claims actually to know the truth about God seem arrogant. And of course religion itself can become an occasion for sinners to show arrogance. What is not so obvious to modern thinking is that the prejudgment of arrogance must presuppose that the religious claims could not actually be true on the basis of a clear message from God. There is arrogance in the supposition that we can make beforehand profound religious judgments about what God can or cannot do. See Timothy Keller, *The Reason for God: Belief in an Age of Skepticism* (New York: Dutton, 2008), 3–21.

Resources Needed in Sociology of Knowledge

Sociology of knowledge can easily make us feel that we cannot really know anything. What we take to be knowledge is only "knowledge" in quotes, that is, what our group or society for social reasons has taken to be knowledge. Playing by these rules, we cannot even know the knowledge offered by the sociology of knowledge.

I am not surprised at this result. It just shows that we need God. God teaches us knowledge (Ps. 94:10). Without him, knowledge would disintegrate.

God offers us an alternative to this skepticism. We may return to the basics. God has authority, control, and presence (chap. 4). God's *authority* includes his authority to specify the true way of life and the meaning of life and to bring judgment on folly. He offers us guidance into the truth in the Bible.

Second, God exercises *control*. He ordains the regularities of each society (chaps. 8–9). The regularities reveal his character, including his truthfulness. Sociology of knowledge that refuses to refer to God ends up with no guarantee that a society could not be almost infinitely immersed in falsehood. But God guarantees the regularities of each society. In spite of sin, truth remains in the world around human beings. Day and night follow one another. Plants grow. Those truths are not merely a human "construction," a product of society with no necessary relation to the "real" world.

Sociology of knowledge worries because human beings and human societies do impart different shapes to knowledge. Some of it is distortion of the truth, but a distortion or counterfeit still does not completely escape the truth. We do not escape the truth that plants grow, even if we think that they grow because we have propitiated the spirits in the soil.

False religion is not merely false but *counterfeit*.[6] Like a counterfeit twenty-dollar bill, it has to be close enough to the truth to be plausible. That closeness shows the continuing dependence on truth and the impossibility of completely escaping truth. We cannot escape because God, who is the God of truth, expresses his truth in the world. God manifests himself in the regularities of society on which we depend when we form our own flawed notions of truth ("knowledge" in quotes).

Third, God is present in the world. Everyone knows God, according to Romans 1:18–25. But we suppress what we know because we are in rebellion. Sociology of knowledge pictures human society as *merely* human. But that is itself a form of suppressing the truth. God is necessarily present in our activities and our social relationships, indeed in every breath (Job 34:14), because he sustains it all.

This book has attempted to highlight some of the ways in which God sustains us. But we are adept at overlooking those ways. And when we overlook them,

---

[6]See Vern S. Poythress, *The Returning King* (Phillipsburg, NJ: P&R, 2000), 16–25.

as sociology of knowledge has committed itself to do in the process of being a religiously "neutral" discipline, we may well despair of thinking that anyone can know God and the truth about him. And then we may use that despair as an excuse to do what we as human beings have been doing ever since the time of Adam, namely, to make ourselves gods and to claim to be a law to ourselves— to be autonomous. Autonomy implies that we will not submit to a later word of God even if it should appear, because, allegedly, we must make up our own mind by our own standards. But of course those standards have become plausible because of the sinfulness of our hearts, combined with the sinfulness of a society around us. Society, or at least the prestigious authorities and professors within the society, assure us that this is the right and logical way of approaching issues when we want to search for truth.

The Value of Sociology of Knowledge

Sociology of knowledge actually has much to offer if we would learn from it the importance of dependence on God to relieve us of our darkness. Unfortunately, using it in this fashion does not seem to be popular at the moment. Such use is implausible according to our current plausibility structures, which leave something to be desired.

APPENDIX G

Sociology and Postmodernism

The one who walks in the darkness does not know where he is going.

—John 12:35

Postmodernism is a wide-ranging and diverse movement.[1] Some of its streams build on insights from linguistics, philosophy of language, and sociology. In particular, sociology of knowledge can contribute to postmodernism, by showing how what a particular culture *counts* as knowledge depends on the culture. Knowledge, it is said, is socially "constructed" (see the previous appendix).

Postmodernism interests itself in the diversity among cultures and groups of human beings. That includes diversity in what people count as knowledge. How then do we propose to live in peace and to practice kindness in the midst of this diversity?

Skepticism

The skeptical strain in sociology of knowledge can influence postmodernism to downgrade expectations that we can know the truth. So one popular form of postmodern thinking proposes that when we differ from other cultures, no one really knows who is right, and in the midst of our uncertainty we agree to

---

[1] Heath White, *Postmodernism 101: A First Course for the Curious Christian* (Grand Rapids: Brazos, 2006); David Lyon, *Postmodernity*, 2nd ed. (Minneapolis: University of Minnesota Press, 1999). I address some aspects in Vern S. Poythress, *In the Beginning Was the Word: Language—A God-Centered Approach* (Wheaton, IL: Crossway, 2009), appendices A and B.

disagree. Chastened by our finiteness, we give up on the modernist vision that neutral reason, untouched by culture, is capable of giving us final truth.

This kind of postmodernism sees itself as passing beyond modernism. According to its view, modernism was characterized by trust in human reason and by hope that through reason human beings could come to fundamental agreement about the important questions of life. René Descartes may be seen as an example of this confidence in reason (see appendix A).

The difficulty, as postmodernism sees it, is partly the difficulty pointed out in the sociology of knowledge. Human reason is never "pure." Or, to put it differently, different cultures have different conceptions of reason, and some may even see mystical insight as superior to rationality.

I basically agree with this criticism of the hopes placed in autonomous reason (see appendix A). These hopes are misplaced because, ever since the fall of mankind into sin, we have temptations, both individual and social, to distort truth in favor of our pride and our autonomy. God provides a remedy in the work of Christ and in the Bible, which instructs us about his redemption.

Postmodernism is indeed a reaction against some of the genuine failures of modernism. But in another respect one strand within postmodernism continues modernism, because it still suppresses the presence of God and desires to continue without reckoning with God's revelation of himself. It continues to be influenced by "knowledge" so-called, the "knowledge" of modern secularism, which assumes that God is absent and irrelevant to our knowledge and our quest for truth. I hope then that this book may serve as an alternative to skepticism.

Postmodernist Impact on Sociology

Postmodernism has also had a reverse impact on sociology. It has insisted that sociology itself, along with all other human activities, takes place within particular cultural environments. Sociologists use assumptions deriving from the general culture, or from a tradition of sociological research that forms a subculture within mainstream academic culture. Sociological reflection is the product of people, and these people are culturally *situated*.

So postmodernism can have the effect of calling on people to reflect explicitly on their situatedness when they do social analysis. They should admit their biases. Sociology outside of a postmodern context has practiced this awareness in limited ways.[2] Postmodernist thinking radicalizes this practice by pointing out that our idea of reason itself is affected by socialization, by studying how desires to obtain or maintain power can affect social analysis, and by exploring how socialization influences standards for evaluating social conditions. Through this kind

---

[2]John J. Macionis, *Sociology*, 11th ed. (Upper Saddle River, NJ: Prentice Hall, 2007), 36–37.

of reflection, social analysis becomes self-conscious about its own social roots, and becomes critical of absolutist claims that lack awareness of their dependence on a social background.

This postmodernist consciousness of social influence can lead to a skeptical atmosphere, as we indicated. A person who follows Christ cannot agree with radical skepticism, because the skepticism itself is socially generated and ill-founded.[3] But a biblical worldview has distinct points of agreement with postmodernists' awareness of human finiteness and social aberrations, both of which point to our need for God and his instruction.

---

[3] See the more expanded discussion in Poythress, *In the Beginning*, appendix B.

APPENDIX H

Postmodern Theology

Some theologians have seen postmodernism as a skeptical deadend and have undertaken to criticize it. Others have undertaken to learn from it. And, as I have indicated in the previous appendix, we *can* learn from it some of the weaknesses of modernism.[1] What disappoints me is that theologians learning from postmodernism have sometimes embraced its deficiencies along with its insights.

Let me explain. Postmodernism analyzes the uncertainty of knowledge due to our dependence on society. Such analysis can indeed be helpful. The remedy, as I have said, is to receive the redemption of God and to listen to the voice of God from outside of and in critique of human society. We need fellowship with God, a "society" with God as the chief person. We can enter into this society through Christ, who gives us the Holy Spirit. When we have entered into this society, we know God, and skepticism is relieved. We need boldly to announce that God is the answer to our social and personal dilemma.

But instead of boldness, what I sometimes hear from contemporary theologians is timidity. They act too much as if they are part of the postmodern dilemma and have never heard the solution. They tell us that we Christians must be modest in our claims for truth, both individually and corporately. They have lost confidence both in the clarity of the Bible and in the ability of God to make his salvation clear in our hearts through the work of the Holy Spirit.

Some people have arrived at these results because, when they understand postmodernist analysis of the limits of knowledge, they then apply it to the Bible, the church, and the Christian faith. And it is true that both the church and human formulations of Christian faith still show the effects of sin. We always need to take sin seriously.

---

[1] See also the numerous points of contact with postmodernism in Vern S. Poythress, *In the Beginning Was the Word: Language—A God-Centered Approach* (Wheaton, IL: Crossway, 2009).

But the general principle concerning the influence of sin does not help us to decide *where in particular* sin has had an influence. Sin does not simply make everything dark and plunge us into total ignorance. For each of us the effects are much more specific. To dig out the particular effects of sin, we have to go back to asking for God's help, reading the Bible, reexamining our theologies, listening respectfully to others who criticize us, and participating in the church, the Christian community. Theologians with some degree of humility have been doing so all along.

But some postmodernists go further and conclude that everything or nearly everything becomes radically uncertain. It has become uncertain because, in the process of understanding sociology of knowledge and linguistics and the other elements that have influenced us, they have also absorbed the modern assumption that God is essentially absent and that Christians are only talking to themselves about theological ideas that they can never know to be true. Theologians have adopted the modern worldview. And so, not surprisingly, they have found the Bible's own claims about the nature of the world incredible (according to their modern plausibility structures, appendix F).

What Is New?

Modernity assumes that God cannot speak and cannot act to redeem us from the spiritual darkness in human understanding in this fallen world. Or if he does speak, he cannot be understood. There is too much uncertainty. There is too much social influence. There are too many views of what the Bible means.

Let me say in return that there is solid agreement about what the Bible teaches, an agreement expressed in the ancient creeds and through centuries of Christian understanding. It is not universal, perfect agreement, but it is substantive agreement on the part of people to whom the Holy Spirit has given a measure of humility, so that they become genuinely willing to *submit* to what God says in the Bible, not merely to read it, to play with it, to twist it in the direction of their ideas, to add to it (Rev. 22:18), to subtract from it (Rev. 22:19), to claim that some later tradition is infallible, or to search high and low for some way in which they may conform it to their autonomous ideas about truth. When believers hear the Bible, the Holy Spirit guides them into the truth (John 16:13) and gives them confidence that they genuinely know God (Rom. 8:15–17; 1 Cor. 2:10–16). The existence of heterodox disagreements about what the Bible means is discussed in the Bible itself, and is quite compatible with its view of sin and its view of its own clarity (2 Cor. 4:1–6).[2]

We should indeed reckon with our finiteness and our remaining sinfulness. We should not claim to be wiser or more mature in the Christian faith than we

---

[2]On the clarity of the Bible, see Wayne A. Grudem, "The Perspicuity of Scripture," Tyndale Fellowship Conference: The John Wenham Lecture 1, July 8, 2009.

are. "For by the grace given to me I say to everyone among you not to think of himself more highly than he ought to think, but to think with sober judgment, each according to the measure of faith that God has assigned" (Rom. 12:3).

Yet God has made himself known in Christ, and we can know him intimately (Rom. 8:14–17). The humility that comes from the Holy Spirit is compatible with boldness in sharing the truth that we know. Humility comes from realizing that we do not deserve anything and are not qualified by innate talents: "Not that we are sufficient in ourselves to claim anything as coming from us" (2 Cor. 3:5). Immediately afterward the biblical text proclaims confidently, "but our sufficiency is from God, who has made us competent to be ministers of a new covenant, not of the letter but of the Spirit" (3:5–6). "Since we have such a hope, we are very bold" (3:12). Through Christ God has brought us out of darkness into light: "He [God] has delivered us from the domain of darkness and transferred us to the kingdom of his beloved Son, in whom we have redemption, the forgiveness of sins" (Col. 1:13–14).

Confidence

I am saying that our confidence needs to be in the right place. We should have confidence in the Lord Jesus Christ, who has saved us, who has revealed himself to us, and whom we have come to know in truth. By contrast, the atmosphere of one popular form of postmodernism encourages us to have little confidence in any religious truth or claim to truth. The paradox here is that the people who encourage us to scale down our confidence tend to be quite confident that we need to scale down our confidence. They have what we might call a second-order confidence.

Their confidence is based on having "seen through" the illegitimate character of first-order confidence, the confidence of ordinary people who know Christ and read their Bibles. Do they look down on these ordinary people? Do they see ordinary people from the superior heights given to them by analysis of the limitations of language or the limitations of societies? Do they think they have transcended the unreflective lives of ordinary people through their analysis?

Pride

Human pride can crop up in strange places. For example, it can crop up among people whom God has saved by his grace. Of all people, we whom God has saved through Christ ought to be least proud, because God and not our own achievement has saved us. But even in the midst of this fundamental reality, we can become proud of our ability to understand the Bible. We can overestimate our understanding and our grasp of truth and underestimate the power of sin to creep in and corrupt it.

Pride can also infect people who have second-order confidence. They engage in critical analysis of pride and "see through" the overconfidence of ordinary people. They become proud of their "superior" standpoint.

I would reply that confidence based on such transcendence is confidence without a firm foundation. Human transcendent analyses have no foundation without fellowship with God. Sin has distorted the confident analyses of language and society. From these distortions we will not recover without submission to Christ. We need confidence in Christ and in his word in order to be delivered from pride and from false confidence in modern and postmodern ideas.

Bibliography

Anderson, Stephen R. *Doctor Dolittle's Delusion: Animals and the Uniqueness of Human Language.* New Haven, CT: Yale University Press, 2004.

Augustine. *The Confessions of St. Augustin.* Vol. 1 of *A Select Library of the Nicene and Post-Nicene Fathers of the Christian Church,* edited by Philip Schaff. Grand Rapids: Eerdmans, 1979.

Berger, Peter L., and Thomas Luckmann. *The Social Construction of Reality: A Treatise in the Sociology of Knowledge.* Garden City, NY: Doubleday, 1966.

Berkhof, Louis. *Systematic Theology.* Grand Rapids: Eerdmans, 1939.

Bromiley, Geoffrey W., et al., eds. *The International Standard Bible Encyclopedia.* Rev. ed. Grand Rapids: Eerdmans, 1988.

Burns, Lanier. *The Nearness of God: His Presence with His People.* Phillipsburg, NJ: P&R, 2009.

Bustard, Ned, ed. *It Was Good: Making Art to the Glory of God.* Baltimore: Square Halo, 2000.

Carson, D. A. *Christ and Culture Revisited.* Grand Rapids: Eerdmans, 2008.

Carson, D. A., and John D. Woodbridge, eds. *Scripture and Truth.* Grand Rapids: Zondervan, 1983.

Chandler, Daniel. *Semiotics: The Basics.* London: Routledge, 2001.

Conn, Harvie M. *Eternal Word and Changing Worlds: Theology, Anthropology, and Mission in Trialogue.* Grand Rapids: Zondervan, 1984.

———. *Evangelism: Doing Justice and Preaching Grace.* Grand Rapids: Zondervan, 1982.

Courtois, Stéphane. *The Black Book of Communism.* Cambridge: Harvard University Press, 1999.

Danesi, Marcel. *Of Cigarettes, High Heels and Other Interesting Things: An Introduction to Semiotics.* London: Macmillan, 1999.

Descartes, René. *Discourse on the Method of Rightly Conducting the Reason and of Seeking for Truth in the Sciences.* Translated by Norman Kemp Smith. In *Descartes' Philosophical Writings,* 115–64. London: Macmillan, 1952.

Edwards, R. B. "Word." In *The International Standard Bible Encyclopedia*. Rev. ed., edited by Geoffrey W. Bromiley et al., 4:1103–7. Grand Rapids: Eerdmans, 1988.

Eliot. T. S. *The Idea of a Christian Society*. New York: Harcourt, Brace, 1940.

Foucault, Michel. *Discipline and Punish: The Birth of the Prison*. New York: Vintage, 1979.

Frame, John M. *Apologetics to the Glory of God: An Introduction*. Phillipsburg, NJ: P&R, 1994.

———. *Christ and Culture: Lectures Given at the Pensacola Theological Institute, July 23–27, 2001*. Accessed December 14, 2009. http://www.thirdmill.org /newfiles/joh_frame/Frame.Apologetics2004.ChristandCulture.pdf.

———. *The Doctrine of God*. Phillipsburg, NJ: P&R, 2002.

———. *The Doctrine of the Christian Life*. Phillipsburg, NJ: P&R, 2008.

———. *The Doctrine of the Knowledge of God*. Phillipsburg, NJ: Presbyterian and Reformed, 1987.

———. *Perspectives on the Word of God: An Introduction to Christian Ethics*. Phillipsburg, NJ: Presbyterian and Reformed, 1990.

Gaebelein, Frank. *The Christian, the Arts, and Truth: Regaining the Vision of Greatness*. Edited by D. Bruce Lockerbie. Portland, OR: Multnomah, 1985.

Graham, Billy. *Peace with God*. Waco, TX: Word, 1984.

Grudem, Wayne A. *Evangelical Feminism and Biblical Truth: An Analysis of More Than One Hundred Disputed Questions*. Sisters, OR: Multnomah, 2004.

———. "The Perspicuity of Scripture," Tyndale Fellowship Conference: The John Wenham Lecture 1, July 8, 2009.

Heddendorf, Russell, and Matthew Vos. *Hidden Threads: A Christian Critique of Sociological Theory*. Lanham, MD: University Press of America, 2010.

Keller, Timothy. *Counterfeit Gods: The Empty Promises of Money, Sex, and Power, and the Only Hope That Matters*. New York: Dutton, 2009.

———. *The Reason for God: Belief in an Age of Skepticism*. New York: Dutton, 2008.

Kline, Meredith G. *Images of the Spirit*. Grand Rapids: Baker, 1980.

———. *The Structure of Biblical Authority*. Grand Rapids: Eerdmans, 1972.

———. *Treaty of the Great King: The Covenant Structure of Deuteronomy: Studies and Commentary*. Grand Rapids: Eerdmans, 1963.

Kline, Meredith M. "The Holy Spirit as Covenant Witness." ThM thesis, Westminster Theological Seminary, 1972.

Knudsen, Robert D. *The Encounter of Christianity with Secular Science: Psychology*. Memphis, TN: Christian Studies Center, 1980.

———. *The Encounter of Christianity with Secular Science: Sociology*. Memphis, TN: Christian Studies Center, 1981.

Köstenberger, Andreas J., and Thomas R. Schreiner, eds. *Women in the Church: An Analysis and Application of 1 Timothy 2:9–15.* 2nd ed. Grand Rapids: Baker, 2005.

Lyon, David. *Christians and Sociology: To the Challenge of Sociology—a Christian Response.* Downers Grove, IL: InterVarsity, 1976.

———. *Postmodernity.* 2nd ed. Minneapolis: University of Minnesota Press, 1999.

Macionis, John J. *Society: The Basics.* 10th ed. Upper Saddle River, NJ: Prentice Hall, 2008.

———. *Sociology.* 11th ed. Upper Saddle River, NJ: Prentice Hall, 2007.

Mead, Margaret. *Cooperation and Competition among Primitive Peoples.* New York: McGraw-Hill, 1937.

Milbank, John. *Theology and Social Theory: Beyond Secular Reason.* Oxford: Blackwell, 1993.

Niebuhr, H. Richard. *Christ and Culture.* San Francisco: HarperSanFrancisco, 2001.

Olasky, Marvin N. *The Tragedy of American Compassion.* Wheaton, IL: Crossway, 1992.

Parsons, Talcott. *The Social System.* Glencoe, IL: Free Press, 1951.

———. *Societies: Evolutionary and Comparative Perspectives.* Englewood Cliffs, NJ: Prentice-Hall, 1966.

———. *Sociological Theory and Modern Society.* New York: Free Press, 1967.

———. *The Structure of Social Action: A Study in Social Theory with Special Reference to a Group of Recent European Writers.* Glencoe, IL: Free Press, 1949.

———. *The System of Modern Societies.* Englewood Cliffs, NJ: Prentice-Hall, 1971.

Parsons, Talcott, and Edward A. Shils, eds. *Toward a General Theory of Action.* Cambridge, MA: Harvard University Press, 1954.

Pike, Kenneth L. *Language in Relation to a Unified Theory of the Structure of Human Behavior.* 2nd ed. Paris: Mouton, 1967.

———. *Linguistic Concepts: An Introduction to Tagmemics.* Lincoln: University of Nebraska Press, 1982.

Piper, John, and Wayne A. Grudem, eds. *Recovering Biblical Manhood and Womanhood: A Response to Evangelical Feminism.* Wheaton, IL: Crossway, 1991.

Polanyi, Michael. *Personal Knowledge: Towards a Post-critical Philosophy.* Chicago: University of Chicago Press, 1964.

———. *The Tacit Dimension.* Garden City, NY: Anchor, 1967.

Porter, Jack Nusan. *Is Sociology Dead? Social Theory and Social Praxis in a Post-Modern Age*. Lanham, MD: University Press of America, 2008.

Poythress, Vern S. "Counterfeiting in the Book of Revelation as a Perspective on Non-Christian Culture," *Journal of the Evangelical Theological Society* 40, no. 3 (1997): 411–18.

———. "Divine Meaning of Scripture," *Westminster Theological Journal* 48 (1986): 241–79.

———. *God-Centered Biblical Interpretation*. Phillipsburg, NJ: P&R, 1999.

———. *In the Beginning Was the Word: Language—A God-Centered Approach*. Wheaton, IL: Crossway, 2009.

———. "The Presence of God Qualifying Our Notions of Grammatical-Historical Interpretation: Genesis 3:15 as a Test Case," *Journal of the Evangelical Theological Society* 50, no. 1 (2007): 87–103.

———. *Redeeming Science: A God-Centered Approach*. Wheaton, IL: Crossway, 2006.

———. *The Returning King*. Phillipsburg, NJ: P&R, 2000.

———. *The Shadow of Christ in the Law of Moses*. Phillipsburg, NJ: P&R, 1995.

———. *Symphonic Theology: The Validity of Multiple Perspectives in Theology*. Grand Rapids: Zondervan, 1987. Reprint, Phillipsburg, NJ: P&R, 2001.

Richards, Jay W. *Money, Greed, and God: Why Capitalism Is the Solution and Not the Problem*. New York: HarperCollins, 2009.

Ryken, Leland. *The Christian Imagination: The Practice of Faith in Literature and Writing*. Colorado Springs, CO: Shaw, 2002.

———. *The Liberated Imagination: Thinking Christianly about the Arts*. Colorado Springs, CO: WaterBrook, 1989.

Sayers, Dorothy L. *The Mind of the Maker*. New York: Harcourt, Brace, 1941.

Schlossberg, Herbert. *Idols for Destruction: Christian Faith and Its Confrontation with American Society*. Nashville: Nelson, 1983.

Sebeok, Thomas A. *An Introduction to Semiotics*. London: Pinter, 1994.

US Census Bureau, *Overview of Race and Hispanic Origin: Census 2000 Brief*. Accessed August 14, 2009. http://www.census.gov/prod/2001pubs/c2kbr01-1.pdf.

Van Til, Cornelius. *The Defense of the Faith*. 2nd ed., rev. and abridged. Philadelphia: Presbyterian and Reformed, 1963.

———. *An Introduction to Systematic Theology: Prolegomena and the Doctrines of Revelation, Scripture, and God*. 2nd ed. Phillipsburg, NJ: P&R, 2007.

———. *A Survey of Christian Epistemology*. n.p.: den Dulk Foundation, 1969.

Van Til, Henry R. *The Calvinistic Concept of Culture*. Grand Rapids: Baker, 1959.

Warfield, Benjamin B. *The Inspiration and Authority of the Bible*. Philadelphia: Presbyterian and Reformed, 1948.

Westphal, Merold. *Overcoming Onto-Theology: Toward a Postmodern Christian Faith*. New York: Fordham University Press, 2001.

———. *Whose Community? Which Interpretation? Philosophical Hermeneutics for the Church*. Grand Rapids: Baker, 2009.

White, Heath. *Postmodernism 101: A First Course for the Curious Christian*. Grand Rapids: Brazos, 2006.

General Index

Scripture Index

Genesis
1—23
1–2—33
1:1—96
1:1–31—98
1:2—99
1:3—74, 84, 250
1:14—84
1:26—18
1:26–27—225
1:26–28—30
1:27—30, 221
1:28—18, 105, 312
1:28–30—46, 86, 100, 117
1:31—45, 240
2:16–17—18, 46
2:17—34, 104, 108, 112
2:18—15, 198
2:18–25—19, 37
2:22—221
2:24—198, 200, 219
3—103, 104, 112
3:1—104, 108, 112, 113
3:4—104, 111
3:4–5—108, 112
3:5—105, 112, 113
3:6—112
3:6–19—200
3:7—112
3:8—46, 106
3:9–13—109
3:9–19—46
3:12—108
3:15—19, 109, 113
3:17–19—113

3:19—103
3:20—262
3:22—113
4:1–24—103
4:1–5:32—19
4:8—108
4:19—108
4:23–24—108
5:1–31—103
5:5—103
6:5–7—103
6:11–12—108
8—117
8:20–22—117
8:21—117
8:21–22—117
9—117
9:5–6—19
10:1–32—123
11:1–9—122, 257n4
12:3—123
15:18—33
16:13—262
17—19
17:1—33
17:1–14—33
17:4—33
17:5—262
17:10—33
17:14—33
22:9—86
23:4—221
24—288
26:28—33, 36
31:44—33, 36

41:37–57—19
45:5—19
50:20—19, 176n

Exodus
3:14—262, 267n
4:11—229
6:4—36
15:3—209
19–20—321
19:5–6—125
20:1–17—34
20:2a—34
20:2b—34
20:3—86
20:3–17—35
20:4–6—83n, 131, 184
20:5–6—35
20:5–7—79
20:7—35
20:12—19, 35, 81, 85, 211
20:14—70
20:15—85, 203
20:16—37
22:16–17—205
22:21–22—222
23:6—221
23:21—262
24—19, 34
24:10—248
24:12—34
25:16—34
25:18–19—248
25:21—34
25:22—34